Trinitarian Theology for the Church

Scripture, Community, Worship

EDITED BY

DANIEL J. TREIER AND DAVID LAUBER

IVP Academic

An imprint of InterVarsity Press
Downers Grove, Illinois

Apollos
Nottingham, England

InterVarsity Press, USA
P.O. Box 1400, Downers Grove, IL 60515-1426, USA
World Wide Web: www.ivpress.com
Email: email@ivpress.com

APOLLOS (an imprint of Inter-Varsity Press, England)
Norton Street, Nottingham NG7 3HR, England
Website: www.ivpbooks.com
Email: ivp@ivpbooks.com

InterVarsity Press®, USA, is the book-publishing division of InterVarsity Christian Fellowship/USA®, a movement of students and faculty active on campus at hundreds of universities, colleges and schools of nursing in the United States of America, and a member movement of the International Fellowship of Evangelical Students. For information about local and regional activities, write Public Relations Dept., InterVarsity Christian Fellowship/USA, 6400 Schroeder Rd., P.O. Box 7895, Madison, WI 53707-7895, or visit the IVCF website at <www.intervarsity.org>.

Inter-Varsity Press, England, is closely linked with the Universities and Colleges Christian Fellowship, a student movement connecting Christian Unions throughout Great Britain, and a member movement of the International Fellowship of Evangelical Students. Website: www.uccf.org.uk

Selected excerpts from Gerald F. Hawthorne, Current Issues in Biblical and Patristic Interpretation ©2008 Wm. B. Eerdmans Publishing Company, Grand Rapids, Michigan. Reprinted by permission of the publisher, all rights reserved.

The lyrics on p. 90 are from "The Servant King / From Heaven You Came" by Graham Kendrick, ©1983 Thankyou Music (admin. by EMI Christian Music Publishing). Used by permission. All rights reserved.

Design: Cindy Kiple

Images: Baptism of Christ, surrounded by the Twelve Apostles, by Byzantine School, 6th Century, Baptistry of Ariani, Ravenna, Italy / Bridgeman Art Library

USA ISBN 978-0-8308-2895-1

UK ISBN 978-1-84474-380-3

Printed in the United States of America ∞

Library of Congress Cataloging-in-Publication Data

Wheaton Theology Conference (2008)
Trinitarian theology for the church: Scripture, community, worship
/ edited by Daniel J. Treier and David Lauber.
    p. cm.
Includes bibliographical references and index.
ISBN 978-0-8308-2895-1 (pbk.: alk. paper)
1. Trinity—Congresses. 2. Bible—Theology—Congresses. 3.
Practical theology—Congresses. I. Treier, Daniel J., 1972- II.
Lauber, David, 1966- III. Title.
BT111.3.W54 2008
231'.044—dc22

                                                                          2008054485

British Library Cataloguing in Publication Data

A catalogue record for this book is available from the British Library.

P   18   17   16   15   14   13   12   11   10   9   8   7   6   5   4   3   2   1

Y   24   23   22   21   20   19   18   17   16   15   14   13   12   11   10   09

Contents

Introduction

DANIEL J. TREIER AND DAVID LAUBER

In the middle of the twentieth century, Western theologians rediscovered the doctrine of the Trinity. In the late twentieth or early twenty-first century, evangelicals began catching up with this rediscovery of the triune God. So goes the standard story. The purpose of this book is to make sense of such a tale for the sake of church life.

This introduction will first sketch the standard narrative, next survey the basics of trinitarian theology to frame what all the clamor is about, then explore some revisionist accounts that challenge the standard narrative and finally look ahead to the contents of this present work.

The Standard Narrative

On the standard account, the twentieth century renewal of trinitarian theology responds to centuries of doctrinal tragedy. The medieval development of heavily systematic, "scholastic" theologies dealing with ever more abstract, speculative questions began to squelch trinitarian dogma. The metaphysical approaches of Western philosophers gave priority to the one substance of the "unmoved mover" who caused the universe. The Father, Son and Holy Spirit played second fiddle to this monotheistic Most Perfect Being, because the history of salvation, in which the particularity of the three persons is revealed, became an afterthought. The structure of Thomas Aquinas's *Summa theologica* is emblematic in this regard: first he speaks of *De Deo uno*, the one God, and only later of *De Deo trino*, the three-personed God. The Protestant Reformers may have resisted scholastic speculation a couple centuries later, but their emphasis on organic biblical theology did not foster a trinitarian renaissance due to the doctrine's lack of explicit development in Scripture.

Accordingly, in the wake of the Enlightenment's quest for a universal, rational and natural religion, the triunity of the Christian God became a source of embarrassment. Out of obligation, conservative theologians continued to demand adherence to the doctrine and unfolded it in their systematic theologies, but they lacked the confidence to develop the doctrine itself or its implications with rigor and verve. More liberal theologians, meanwhile, increasingly hid the doctrine from public focus or considered it to be unnecessary speculation and denied it entirely. An oft-cited example is Friedrich Schleiermacher. Considering the Trinity to be unnecessary in accounting for the pious experience of redemption, Schleiermacher thus relegated the doctrine to a thirteen-page conclusion at the end of nearly eight hundred pages and, furthermore, rejected its orthodox formulation to some degree or another.[1]

Early in the twentieth century, however, Karl Barth embraced the revelatory scandal over trinitarian theology instead of cowering with embarrassment. Barth's tendency to think of everything in relation to Jesus Christ as divine revelation brought trinitarian dogma back to the forefront of theological agendas.[2] Beginning at mid-century, Wolfhart Pannenberg, Jürgen Moltmann and others followed Barth by developing Trinity-rich approaches to history and eschatology. Feminist and Global South theologians such as Catherine Mowry LaCugna and Leonardo Boff explored the possibilities of trinitarian doctrine for connecting God more closely to the world and its suffering, as well as for constructing models of human community.

The resulting forms of what is often called "social trinitarianism" began to influence evangelicals late in the twentieth century, as Western individualism came under ever more intense criticism. The "postmodern" urge to seek community prodded pastoral accounts of divine fellowship as not only the motivation but also the model for such human communion. Forms of the social emphasis vary widely, as do the ways theologians apply it to the church and society, but at times the appeal to relationality itself seems ubiquitous.

---

[1]See F. D. E. Schleiermacher, *The Christian Faith* (Edinburgh: T & T Clark, 1999).
[2]See Claude Welch, *In This Name: The Doctrine of the Trinity in Contemporary Theology* (1952; reprint, Eugene, Ore.: Wipf & Stock, 2005).

Yet, with rare exceptions, the apparent popularity and pastoral appeal of trinitarian theology for evangelicals has not elicited much depth of doctrinal reflection among us.[3] Hence we took up the subject at the 2008 Wheaton Theology Conference, from which the essays in this book have been collected. Before providing an overview of the chapters themselves, however, it will help to step back and consider what we mean by "trinitarian theology" in the first place, as well as how one might challenge the standard story we have just told.

THE BASICS OF TRINITARIAN THEOLOGY

The doctrine of the Trinity has a history with its roots in Jewish monotheism. The basic pattern of biblical teaching about God starts with the *Shema* of Deuteronomy 6:4: "Hear, O Israel: The LORD our God, the LORD is one" (NIV). What were the early Christians to make of their worshiping Jesus Christ in light of such Old Testament teaching—in light of the Bible as they knew it? Moreover, just when and how may we speak of "worshiping" Jesus Christ? If there is evidence of such worship in the New Testament,[4] were the early Christians indeed worshiping Jesus as "fully divine" in the sense of which the later creeds speak? The church fathers used the phrase

---

[3]An evangelical survey of the renaissance in trinitarian theology, according to the standard view, comes from Stanley J. Grenz, *Rediscovering the Triune God: The Trinity in Contemporary Theology* (Minneapolis: Fortress, 2004). Among the substantial, scholarly evangelical contributions to trinitarian theology are Miroslav Volf, *After Our Likeness: The Church as the Image of the Trinity*, Sacra Doctrina (Grand Rapids: Eerdmans, 1997), whose work garnered much discussion at our conference; Robert Letham, *The Holy Trinity: In Scripture, History, Theology, and Worship* (Phillipsburg, N.J.: Presbyterian & Reformed, 2005). The nonevangelical literature is far too broad to survey, but Grenz's primer provides access to some of it, as does Roger E. Olson and Christopher A. Hall, *The Trinity*, Guides to Theology (Grand Rapids: Eerdmans, 2002). Colin Gunton's trinitarian emphasis proved stimulating for many evangelicals, as is evident in Paul Louis Metzger, ed., *Trinitarian Soundings in Systematic Theology* (London: T & T Clark, 2006). Note also that Fred Sanders authored the chapter on the Trinity in the recent *Oxford Handbook of Systematic Theology*, ed. John Webster, Kathryn Tanner and Iain Torrance (Oxford: Oxford University Press, 2007), pp. 35-53. Finally, ours is not the only recent conference on trinitarian theology; see, e.g., Timothy George, ed., *God the Holy Trinity: Reflections on Christian Faith and Practice* (Grand Rapids: Baker Academic, 2006).

[4]See, e.g., Larry W. Hurtado, *Lord Jesus Christ: Devotion to Jesus in Earliest Christianity* (Grand Rapids: Eerdmans, 2003); David Yeago, "The New Testament and the Nicene Dogma," reprinted in *The Theological Interpretation of Scripture: Classic and Contemporary Readings*, ed. Stephen E. Fowl (Oxford: Blackwell, 1997), pp. 87-100; Richard Bauckham, *God Crucified: Monotheism and Christology in the New Testament* (Grand Rapids: Eerdmans, 1999).

lex orandi lex credendi to say that the "law of prayer" should be the "law of faith": what we say about God in our creeds should match our worship practices. But is the trinitarian theology toward which the Nicene (Constantinopolitan) Creed points a philosophical imposition over the simplicity of Scripture, an imposition deriving from the later clash of Judaism and a form of "Christianity" moving in a Greco-Roman direction?

To the contrary, there is, in fact, New Testament evidence of triadic thinking about God as Father, Son and Holy Spirit. Passages such as 1 Peter 1:2; the baptismal formula of Matthew 28:19-20; 2 Corinthians 13:14 and a host of such Pauline texts clearly evince a conviction of some threeness in God, giving at least some "divine" significance to the Son and Spirit. Furthermore, the New Testament seems to draw on certain Old Testament hints about plurality or relationality in God, at least about divine self-expressiveness toward the created order: the figures of Wisdom, Word and Spirit are especially relevant in this connection. Perhaps this should be enough to conclude that the earliest Christian teaching, fixed in the New Testament, identifies Jesus with God. But in any case the Gospel of John in places such as 1:1-18 and 8:58 makes this identification more explicitly. And when it comes to the Holy Spirit, the early Christians clearly built on Old Testament texts identifying the Spirit with divine power. Eventually the church concluded as well that the Spirit participates personally in divine identity, as verses such as Acts 5:3 and Romans 8:14-16 seem to indicate with regard to the Spirit's communicative actions.

From the biblical texts and the arguments about them in light of the Christ event, which initiate this Christian tradition of worship, we gain a strange sense of living in freedom *by way of* basic rules that exclude error—not excluding disagreements, mind you, but ruling out divisive heresies. For many of us, who know only two ways of handling disagreements—either dividing over them or else dismissing them as irrelevancies due to common piety—this could seem to be a new way of life. Some disagreements are indeed not worthy of division but may nevertheless be discussed and debated as very relevant. Other disagreements, though, are so relevant to Christian life and worship that they require division; otherwise they would rend apart the common fabric of piety. Hence we need creedal language—to set the basic rules within which the community can think and live, rules by which extreme errors are excluded.

Two sets of rules pertaining to the Trinity will illustrate. First, a number of rules developed for proper speech about Jesus Christ. He is fully divine—not just human, as the Ebionites said; and not just a partly divine mediating creature, as the Arians said. He is fully human—not just divine, as the Docetists said; and not just partly human, as the Apollinarians said (he does not merely have a human body and soul with a divine mind or nature). And as to the relation of his full divinity and humanity, one may not say that he is fundamentally schizophrenic (two persons, or two natures only incidentally united); nor may one say that in the unity of his person these natures are confused with each other. We do not, on account of the story of Jesus Christ, start to mix what it means to be the Creator with what it means to be dependent creatures.

Second, when we broaden from considering the identity of Jesus Christ and his relation with the Father to consider the import of such language for the identity of God and for the relation of Father and Son also to the Holy Spirit—then we develop properly trinitarian rules for speech. Here again, we have great freedom within generous boundaries that prevent error and protect the essentials. One may not say that there are three gods or in any way three separate individuals who simply share a "divine" nature. Nor may one say, to protect the divine oneness with folks like the Sabellian modalists, that God simply appears to us in three different modes at different moments of salvation history, or in three different forms of appearance related to different functions at any one moment. Father, Son and Holy Spirit are proper names, not just masks the one God wears—whether in the Old Testament, New Testament and post-Pentecost age or in aspects of transcendence, mediation and immanence.

These rules are indebted to the defeat especially of Arian Christology at the Councils of Nicaea (325) and Constantinople (381) that resulted in the Nicene (Constantinopolitan) Creed and to the Cappadocian fathers—Basil of Caesarea, Gregory of Nazianzus and Gregory of Nyssa—who gave us two crucial concepts for trinitarian thinking: (1) the distinction between *ousia* (one substance or essence or being) and *hypostasis* (three persons or subsistences); and (2) the concept of *perichōrēsis* (mutual indwelling) for talking about the nature of the three persons' communion. As you will see in some of the succeeding chapters, the precise legacy of the Cappadocian thinkers remains under dispute. In any case, finally, we should also mention the Chalcedonian Definition of 451 regarding the "hypostatic union": the integral relation of two natures, full divinity and humanity, in one person, Jesus Christ.

For a long time, Western thinking about the Trinity was largely a series of footnotes to the work of Augustine. In contrast to the East, Augustine is famed for emphasizing the unity or oneness of the Godhead. Moreover, he developed a series of "psychological" analogies, which related the Trinity to the human person: for example, the mind, knowledge and love; or a lover, the beloved and the bond of love between them. It is important to note that he discarded nearly all of these analogies on further inspection, and that he regarded them only as analogies in a rather weak sense.[5]

The Cappadocian fathers who influenced Eastern Christianity, by contrast, are known for using more "social" analogies than Augustine. For instance, Peter, James and John are all persons who share a single, common humanity and could form a community. In addition, whereas the West emphasized divine oneness so as to emphasize the equality of the three persons, the East is often viewed as emphasizing the monarchy or hierarchy of the Father along with the threeness of the persons. The resulting dispute over the *filioque* clause in the Nicene (Constantinopolitan) Creed was one of the principal issues that led to formal division between the Eastern and Western churches usually dated to 1054. The West gradually added the words "and the Son" *(filioque)* to the third article of the creed (so that the Spirit "proceeds from the Father and the Son") in public worship. Formalization of this Augustinian concept and church practice by the pope seemed schismatic to the Eastern churches, which rejected the papal authority involved. Of course, much was politically sordid throughout this evolving schism. But, theologically, the Eastern perspective worried that the *filioque* clause weakened the monarchy of the Father as well as the full personhood of the Spirit, who seemed to become merely an impersonal "bond of love" between Father and Son.

Though the *filioque* clause manifests real distinctions between Eastern

---

[5] See, e.g., Augustine of Hippo, *The Trinity*, trans. Edmund Hill, ed. John E. Rotelle (Hyde Park, N.Y.: New City Press, 1991), 15.39.

and Western trinitarian thought, on closer inspection the differences have probably been overplayed. The textbook categories—East: threeness, monarchy, social analogies; West: oneness, equality, psychological analogies—come largely from a nineteenth-century Frenchman, Théodore de Régnon.[6] Each communion likely emphasized different analogies without denying the importance of both—for example, Augustine and Gregory of Nyssa each used both the psychological and social analogies. Thinkers on both sides heavily qualified their claims by noting that these were *only* analogies. And thinkers on both sides primarily concerned themselves with rejecting heresies such as Arianism.[7]

Western thinking about the Trinity is often said to have languished in excessive abstraction and speculation during the Middle Ages. Yet here again the textbook stereotypes are breaking down. The work of Richard of St. Victor is one illustration that might belie this charge, as does the recent recovery of Thomas Aquinas as a biblical, not just philosophical, thinker.[8] In any case, the Protestant Reformation (only to some extent and at least somewhat unintentionally) paved the way for the modern age, with its apparent eclipse of the doctrine of the Trinity. This too is a story that we are still figuring out how to tell and what it means. Certainly one cannot draw a straight line from the relative biblicism of the Reformers to philosophers such as Immanuel Kant, who rejected trinitarian teaching, as well as theologians such as Schleiermacher, who in some sense relegated the doctrine to minor status if they retained it at all.

---

[6]See, e.g., Michel René Barnes, "Rereading Augustine on the Trinity," in *The Trinity: An Interdisciplinary Symposium on the Trinity*, ed. Stephen T. Davis et al. (Oxford: Oxford University Press, 1999), pp. 145-75; idem, "The Use of Augustine in Contemporary Trinitarian Theology," *Theological Studies* 56 (1995): 237-51; idem, "De Régnon Reconsidered," *Augustinian Studies* 26 (1995): 51-79.

[7]The importance of Ex 3:14 and the "divine names" throughout the Christian tradition further supports the notion that East and West were not as distinct as they have sometimes appeared to be. See, e.g., Janet Martin Soskice, "The Gift of the Name: Moses and the Burning Bush," in *Silence and the Word: Negative Theology and the Incarnation*, ed. Oliver Davies and Denys Turner (Cambridge: Cambridge University Press, 2002), pp. 61-75; idem, "Naming God: A Study in Faith and Reason," in *Reason and the Reasons of Faith*, ed. Paul J. Griffiths and Reinhard Hütter (New York: T & T Clark, 2005), pp. 241-54.

[8]E.g., Matthew Levering, *Scripture and Metaphysics: Aquinas and the Renewal of Trinitarian Theology*, Challenges in Contemporary Theology (Oxford: Blackwell, 2004); Jean-Pierre Torrell, O.P., *Saint Thomas Aquinas: The Person and His Work* (Washington, D.C.: Catholic University of America Press, 2005); Nicholas M. Healy, *Thomas Aquinas: Theologian of the Christian Life*, Great Theologians (Aldershot, U.K.: Ashgate, 2003).

Which God were these moderns rejecting? On one hand, they rejected the triune God of Christian faith because they could not reconcile this God—and the inescapability of revelation and redemption being *particular* if this God were to be known—with the requirements of universal reason. Yet on the other hand, moderns may have been rejecting the lordly God of Western philosophical reason—the God of the later Middle Ages and of Protestant scholastic Calvinists, who seemed to stand in the way of human autonomy and to be increasingly unnecessary in light of scientific progress.[9] Rival tellings of this story abound, and so do judgments about its significance for us today. At minimum we can say that the doctrine of God—and what role a trinitarian version should play—has become crucial to intellectual history from a Christian perspective.

REVISIONIST HISTORY

To some degree this overview of basic trinitarian theology reflects the shape of the standard narrative, but it also reflects some emerging weaknesses within that story. If the textbook distinctions between East and West or criticisms of the medieval West are overdrawn, then our reading of the modern eclipse of trinitarian theology may need some revisions as well.

Bruce Marshall suggests that the oft-claimed twentieth-century "renewal" of trinitarianism should manifest itself in terms of both novelty and quality. Yet in fact neither is the case. To demonstrate this, Marshall examines six theses emerging from Karl Barth (Protestant) and Karl Rahner (Roman Catholic) as crucial representatives of the supposed renewal. First, the Trinity is the most essential or basic Christian doctrine. Second, the doctrine of the Trinity "is the Christian way of identifying God."[10] Third, "Rahner's Rule" holds that "the immanent Trinity [God in himself, apart from the world] is strictly identical with the economic Trinity [God creating and redeeming] and vice versa."[11] Fourth, "Father, Son and Spirit are genu-

---

[9]See, e.g., Colin E. Gunton, *The One, The Three and the Many: God, Creation and the Culture of Modernity* (Cambridge: Cambridge University Press, 1993); Michael J. Buckley, *At the Origins of Modern Atheism* (New Haven: Yale University Press, 1987); William Placher, *The Domestication of Transcendence: How Modern Thinking About God Went Wrong* (Louisville, Ky.: Westminster John Knox Press, 1999).

[10]Bruce D. Marshall, "Trinity," in *Blackwell Companion to Modern Theology*, ed. Gareth Jones (Oxford: Blackwell, 2004), p. 187.

[11]Cited in Paul Molnar, *Divine Freedom and the Doctrine of the Immanent Trinity: In Dia-

ine *persons*, agents who address and interact with one another in love and mutual knowledge," a point at which contemporary trinitarianism largely departs from Barth and Rahner.[12] Fifth, every Christian doctrine should bear a distinctive trinitarian stamp; accordingly it is unwise or inconsistent to start one's theology with "the one God" if one holds to the first four theses. Sixth, one ought to start with "the" Eastern approach because it begins with the economy of salvation, whereas the West starts more philosophically, with the divine essence and attributes.

What ought we to make of these theses? Marshall points out that the first is not all that novel, citing a wide variety of classic figures in Western theology who say something like it. Likewise, the second thesis, in a certain way, is widespread throughout the tradition. In its weaker forms it may not go very far at all, yet in its stronger forms it causes problems for Christians trying to respect their connection with the God of Israel as seen in passages such as Romans 11. Marshall further points out that connecting these two theses with a story of contemporary renewal can run counter to the supposed importance of the doctrine they try to protect. If the doctrine has been so thoroughly eclipsed, then how important could it really be to Christian identity and practice in the first place? Perhaps the doctrine operates tacitly, with Christians worshiping better than they—or theologians!—know.[13]

The third thesis again has a welter of possible versions and multiplies confusion. Some of the stronger versions threaten to lose divine freedom and moreover were available in the nineteenth century, before the supposed renewal. In addition, it is not as if the economy of salvation is transparently clear in the first place; the Son and the Spirit have a variety of interactions that do not obviously construe their relationship in one and only one way.[14]

The fourth, fifth and sixth theses tend to focus on how we start our theology in general or trinitarian doctrine in particular—whether to start with classically "essentialist" or instead with more contemporary "person-

---

logue with Karl Barth and Contemporary Theology (London: T & T Clark, 2002), p. xi.
[12]Marshall, "Trinity," p. 188.
[13]Ibid, pp. 192-93.
[14]Ibid, pp. 193-97.

alist" approaches. In addressing this question, Marshall tries to show that the task of relating "three persons" and "one God" does not hang on the order of presentation. Whatever the pedagogical significance of this decision, it does not put the logical coherence or justification of one's position at stake.[15] Furthermore, the sixth thesis relies on the East versus West distinctions that (as noted above) appear to be overdrawn.

Marshall then questions both the quality of several versions of the confusing theses and the novelty of those that withstand scrutiny. And he is not alone in his worries about the oft-proclaimed "renewal" of contemporary trinitarian theology. Several others have questioned the value of recent appeals to perichoresis as a divine model for human social orders.[16] In another recent essay, for instance, Kathryn Tanner rejects a multitude of strategies for making such a move. Against its apparent communitarian appeal, she suggests that in fact political "trinitarianism can be every bit as dangerous as monotheism; everything depends on how that trinitarianism (or monotheism) is developed and applied"[17]—or else we reject any "progressive political potential" for Judaism and Islam, for example. While granting the value of recent focus on the divine economy of salvation, Tanner also asserts that this can be rightly or wrongly pursued. We should not focus on the economy simply to learn the formal character of relations between divine persons and apply that to ourselves; we ought rather to learn from the economy what the divine persons are doing for the sake of humans, which will then have implications for how we relate to each other. Hence, Tanner does not believe we should model ourselves on the Trinity; instead, we should seek to understand what it means to participate in the fellowship of the triune God, in which our humanity is transformed into that for which God made us.[18] We learn about the Father, Son and Holy Spirit not to reproduce trinitarian relations, but to participate in appropriate human relations with the triune God and accordingly with each other.

---

[15]Ibid, pp. 198-99.

[16]See, e.g., Randall E. Otto, "The Use and Abuse of Perichoresis in Recent Theology," *Scottish Journal of Theology* 54 (2001): 366-84; Karen Kilby, "Perichoresis and Projection: Problems with Social Doctrines of the Trinity," *New Blackfriars* 81 (2000): 432-45.

[17]Kathryn Tanner, "Trinity," in *Blackwell Companion to Political Theology*, ed. William T. Cavanaugh and Peter Scott (Oxford: Blackwell, 2003), p. 323.

[18]Tanner, "Trinity," esp. pp. 328-29.

The point of these revisionist voices is not to diminish the importance of the present book, but to situate the need for it. Marshall, Tanner and others have demonstrated the sloppiness of much enthusiasm regarding a trinitarian renaissance, even if one does not embrace all of their conclusions and hesitations. We do not need to dispense with conversation about trinitarian theology; rather, we need to pursue it all the more carefully. This contemporary phenomenon may be a bit like the stock market: even if there are strong elements of hype, the perception itself comes to influence reality. The wealth of books about trinitarian theology no doubt participates in the proliferation of books about everything; nevertheless, we seem to have an opportune trickle-down moment for the doctrine of the Trinity to influence church life more explicitly and intentionally.[19]

A SNEAK PREVIEW

With that goal in mind, we turn specifically to the contributions of this book. Our conference themes organize naturally under three headings: Scripture, community and worship—with each of these oriented toward a larger theme that emerged: mission. For we discovered that the *missio Dei*—the mission of the triune God—kept cropping up in essays under all three headings. The Father sent the Son as self-revelation to redeem the fallen, cursed creation; now the Spirit is sent, in order to send the church as a witness to the divine mission.

If the doctrine of the Trinity means getting our redemptive story straight, then as evangelical Protestants we must first turn to Scripture. We do so in two ways: Kevin Vanhoozer primarily unfolds the implications of trinitarian theology for how we approach the ontology of Scripture; Edith Humphrey follows with how the doctrine of the Trinity unfolds from Scripture itself.

Vanhoozer's trinitarian understanding of Scripture develops in two parts. His first chapter begins with a glance at the Evangelical Theological Society's identity markers: belief in biblical inerrancy and the doctrine of the Trinity. Vanhoozer desires to understand how these go together to es-

---

[19]In his essay for the conference, Fred Sanders suggested that evangelicalism has been tacitly trinitarian even in low-church sectors that do not emphasize formal liturgy, tradition and sacraments. What needs to happen is making explicit the trinitarian theological framework of our understandings of the gospel, even (or especially) those centered in phrases such as a "personal relationship with Jesus."

tablish an authority principle. Worrying about functional deism in modern biblical hermeneutics, Vanhoozer considers a series of possible headings under which theologians might place the doctrine of Scripture in order to understand it *theologically*: inspiration and providence, inspiration and incarnation, inspiration and revelation. Each has its insightful adherents but also its problems. After highlighting these problems, the essay closes by considering two alternatives: Karl Barth's distinctly theological appeal to the doctrine of the Trinity alongside Nicholas Wolterstorff's philosophical appeal to speech-act theory. Vanhoozer's intention is to mine insights from each while addressing their respective weaknesses.

The second chapter thus begins by foregrounding the prominence of divine speaking as a biblical theme. The one God speaks, but so also speech activity is appropriated to each of the three persons. Vanhoozer thus explores divine dialogue in the immanent Trinity and divine rhetoric in the triune economy. This trinitarian focus helps us to avoid some (though not all!) of the either-or polarizations in debates over the doctrine of Scripture. Some of the alternatives for housing the doctrine are better than others; the incarnational analogy, for example, needs considerable alteration. Traditional evangelical affirmations about the ontology of Scripture do not disappear from this account, but they are reaffirmed within the larger context of the triune economy of covenant communication.

Finally regarding Scripture, Edith Humphrey's chapter turns our attention to the content of the Bible itself regarding the identity of the triune God. She undertakes a possibly counterintuitive thought experiment regarding the God of the Old Testament being identified with the incarnate divine Son of the New Testament—the way many ancient theologians read the Scriptures. Weaving a rich tapestry of biblical and liturgical materials into her portrayal of "the gift of God," she advocates renewed attention to the meaning of being God's children, who have received the gift of divine presence itself.

Through Scripture as divine self-communication, we are called into fellowship with God and each other. Thus our second major theme, community, follows as a focus of trinitarian theology. The first two chapters under this heading provide contrasting perspectives on debates over "social trinitarianism." John Franke advocates a "relational turn" favoring a more social understanding of the Trinity. Exploring apparent contrasts between East and West, he finds Richard of St. Victor to provide a Western instance of a more relational, less psychological approach than Augustine's. The recent relational turn offers the possibility of escape from the static God-concepts that result from a substantialist focus on the shared divine essence. The relational turn prioritizes the recognition that "God is love," with a resulting emphasis on the missional divine character as self-giving. But Mark Husbands is not convinced: he aims to demonstrate that social trinitarians consistently misread the Cappadocian tradition to which they appeal, and in particular Gregory of Nyssa. According to Husbands, it is actually Karl Barth—often accused of overemphasizing divine oneness even to the point of modalism—who is the more faithful inheritor of the Cappadocian legacy. Moreover, Husbands claims that some social trinitarians, such as even the more conservative Miroslav Volf, obscure the vital ontological distinction between God and humanity.

The other two chapters addressing community concern the connection between divine relationality and human religion. Several contemporary theologians have sought to apply trinitarian theology, construed along relational lines, to the question of Christian responses to religious pluralism. Keith E. Johnson surveys three of these thinkers: Amos Yong, Mark Heim and Jacques Dupuis. Continuing a theme that surfaced in Mark Husbands's preceding chapter, Johnson shows the inconsistency of these thinkers with the patristic tradition, focusing on Augustine. Yet Robert Lang'at follows up these two chapters of critical engagement with relationality by offering a more positive appraisal. Lang'at sees the perennial problem of "the one and the many" as a matter with missional import, which he illustrates with reference to African theological debates. According to Lang'at, Isaiah 6 is an instance of the Bible itself rendering God in relational and missional terms simultaneously. Pauline apostolic greetings similarly connect these concepts. The early church's trinitarian controversies were actually missional queries as the relational gospel encountered its Greco-Roman context. Christian faith is inherently missional because the triune God is missional.

Third, then, the community called into existence by the Holy Spirit and through the divine Word in Scripture worships a relational, missional God.

How might our worship more adequately draw us into fellowship with this triune God? Gordon Smith suggests first of all that via the sacraments we embody our trinitarian faith. He expounds this theme with particular reference to the ecumenical document *Baptism, Eucharist and Ministry*. Once again, it is striking to note that Smith's chapter ends by relating the sacraments to mission—its beginning and end.

Next we focus more directly on proclamation. Philip Butin unfolds a trinitarian theology of preaching. This involves a delicate balance between Word and Spirit as well as the interplay between preaching, Scripture and Jesus Christ as three forms of the one divine Word. Such a theology is necessary in order to relate the divine Word to human words, and Butin offers practical resources for approaching this via, for instance, trinitarian, pneumatological prayers for illumination. Leanne Van Dyk's chapter seeks to expand our concept of proclamation beyond preaching and evangelism, narrowly construed. She links proclamation to all dimensions of the church's life as a missionary community in the world. Raising the question of whether visible practices can be proclamatory in some sense, such a theology views the church's life as missional because it participates in divine communion and self-giving.

With John Witvliet's closing chapter we encounter a fitting recapitulation of several issues in the book, as well as more concrete reflections on the practice of ministry. Witvliet offers specific examples of how trinitarian doctrine might play out in the practices of Christian worship. He then pursues the additional question of how catechesis might enable worshipers to be more aware of what is transpiring in worship so that their awareness of the triune God might be more explicit. Thus, he moves beyond the decisions of worship leaders to consider the pedagogy necessary for preparing our congregations to engage the triune God in prayer and praise.

So much of church life, of course, has to do with words, and this brings us full circle. The triune God calls the church into existence by the Word and Spirit, so that we might be a community whose worship reflects the self-giving, missional character of this God. To be intentionally trinitarian means paying attention to how our words can bear witness to the divine Word—not least by being part of lives that are consistent with the self-giving love of our God, whose being is in communion.

ACKNOWLEDGMENTS

We hope that this brief introduction and the essays themselves can convey a small sense of the rich fellowship and spirited conversation we enjoyed in April 2008 at the conference itself. Beyond the contributions appearing here, we also heard fine presentations from Craig Carter, John Flett, Fred Sanders, Steven Studebaker and Jonathan Wilson. Unfortunately, contractual and spatial limitations prevented their inclusion in this volume, but we are very grateful for their contributions to the conference and expect to see their essays appear in some form elsewhere.

Furthermore, we express heartfelt gratitude to others besides the speakers whose gracious support and encouragement make the Wheaton Theology Conference possible. For particular assistance we thank Liz Klassen and Kevin Jones, as well as Bruce Knowlton and the staff at the Media Resources department along with numerous student workers. Fellow theologians at Wheaton continue to provide wise counsel and ongoing support in various ways. Yet we acknowledge especially that without the graduate office coordinator Rebekah Canavan cheerfully and capably managing the numerous details of this year's conference, it would have been impossible. Along with Rebekah, Emily Bergen then helped in the production of this volume. Uche Anizor helped compile the index.

Ultimately, the conference and work of scholarship represented here would simply not happen without the financial assistance of InterVarsity Press and, in particular, the friendly advice of Bob Fryling, Publisher, and Gary Deddo, Senior Editor for InterVarsity Press Academic. Moreover, once again we express our thanks to the Dean of Humanities and Theological Studies, Jill Peláez Baumgaertner, and the Associate Dean of the Biblical and Theological Studies Department, Jeffrey Greenman, for their ongoing care and attention to fostering theological scholarship at Wheaton College.

PART ONE

SCRIPTURE

The Bible and the Triune Economy

1

Triune Discourse

Theological Reflections on the Claim That God Speaks (Part 1)

KEVIN J. VANHOOZER

*The highest proof of Scripture derives in general
from the fact that God in person speaks in it.*

CALVIN *INSTITUTES* 1.7.4

INTRODUCTION: IS THE ETS DOCTRINAL STATEMENT (IN)COHERENT?

At the heart of Christian faith lie neither principles, piety nor practices but rather the work of three persons: Father, Son and Spirit. The theologically correct term for this work is "economy," from two Greek terms roughly meaning household management—*oiko-* (house) + *nomia* (law). To speak of the economy is to refer to the way in which the persons of the Trinity work out the "plan" *(oikonomia)* of salvation (Eph 1:10). My assignment, to write on Trinity and Scripture, thus involves home economics: redemptive history as divine housekeeping.

Once upon a time the only thing one needed to sign in order to join the Evangelical Theological Society (ETS) was a brief statement affirming that "the Bible alone, and the Bible in its entirety, is the word of God written and is therefore inerrant in the autographs." A few years ago the society saw fit to add a second statement: "God is a Trinity, Father, Son, and Holy Spirit, each an uncreated person, one in essence, equal in power and glory." Nothing is said about how to connect these two articles of evangelical faith.

Since it is *not* written, "Let no man put asunder what ETS has joined together," we are free critically to examine this extraordinary pairing at the doctrinal core of the ETS. My purpose is not to put asunder but to put *together* what appears to be an unstable juxtaposition. In questioning the explicit coherence of the ETS, then, I am not suggesting that its members are insane—only that its doctrinal statement leaves something to be desired: logical and theological cohesion. I wish to conduct an Anselmic exercise—faith seeking understanding—that would demonstrate not simply the compatibility of the two parts of the ETS doctrinal statement but, if possible, their intrinsic *necessity*.[1]

This chapter makes no attempt to justify the doctrine of the Trinity from Scripture. The church has been there and done that: read the Nicene Creed. By contrast, there is neither creed nor ecumenical consensus concerning Scripture. What confessional statements there are typically identify Scripture as the word of God without deploying the resources of trinitarian theology. The ETS doctrinal statement simply calls attention to a widespread, though nonetheless puzzling, lacuna. Because the God in whom Christians believe is Father, Son and Spirit, one might think that the identity of this God would be relevant as we seek to understand the Bible as God's word.

We find a third of a trinitarian theology of Scripture in Bernard Ramm's formulation of the Protestant principle, according to which the ultimate authority in the church is *"the Holy Spirit speaking in the Scriptures."*[2] Coming from the opposite direction, N. T. Wright observes that biblical authority only makes sense if it is shorthand for "the authority of the triune God, exercised somehow *through* Scripture."[3] Ramm rightly identifies

---

[1]Since Anselm, one aspect of the theological task of "faith seeking understanding" is a kind of conceptual elaboration of the gospel that demonstrates the rationality of faith by clarifying how one thing necessarily relates to another. What rational argument ensues in the present chapter therefore partakes of the nature of conceptual elaboration (i.e., clarification) rather than proof (for this distinction between two kinds of theological reason, see Norman Kretzmann, "Trinity and Transcendentals," in *Trinity, Incarnation, and Atonement: Philosophical and Theological Essays*, ed. Ronald J. Feenstra and Cornelius Plantinga [Notre Dame, Ind.: University of Notre Dame Press, 1989], p. 81). My hope is that this strenuous exercise of reason might yield a firmer grasp of the nature and authority of Scripture in the church.

[2]Bernard Ramm, *The Pattern of Religious Authority* (Grand Rapids: Eerdmans, 1957), p. 28, with his emphasis.

[3]N. T. Wright, *The Last Word: Beyond the Bible Wars to a New Understanding of the Au-*

speaking as the means but limits its agency to the Spirit; Wright rightly identifies the triune agent but is vague about the way in which Scripture is the medium of divine authority. I want to combine these thoughts and think of the ultimate authority for Christian faith, life and thought as *the triune God speaking in and through the Scriptures.*

The doctrine of the Trinity is first and foremost a vital safeguard of the gospel, a necessary implication of the story of salvation. Unless the Son and Spirit are fully divine, the logic of the gospel—that God reconciles creation to himself through Christ—collapses. The material principle of evangelical theology requires the Trinity. But can we not say the same about the formal principle of evangelical theology (i.e., the doctrine of Scripture)?[4] We can and we must! While the primary function of the doctrine of the Trinity is to serve and preserve soteriology, that it further helps us to develop a doctrine of Scripture may be a secondary, though nonetheless welcome, benefit.

The questions now come thick and fast, and we will be able to do no more with some of them than wave as we drive by: (1) What concrete difference does it make to the doctrine of Scripture whether or not we discuss it in relation to the doctrine of the Trinity? (2) Is speaking in Scripture really the work of the Spirit only, as the creed suggests in placing the words *qui locutus est per prophetas* (who has spoken through prophets) under the third article? (3) Is the finite capable of the infinite? Specifically, are human voices capable of the voice of God? Are human ears? (4) Is the Bible the word of God because it reveals God? (5) Is Calvin right when he says, "We owe to the Scripture the same reverence we owe to God"?[5]

My working hypothesis is that we will have a better purchase on all five of these questions if we approach them in trinitarian perspective.

---

thority of Scripture (San Francisco: Harper, 2005), p. 23.

[4]Thomas Aquinas suggests that "spiration" may be more apt than "procession" as the proper attribute of the Spirit (see his *Summa theologica* Ia q. 27, a. 4 ad. 3).

[5]Cited in Donald Bloesch, *Holy Scripture: Revelation, Inspiration and Interpretation* (Downers Grove, Ill.: InterVarsity Press, 1994), p. 86. The quote comes from *Calvin's Commentary on Epistles to Timothy, Titus, and Philemon,* trans. William Pringle (Grand Rapids: Eerdmans, 1948), p. 249. Kern Robert Trembath complains that "inerrancy discussions ascribe to the words of the Bible an attribute which only God may be said to possess: intrinsic freedom from error" (*Evangelical Theories of Biblical Inspiration: A Review and Proposal* [New York: Oxford University Press, 1987], p. 99).

TWO DOCTRINES DIVERGE IN A MODERN WOOD: DETRINITIZING SCRIPTURE

Back to household management. If theology were a house, in what room should one put the doctrine of Scripture? David Kelsey's observation—that we must house "a 'doctrine of Scripture' in the context of a doctrine of God"[6]—appears almost self-evident to Protestants nurtured on confessional statements that identify Scripture as the "word of God." The chief purpose of a doctrine of Scripture is to further the church's understanding of just how the Bible is "of God."

The Fathers specified the contents of the canon but did not produce a doctrine of Scripture as such. This did not stop them from producing rich, God-saturated interpretations. For example, Augustine believed that Scripture was given by God in order to lead us back to God.[7] Scripture tells the story of the triune God in which the Father reaches down with both hands, Son and Spirit, so that we can reach back to God.[8]

How Scripture and the Trinity came apart is too long and tortuous a tale to recount in this context. It has to do with how theologians lost interest in theology, to use my doctoral supervisor Nicholas Lash's paradoxical expression.[9] What does it mean to say that theologians lost interest in theology, when did it happen, and why would they do that? Some blame the Reformers and their sixteenth-century successors. They were the ones who first made the doctrine of Scripture into an independent locus and, in so doing, turned the wine of the canon as a means of grace into the tasteless water of an epistemic criterion.[10] On this rather tendentious account, Lu-

---

[6]David H. Kelsey, "The Bible and Christian Theology," *Journal of the American Academy of Religion* 48 (1980): 396.

[7]Cf. Jason Byassee's comment about reading like Augustine: "Allegory might best be described as a habit of remaining open to God while reading Scripture" (*Praise Seeking Understanding: Reading the Psalms with Augustine* [Grand Rapids: Eerdmans, 2007], p. 249). Cf. Richard A. Norris Jr., "Augustine and the Close of the Ancient Period of Interpretation," in *A History of Biblical Interpretation*, vol. 1, *The Ancient Period*, ed. Alan J. Hauser and Duane F. Watson (Grand Rapids: Eerdmans, 2003), pp. 380-408; Pamela Bright, "St. Augustine," in *Christian Theologies of Scripture*, ed. Justin Holcomb (New York University Press, 2006), pp. 39-59.

[8]Lewis Ayres, "On the Practice and Teaching of Christian Doctrine," *Gregorianum* 80 (1999): 44.

[9]Nicholas Lash, "When Did Theologians Lose Interest in Theology?" in *The Beginning and the End of "Religion"* (Cambridge: Cambridge University Press, 1996), pp. 132-49.

[10]William J. Abraham, *Canon and Criterion in Christian Theology* (Oxford: Clarendon, 1998). See Daniel J. Treier's review for a critique of this historiography ("A Looser 'Canon'? Relating William Abraham's *Canon and Criterion in Christian Theology* to Biblical Inter-

ther and Calvin are "canonical foundationalists," more intent on proving doctrine than on knowing God.[11]

Lash himself charts an alternative and, to my mind, more plausible genealogy, more or less in line with Michael J. Buckley's influential book *At the Origins of Modern Atheism*.[12] On this view, things began to go wrong when Christian theologians no longer relied upon the internal resources of Christian faith to respond to challenges from science and philosophy and decided instead to fight with their opponents' weapons. They treated the problem of atheism as though it were a philosophic rather than a religious issue and tried to prove the existence of God with evidence drawn from nature rather than grace, from the cosmos rather than from Christ. A doctrine of God cannot be counted as Christian, however, if it does not include reference to Jesus. Losing interest in theology means forgetting about the Trinity when one speaks of God (or God's word).

To speak of God as Supreme Being is to change the subject of Christian theology.[13] Two doctrinal roads—two ways of thinking about God—thus diverged in a seventeenth-century wood, and the doctrine of Scripture paired off with *Deo uno* (i.e., the one God; the Supreme Being).[14] If it did not exactly languish there, neither did it flourish. Theologians did more than lose interest in theology then; they lost the subject matter! For the doctrine of the Trinity is "the grammar and summation of the entire Christian mystery of salvation."[15] Call it the "great reversal" of systematic theology.

We can link this great reversal in systematics to what Hans Frei dubs the great reversal of hermeneutics, that fateful modern moment when reading Scripture became "a matter of fitting the biblical story into another world

pretation," *Journal of Theological Interpretation* 2, no. 1 [2008]: 101-16).

[11]Abraham, *Canon and Criterion*, p. 137. There is an alternative explanation. The Reformers and their successors were not altering the substance of what Christian theologians had previously believed so much as putting it into a more serviceable form, not least to clarify the dispute with Roman Catholicism over the locus of theological authority. See Richard Muller, *Post-Reformation Reformed Dogmatics*, vol. 2, *Holy Scripture*, 2nd ed. (Grand Rapids: Baker, 2003), pp. 95-97.

[12]Michael J. Buckley, *At the Origins of Modern Atheism* (New Haven: Yale University Press, 1987).

[13]Lash, "When Did Theologians?" pp. 136-37.

[14]Elizabeth Johnson speaks in terms not of roads diverging but of a breach between the one God *(Deo uno)* and the triune God *(Deo trino)* (*Quest for the Living God* [New York and London: Continuum, 2007], p. 206).

[15]Walter Kasper, *The God of Jesus Christ* (New York: Crossroad, 2000), p. 311.

[the one categorized by philosophy and colonized by science] rather than incorporating that world into the biblical story."[16] That both the doctrine of Scripture and the practice of biblical interpretation became separated in modernity from the doctrine and the activity of the triune God is a striking event of first theological importance.

To some degree we all are heirs of this genetic mutation, this cancer, as it were, in the marrow of modern divinity: the tendency to be nominally but not operationally trinitarian. Such is Mark Bowald's contention in his recently published book on theological hermeneutics, where he baldly declares with the boldness of youth: "most contemporary accounts of biblical hermeneutics are deistic."[17] By this he means that they require no further action on God's part besides his maintaining the created order of language.[18] For all interpretative intents and purposes, then, reading the Bible is like reading any other text: we labor to extract from the text what its human authors put into it. Biblical inspiration is simply the answer as to why we read *this* book (it is authoritative); it is not a mandate for reading the Bible differently. Hermeneutics remains functionally deistic when God is viewed as the *cause* of the canon, as he is of creation, and nothing more.

In light of this modern detrinitizing, we can be grateful that the ETS doctrinal statement is explicitly trinitarian. And yet the question continues to nag: do God's being and activity as Father, Son and Spirit make any operational difference to what we believe about the nature, authority and interpretation of the Bible and its truth?

ON THE DOGMATIC LOCATION OF THE DOCTRINE OF SCRIPTURE

As the question "Who do we say that he is?" gives rise to and orients Christology, so the query that provokes the development of the doctrine of Scripture is, "*What* do we say that it is, and *where* do we say it?" Under what doctrinal locus do we place a doctrine of Scripture or, if we accord it an independent heading, with what other doctrines does it connect?

---

[16]Hans W. Frei, *The Eclipse of Biblical Narrative: A Study in Eighteenth and Nineteenth Century Hermeneutics* (New Haven: Yale University Press, 1974), p. 130.

[17]Mark Bowald, *Rendering the Word in Theological Hermeneutics: Mapping Divine and Human Agency* (Aldershot, U.K.: Ashgate, 2007), p. 173.

[18]See also Bowald, "Rendering Mute the Word: Overcoming Deistic Tendencies in Modern Hermeneutics," *Westminster Theological Journal* 69 (2007): 367-81.

Now we turn to consider some of the ways in which evangelicals and others have confessed Scripture to be "of God." What follows is not a comprehensive but a representative survey.[19] I want especially to highlight three ways in which theologians describe biblical inspiration in doctrinal terms that tend to be only nominally trinitarian: the activity or economy of the Trinity makes no concrete difference.

Inspiration and providence: "Guide me, O thou great Jehovah." We begin with what has become something of the default account of inspiration in evangelicalism: the suggestion that the Bible is "of God" because it is the result of divine providence.

Benjamin B. Warfield defines inspiration as "that extraordinary, supernatural influence . . . exerted by the Holy Ghost on the writers of our Sacred Books, by which their words were rendered also the words of God."[20] Inspiration is a special case of divine providence, of that divine "oversight" whereby God confirms, cooperates with and ultimately controls created things so that they conform to his purpose.

The standard evangelical textbooks more or less repeat Warfield's classic formulation of the doctrine. Rounding up the usual evangelical suspects, we see, for example, that Millard Erickson defines inspiration as "that supernatural influence of the Holy Spirit on the Scripture writers which . . . resulted in what they wrote actually being the Word of God."[21] This is the testimony of Scripture itself. Peter, for example, says of the prophetic word that it is more than the product of mere human willing because those who "spoke from God . . . were carried along by the Holy Spirit" (2 Pet 1:21 NIV).

At this point the specter of mechanical inspiration—the "dictation theory"—usually rears its ugly head. Yet "the real issue here is what confounds scholars in so many areas: the manner in which individual human events are jointly caused by both God and man."[22] If the Spirit makes use

---

[19]For example, space does not permit an examination of the claim that the doctrine of Scripture is a species of the genus "sacraments" (see Geoffrey Wainwright, *Doxology: The Praise of God in Worship, Doctrine, and Life* [New York: Oxford University Press, 1980], chap. 5).

[20]B. B. Warfield, *The Inspiration and Authority of the Bible* (Phillipsburg, N.J.: Presbyterian & Reformed, 1979), p. 420.

[21]Millard Erickson, *Christian Theology*, 2nd ed. (Grand Rapids: Baker, 1998), p. 225.

[22]James Burtchaell, *Catholic Theories of Biblical Inspiration Since 1810* (Cambridge: Cambridge University Press, 1969), p. 279.

of the biblical authors the way a flutist breathes into a flute,[23] then we have a vivid image of how the Bible could be said to be the word of God, but it comes at the cost of denying its real humanity. This is probably the reason that few theologians, if any, have actually held a dictation view.

Providence is not dictation. Herman Bavinck rightly says that "God never coerces anyone. He treats human beings, not as blocks of wood, but as intelligent and moral beings."[24] Inspiration for Bavinck is an *organic* process by which the Spirit works with, and respects, the historical and psychological reality—the life—of the Bible's human authors.[25] On this point there is a broad consensus that includes Pope Leo XIII, Warfield, J. I. Packer and many others. The consensus centers on concursus: the Spirit's efficient causality working through the human authors as instrumental causes without overriding their own personality or freedom of action.[26] Inspiration, says Erickson, "presupposes a long process of God's providential working with the author."[27] In Warfield's more eloquent words, "If God wished to give His people a series of letters like Paul's, He prepared a Paul to write them, and the Paul He brought to the task was a Paul who spontaneously would write just such letters."[28]

To be sure, the prophetic paradigm—according to which an individual receives the word of the Lord—works better for some books of the Bible than others. Peter comments in Acts 1:16 that "the Scripture had to be fulfilled, which the Holy Spirit spoke beforehand by the mouth of David." Prophets and kings may be mouthpieces for God, yet Luke evidently undertook his own research before writing his Gospel (Lk 1:1-4). Moreover, bib-

---

[23]The image comes from Athenagoras, *A Plea for the Christians* 9.

[24]Herman Bavinck, *Reformed Dogmatics*, vol. 1, *Prolegomena*, trans. John Vriend (Grand Rapids: Baker, 2003), p. 432.

[25]"The Holy Spirit, in the inscripturation of the Word of God, did not spurn anything human to serve as an organ of the divine" (ibid., 1:442).

[26]Warfield, *Inspiration*, p. 83. Bruce Vawter calls this the "scholastic synthesis" (*Biblical Inspiration* [Philadelphia: Westminster Press, 1972], p. 44). In Roman Catholicism, it was Pope Leo XIII who urged theologians to deploy Aquinas's notion of instrumental causality for the sake of the doctrine of biblical inspiration.

[27]Erickson, *Christian Theology*, p. 243. Note that Erickson is ambivalent as to whether inspiration applies to the writer or the writing; 2 Pet 1:20-21 refers to authors while 2 Tim 3:16 refers to what they wrote: "In the primary sense, it is the writer who is the object of the inspiration. As the writer pens Scripture, however, the quality of inspiredness is communicated to the writing as well" (p. 244).

[28]Warfield, *Inspiration*, p. 155.

lical scholars now believe that many biblical books, far from coming out of the authorial oven fully baked by a single individual, actually had a number of sous-chefs (i.e., redactors).[29] Not to worry: the doctrine of providence can handle it. If we define "author" as "that person (or persons) responsible for the content and final form of the text," we can then assert the Spirit's superintendence over the whole process of Scripture's composition: "the concursive action of the Spirit is not tied to one particular understanding of how the books of the Bible were written. Rather, God was at work in the whole process of composition."[30]

Two questions continue to nag those who would place the doctrine of Scripture under the doctrine of divine providence: (1) does it successfully rebut the charge of Bible deism? (2) Does it say enough to ensure divine authorship? Lurking behind both questions is the issue of divine agency, its nature and its function.

John Webster expresses the first concern this way: "Accounts of scriptural inspiration are not infrequently curiously deistic, in so far as the biblical text can itself become a revelatory agent by virtue of an act of divine inspiration in the past."[31] Clearly this is not your great-great-great-grandmother's deism: Warfield and company clearly affirm God's historical action. Webster surely knows this but nevertheless sees a certain parallel between God's creating and authoring. Both cases invoke God as the ultimate explanation as to why there is something—a cosmos and a canon, respectively—rather than nothing. The crucial question is whether God is nothing more than a creator-author. Are we content with a doctrine of Scripture that affirms the Bible as God's providentially spoken word yet

---

[29] Paul J. Achtemeier, *Inspiration and Authority: Nature and Function of Christian Scripture* (Peabody, Mass.: Hendrickson, 1999), pp. 99-104. Providence is thus involved in the whole process of composition and, according to Karl Barth, even in the formation of the canon (*Church Dogmatics* 3/3, ed. Geoffrey W. Bromiley and T. F. Torrance, trans. Geoffrey W. Bromiley and R. J. Ehrlich [Edinburgh: T & T Clark, 1960], p. 201).

[30] I. Howard Marshall, *Biblical Inspiration* (Vancouver: Regent College Publishing, 2004), p. 36. After all, the other key text, 2 Timothy 3:16 attributes inspiration to the writings, not their authors: "All *Scripture* is *theopneustos*"—God-breathed. Andrew McGowan proposes that we drop the misleading term "inspiration" and speak instead of divine "spiration" (see his *The Divine Authenticiy of Scripture* [Downers Grove, Ill.: InterVarsity Press, 2007]).

[31] John Webster, *Holy Scripture: A Dogmatic Sketch* (Cambridge: Cambridge University Press, 2003), p. 36.

limits God's agency in connection to Scripture to the past only?[32]

Others have raised a second concern about the inspiration-as-providence model, wondering whether it goes far enough. It is not enough to say that God guided those who produced the books of the Bible for the simple reason that divine providence is the ultimate factor—the remote cause—behind *all* the books that have been produced! The issue is not whether God is provident over Scripture but whether he is its author.[33] From a slightly different angle, Bavinck reminds us of the importance of the actual content of Scripture: "Inspiration alone would not yet make a writing into the word of God in a Scriptural sense. . . . Scripture is the word of God because the Holy Spirit testifies in it concerning Christ, because it has the Word-made-flesh as its matter and content."[34]

Warfield himself anticipates these objections. Toward the end of his essay "The Biblical Idea of Inspiration," he asks whether anything else is needed besides the providential government of God to produce books that would accord with his will. In reply, Warfield says, "Nothing is needed beyond mere providence to secure such books"[35]—assuming that God is content for everything in them to be what humans alone could put there. However, "If heights are to be scaled above man's native power to achieve, then something more than guidance, however effective, is necessary."[36] What Warfield calls "that extraordinary, supernatural influence exerted by the Spirit" turns out to be something *more* than providence after all. *Theopneustos* means that "these books become not merely the word of godly men, but the immediate word of God himself."[37] Warfield here tackles the deistic objection head-on. In the final analysis, the biblical idea of inspira-

---

[32]The Spirit's illumination of the reader in the present is another matter that has to do with the Bible's right interpretation, not its constitution. As such, it is an epistemological work, not an ontological one. Webster warns of the "objectification" of inspiration whereby inspiration becomes a formal property of the text insufficiently coordinated with God as author. When this happens, "the gap left by the withdrawal of the self-communicative divine presence is filled by readerly activity" (ibid., p. 35).

[33]See Frame's review of N. T. Wright, *The Last Word*, in *Penpoint* 17, no. 4 (August 2006). Similarly, John Goldingay observes that "Providence is a necessary but not sufficient condition for God's inspired word to be spoken" (*Models for Scripture* [Grand Rapids: Eerdmans, 1994], p. 249).

[34]Bavinck, *Reformed Dogmatics*, 1:443.

[35]Warfield, *Inspiration*, p. 157.

[36]Ibid., p. 158.

[37]Ibid.

tion involves more than providence, and this "more" is what enables Warfield to conclude that God's activity is not merely past but present. Whatever inspiration is, it allows us to think of God's word as active and alive in Scripture. Readers no longer have to go on exegetical digs into the linguistic past because they "can listen directly to the Divine voice itself speaking immediately in the Scripture word."[38]

Perhaps Warfield's view of inspiration eludes this dogmatic location after all. I leave that judgment to the experts. To return to our main question: Is the doctrine of the Trinity doing any heavy lifting yet? If not, should that bother us? My answer: Not yet, and yes, it should.

Inspiration and incarnation: "And the word became text . . ." Now we come to a second possible dogmatic home for the doctrine of Scripture, one that proceeds from the perception of a certain likeness between the Word's becoming flesh (incarnate) and the word's becoming text (being inscripturated). Might Christology be the best way to discover the connection between Scripture and the Trinity? A number of thinkers, past and present, find the comparison irresistible. After all, both Jesus and the Bible are not only human but also divine: two natures in one person, or should I say, two natures in one *papyrus?*

Listen to Balthasar: "The Word that is God took a body of flesh, in order to be man. . . . He took on, at the same time, a body consisting of syllables, scripture, . . . verbal utterance."[39] The chapter on inspiration in *Dei Verbum,* the Vatican II document that deals with revelation, quotes John Chrysostom's comment about God condescending to adapt his language to our human nature and then is similarly explicit: "For the words of God expressed in human language, have been made like human discourse, just as of old the Word of the eternal Father, when he took to Himself the weak flesh of humanity, became like other men."[40]

Not to be outdone, the evangelical authors of the 1982 Chicago Statement on Biblical Hermeneutics declare: "We affirm that as Christ is God and Man in One Person, so Scripture is, indivisibly, God's Word in human

---

[38]Ibid.

[39]Hans Urs von Balthasar, "The Place of Theology," in *Explorations in Theology,* vol. 1, *The Word Made Flesh* (San Francisco: Ignatius Press, 1989), p. 149.

[40]*Dei Verbum* 3.13.

language." In both cases, something in humanity is conceived by the Holy Spirit. Bernard Ramm speaks of "revelation in the flesh and blood of human language."[41] Recent years have seen a spate of evangelical proposals that mine the incarnational model of Scripture.[42] Peter Enns, an Old Testament scholar, uses the incarnational analogy to remind us to take the Bible's historical and cultural conditionedness—its *humanity*—with the utmost seriousness: "That the Bible, at every turn, shows how 'connected' it is to its own world is a necessary consequence of God incarnating himself."[43]

The incarnational analogy offers a way of thinking about the relation between the Word of God and the words of Scripture: "The incarnation becomes an analogy for the Bible in its divine and human identity."[44] The relation is analogical rather than univocal because the words of the Bible are not exactly the same as the Word that was with God as mentioned in the Prologue to the Fourth Gospel. N. T. Wright knows that the analogy between the Bible and Jesus is not exact, but he believes that "provided it is seen *as an analogy*, not as a precise two-way identity, it remains helpful."[45]

To say that it is only an analogy acknowledges that it can be pressed too far. This will be helpful to keep in mind. Let us agree that every version of what I am calling the "incarnational analogy" eventually equivocates or breaks down. The challenge will be to follow the parallel between inspiration and inscripturation as long as it is illumining but no farther.

The analogy is clearer in what it denies than in what it affirms. Theolo-

---

[41]Bernard Ramm, *Special Revelation and the Word of God* (Grand Rapids: Eerdmans, 1961), p. 150.

[42]Besides the ones mentioned in this paragraph, see especially Jens Zimmerman, *Recovering Theological Hermeneutics: An Incarnational-Trinitarian Theory of Interpretation* (Grand Rapids: Baker, 2004).

[43]Peter Enns, *Inspiration and Incarnation: Evangelicals and the Problem of the Old Testament* (Grand Rapids: Baker, 2005), p. 20. Enns suggests that if God speaks at a certain time and place, he does so in ways that make sense to the people where they are, and that may mean speaking in terms of ancient Near Eastern mythology (p. 56). See also his "Preliminary Observations on an Incarnational Model of Scripture: Its Viability and Usefulness," in *Calvin Theological Journal* 42 (2007): 219-36. In this article Enns seeks to appropriate Warfield and Hodge to his cause, but from the passages that he cites, it is not clear to me that they would espouse the incarnational paradigm even if they were to affirm, as Warfield does, that Scripture is "at once divine and human in every part" (Warfield, "The Divine and Human in the Bible," *Presbyterian Journal*, May 3, 1894; cited in Enns, "Preliminary Observations," p. 221).

[44]Jeannine K. Brown, *Scripture as Communication* (Grand Rapids: Baker, 2007), p. 253.

[45]Wright, *The Last Word*, p. 130.

gians regularly cite christological heresies to criticize inadequate views of Scripture. For example, views that deny the contributions of human authors are routinely dismissed as "Docetic" (i.e., Jesus/Scripture only *appears* to be human). Similarly, the verbal dictation theory is deemed "Monophysite"[46] (one-natured) or Apollinarian insofar as the divine Logos replaces the human mind/voice.[47]

Other theologians, however, use the incarnational analogy in order to affirm inerrancy. The 1943 papal encyclical, *Divino Afflante Spiritu*, states: "For as the substantial Word of God became like to men in all things, 'except sin,' so the words of God, expressed in human language, are made like to human speech in every respect, except error."[48] On the Protestant side, Richard Gaffin describes the "Old Amsterdam" theologians in much the same way: "The correlate to the sinlessness of Christ is that Scripture is without error."[49] Bavinck takes this analogy and runs with it: "But just as Christ's human nature, however weak and lowly, remained free from sin, so also Scripture is 'conceived without defect or stain'; totally human in all its parts but also divine in all its parts."[50] Bavinck here posits an analogical connection between biblical inerrancy and Jesus' impeccability.[51] If we

---

[46]See Aidan Nichols, *The Shape of Catholic Theology* (Collegeville, Minn.: Liturgical Press, 1991), pp. 114-30.

[47]Though recent theologians have flocked to the incarnational analogy, many who hold an equally high view of Scripture resist the temptation to tie the doctrine of Scripture to the mast of Christology, preferring instead to use the category of divine accommodation. Bruce Vawter notes that the Fathers recognized the "divine condescension" involved in the production of Scripture. Chrysostom in particular spoke of "accommodation." Calvin too speaks of divine accommodation and avoids mention of incarnation in connection with the Bible as the word of God. Finally, though Bernard Ramm sees the incarnation as the supreme instance of accommodation, he stops short of describing inscripturation in terms of incarnation. At the core of the phenomenon of inspiration is not a christological but an anthropological principle: "By *anthropic* we mean accommodated to man, his language, his culture, and his powers" (Ramm, *Special Revelation and the Word of God*, p. 33).

[48]*Divino Afflante Spiritu*, §37.

[49]Richard Gaffin, "Old Amsterdam and Inerrancy?" *Westminster Theological Journal* 45 (1983): 268.

[50]Bavinck, *Reformed Dogmatics*, 1:435.

[51]Still other theologians focus on kenosis. Abraham Kuyper writes: "As the Logos has not appeared *in the form of glory*, but in the form of a servant," so as "a product of writing, the Holy Scripture also bears on its forehead the mark of the form of a servant" (*Principles of Sacred Theology* [Grand Rapids: Eerdmans, 1954], p. 479). Balthasar goes further than Kuyper and suggests that kenosis involves a certain "emptying out" of divine prerogatives that has an effect of Scripture's truth: "The Bible's humiliated form, with its historical errors and stylistic infelicities, is an analogue of Jesus Christ's humiliation on the cross"

press this analogy too far, inerrancy ends up requiring a kind of textual equivalent to the Immaculate Conception, a miracle that guarantees the flawless humanity of what is conceived.[52] The incarnation, however, is a unique and particular event, not a general principle that we can apply to other phenomena, not even biblical inspiration.

To be sure, invoking incarnation does appear to move one's doctrine of Scripture closer to the doctrine of the Trinity. But is this the best way to connect the doctrinal dots? How far may we apply the Chalcedonian formula to our doctrine of Scripture? It is time to get down to the conceptual nuts and bolts, or rather, persons and natures. "Two natures in one person . . . without confusion or separation." Does Chalcedon's formula stretch or does it break? May we say of Scripture that it is "fully divine" and "fully human"? And is there only one person speaking in it (e.g., the Holy Spirit) or two or more?

Consider first the two natures. To what in Scripture do we wish to ascribe divinity, and which divine properties in particular do we have in mind? According to the Lutheran doctrine of *communicatio idiomatum*, there is a transfer or properties from the Son's divine nature to the human. (This is the idea that allowed Lutherans to affirm that Christ's body is "ubiquitous" and thus consubstantial with the bread in the Eucharist.) Does this work with Scripture?

Well, the Bible clearly lacks some of the so-called incommunicable attributes of God. It is hard to see how the Bible could be said to be "infinite," "eternal" or "omnipresent." Yet the Bible does say that the law of the Lord is "perfect" (Ps 19:7) and that "the word of the Lord endures forever" (1 Pet 1:25 NASB), so perhaps there is a sense in which Scripture *is* eternal and immutable. On balance, however, when we think of Scripture as di-

---

(see W. T. Dickens, *Hans Urs von Balthasar's Theological Aesthetics: A Model for Post-Critical Biblical Interpretation* [Notre Dame, Ind.: University of Notre Dame Press, 2003], p. 180).

[52]Some Roman Catholics appeal to the Immaculate Conception—the doctrine that Mary was conceived without original sin—in order to explain why Jesus did not inherit sinful humanity. The parallel, then, is between Mary's sinless womb (a result of her immaculate conception) as the condition of Jesus' impeccability and Scripture's equally pure words (Scripture's "immaculate conception") as fitting containers or conveyors of the inerrant textual message concerning Jesus Christ. In both cases—Mary and the authors of Scripture, respectively—the Spirit is present and active at the moment of conception.

vine, we typically think in terms of God's communicable attributes—goodness and truthfulness, for example.

Reformed theologians, by contrast, insist that it is the *person* to whom the properties of each nature should be ascribed. Is there an equivalent in Scripture to the Chalcedonian "in one person": one *hypostasis?* In asking whether there is a kind of hypostatic union in Scripture, we take the incarnational analogy to the limit. Christ is one person with two natures, but Scripture is one text with (at least) two authors. What is singular in Christ (one speaking subject or hypostasis) is plural in Scripture. There is a "voicing" problem.

Some who see the problem try nevertheless to salvage the analogy. According to Gaffin "Inscripturation arises necessarily from the incarnation and would not exist apart from it. This reality . . . gives Scripture a unique theanthropic character ('everything divine and everything human'), without, however, involving some sort of hypostatic union between divine and human elements."[53] But this leaves unanswered the question *Who* is speaking to the church in and through Scripture (and how many speakers are there)? If the parallel with incarnation is to work, "there must be some verbal analogue to the hypostatic union."[54]

And now for something completely etymological. *Hypostasis* means "standing under" and in the formula of Chalcedon refers to the person who undergoes the life of Jesus Christ. That person is the second person of the Trinity, the eternal Word. To posit the eternal Word as the hypostasis of Scripture as well would jeopardize the uniqueness of the incarnation. This is perhaps why the *Westminster Confession of Faith* says not that the Spirit *becomes* Scripture but that he is the supreme authority "speaking in the Scripture."[55]

The operative term, then, is not "standing under" *(hypostasis)* but "speaking in." Eureka! We have found it, the key equivocation in the incar-

---

[53]Gaffin, commenting on Ridderbos and Bavinck, in "Old Amsterdam and Inerrancy?" p. 268.

[54]Telford Work, *Living and Active: Scripture in the Economy of Salvation* (Grand Rapids: Eerdmans, 2002), p. 82. In context, Work is examining Barth's version of the christological analogy.

[55]*Westminster Confession of Faith,* I.x. Cf. T. F. Torrance's charge that Warfield's theory of verbal inspiration "incarnates" (or perhaps "incarcerates") the third divine person in the Bible (so Work, *Living and Active,* p. 29).

national analogy. The watchword is no longer "two natures in one person" but "two voices in one text." For the Bible is not a person but a work, a text made up of words. Speech, whether oral or written, is a kind of extension of a person. My speech is neither wholly me nor is it wholly other than me. The present talk is neither begotten nor made, but *done* by me.[56] What authors do with words often comes to be identified with them: "That's Dostoyevsky," "That's Dickens," "That's Dickinson," we might say after hearing a passage from *The Brothers Karamazov* or *David Copperfield* or "I heard a fly buzz—when I died," respectively.

In a biblical example, Paul writes to the Corinthians: "For though absent in body I am present in spirit, and as if present, I have already pronounced judgment" (1 Cor 5:3 RSV). Or again: "I do not want to appear to be frightening you with my letters. For they say, 'His letters are weighty and strong, but his bodily presence is weak. . . .' Let such a person understand that what we say by letter when absent, we do when present" (2 Cor 10:9-11 ESV). These examples show how Paul's written words extend Paul's personal presence even though they do not contain Paul's personhood.[57]

Speaking of words, let me introduce another Greek term: *phaskō*, "to state something with confidence."[58] Paul does this in Acts 25:19, where we read about "a certain Jesus, who was dead, but whom Paul asserted [*ephasken*] to be alive" (ESV). In its noun form, *phasis* means "information concerning a person or event; a report" (as in Acts 21:31). If I belabor the etymological point, it is because Roman Jakobson, the linguist, christens one of the six functions of language the *phatic*.[59] For Jakobson, however, the phatic function of language has less to do with stating things than with establishing and maintaining a relationship between addresser and addressee. That, too, is part of communication, and it is one of the reasons that Paul wrote his epistles.

But we were talking about the hypostatic union. The point of my digres-

---

[56]For a fuller development of these distinctions, see my *Is There a Meaning in This Text?* (Grand Rapids: Zondervan, 1998), pp. 225-26.

[57]I am indebted to Work, *Living and Active*, pp. 95-96, for this way of formulating the matter.

[58]Cf. *phēmi*, the Greek verb for "to say; to state something orally or in writing."

[59]Roman Jakobson, "Closing Statement: Linguistics and Poetics," in *Style in Language*, ed. Thomas A. Sebeok (Cambridge, Mass.: MIT Press, 1960). See also John Fiske, *Introduction to Communication Studies*, 2nd ed. (New York: Routledge, 1990), pp. 35-37.

sion was to suggest that inscripturation involves personal presence, but not personhood: "Verbal union is not hypostatic union in that language is not full personhood. Inlibration is not incarnation because words are not flesh."[60] What we have in Scripture is Paul and the Spirit doing things—stating things with confidence; establishing and maintaining relationships—with words that are not begotten (and thus of the same substance as the speaker) but rather bespoken. Ladies and Gentlemen, I give you the *hypophatic* union: the concept of two voices speaking in the same stretch of words.

Still, I cannot help thinking that the incarnational analogy may be more trouble than it is worth. Chalcedon was designed to clarify the being of Jesus Christ, not Scripture. Please do not misunderstand: there is nothing wrong with Chalcedon, just as there was nothing wrong with the paper clip I used so cleverly in my skateboard to replace a screw. However, that improvisation ended with a broken arm. I wonder, then, about the wisdom of using language formulated for one truth to express another.[61]

Inspiration and revelation: "Guard the good deposit." And so to a third possible home for Scripture: the doctrine of revelation. We can proceed quickly over this more familiar ground; many if not most of us have probably learned to think of Scripture as an aspect of the doctrine of the knowledge of God. God makes himself known in a general way through nature and conscience, in a special way through words and deeds, and definitively in Jesus Christ. Scripture is tied to revelation because the canonical testimony of the prophets and apostles is the only authorized record of Jesus' life and work we have.

The term *revelation* refers both to the event and to the result: the truth made known. Revelation, at least according to the dominant evangelical view in the twentieth century, consists in information about the nature and works of God that could not otherwise be known. What inscripturation preserves is not the event of revelation but its meaning, its cognitive content. Inspiration thus serves to preserve divine revelation in written form.

---

[60]Work, *Living and Active*, p. 95.

[61]For other critiques of the incarnational analogy, from theologians as diverse as Markus Barth and James Barr, see ibid., pp. 27-31. See also Webster: "It has to be asserted that no divine nature or properties are to be predicated of Scripture; its substance is that of a creaturely reality" (*Holy Scripture*, p. 23).

The evangelical understanding of the Bible as revelation was hammered out largely in debate with neo-orthodox theologians who claimed that God revealed himself, not information about himself. In the highly charged epistemological atmosphere of modernity, the claim that revelation was personal rather than propositional led evangelicals to defend the traditional view of the Bible as a treasure house of divinely given information. Carl F. H. Henry insisted on the propositional nature of special revelation in Scripture: "God supernaturally communicated his revelation to chosen spokesmen in the express form of cognitive truths, . . . in sentences that are not internally contradictory."[62]

What comes to the fore in many evangelical doctrines of Scripture is an insistence that the Bible is the word of God because it contains propositional revelation: the good deposit of verbal-conceptual doctrinal truth. I am in substantial agreement with the intentions of the historical defenders of this notion. Whether this is the sum and substance of the doctrine of Scripture is another question. Let me mention a few concerns about the emphasis on revelation as a deposit of divinely given true statements about God and his dealings with the world: (1) It may lead some to do less than justice to the literary and poetic dimensions of Scripture by seeking to translate the variety of biblical discourse into propositional form.[63] (2) It may exaggerate the informative dimension of language to the detriment of other legitimate dimensions. Finally and most pointedly for present purposes, (3) it may lead some to detach Scripture from the history of redemption from which it arose. But this cuts Scripture off from its life-source and makes Scripture a theologically "inorganic" product that can stand on its own. Bavinck complains that, for such theology, "it seemed as if there was nothing behind Scripture."[64] Webster concurs: "In an objectified account of revelation, the inspired *product* is given priority over the revelatory, sanctifying, and inspiring activities of the divine agent."[65]

Well, why not? After all, as the angel tells the author of the book of Revelation at the very end of the Bible, "These words are trustworthy and true"

---

[62]Henry, *God, Revelation, and Authority* (Waco, Tex.: Word, 1979), 3:457.

[63]So Ramm, *Special Revelation and the Word of God*, p. 155. For an example of this tendency, see Henry, *God, Revelation, and Authority*, 3:417, 453, 463, 477.

[64]Bavinck, *Reformed Dogmatics*, 1:381.

[65]Webster, *Holy Scripture*, p. 33.

(Rev 22:6 ESV). That revelation is the logical home for a doctrine of Scripture is the implied thesis of a recent book titled *The Trustworthiness of God: Perspectives on the Nature of Scripture.*[66] According to Francis Watson, who wrote a response to the book and served as a kind of external examiner, "The correlation of divine and scriptural trustworthiness is regarded as constitutive of evangelical identity. What Scripture says is what God says, and to be 'evangelical' is to commit oneself to that equation."[67]

But is this, asks Watson, the best we can do? Is there anything *distinctly Christian* in the concept of trustworthy words of a trustworthy God? On a formal level, could one not say something similar about the Qur'an? Watson encourages us to be more evangelical by developing our doctrine of Scripture in light of the *euangelion* that lies at its heart: "According to the gospel, God is *triune*; that is to say, the word 'God' is properly used only when supplemented by reference (explicit or implicit) to Jesus and his Spirit."[68] Watson's verdict on the idea that Scripture is a deposit of divinely revealed truth is rather harsh: "'Evangelical' discussions of the trustworthiness of Scripture often seem to bypass the *euangelion* [gospel]. . . . The result is a doctrine of scriptural . . . 'authority' in which Jesus himself is relatively marginal."[69] Is this indeed the best we can do? Watson thinks not and thus points us in the direction of our next stop with his own answer: "God has shown himself faithful or trustworthy by uttering in Jesus the single word: Yes!"[70]

"GOD SPEAKS": TWO KINDS OF CONCEPTUAL ELABORATION

Karl Barth's trinitarian theology of the Word. If the Trinity is conspicuous by its absence in traditional evangelical doctrines of Scripture, it is conspicuous by its dominating presence in Karl Barth's treatment of the subject. This is not the place to summarize Barth's *Church Dogmatics*, not even the first half-volume. Suffice it to say that Barth, too, locates the doctrine of Scripture under the rubric of revelation, though for him revelation is less a deposit than a dynamic, the free act of God making himself known

---

[66]Paul Helm and Carl R. Trueman, eds., *The Trustworthiness of God: Perspectives on the Nature of Scripture* (Grand Rapids: Eerdmans, 2002).
[67]Watson, "An Evangelical Response," in ibid., p. 287.
[68]Ibid.
[69]Ibid., p. 288.
[70]Ibid., p. 289.

through himself: "God's Word is God Himself in His revelation."[71] The Father is the Revealer, the Son the Revelation, the Spirit the Revealedness (i.e., revelation successfully received). The triune God is identical with the revealing agent, the revealed content and the effect of revelation. As to Scripture, it is one of the three forms of revelation, the others being preaching and, the definitive form, Jesus Christ.[72]

For Barth, everything in Christian theology begins, and begins again, with God's revelation in Jesus Christ: "We arrive at the doctrine of the Trinity by no other way than that of an analysis of the concept of revelation."[73] The key premise, the root of Barth's doctrine of the Trinity, is that "in God's revelation God's Word is identical with God himself,"[74] for only God can make God known. Note Barth's insistence that it is the Trinity, not Scripture, that explains what we mean by "Word of God." The primary medium of God's speech is not language but Logos: the living and personal speaking subject, Jesus Christ. As Lord of his "wording," the Logos is free to reveal himself to others or not. For Barth, to say that "God speaks" is to refer to the sovereign act by which Jesus Christ presents himself to another. Barth concludes: "We cannot regard the presence of God's Word in the Bible as an attribute inhering once for all in this book."[75]

Where, then, does this leave Scripture? The standard Barthian formulas are well known: the Bible is not itself revelation but *becomes* so when God in his freedom uses it to present Christ. For Barth, "the Word of God is a *happening*, not a thing."[76] This explains his hostility to the notion of Scripture as a deposit of revealed truth. Such a deposit, even if originally given by God, is now separated from God's free agency. To "propositionalize" revelation makes it a noun rather than a verb, a worldly entity rather than

---

[71]Karl Barth, *Church Dogmatics* 1/1 (Edinburgh: T & T Clark, 1975), p. 295.

[72]Interestingly, the only analogy to this threefold form of the Word of God is the triunity of God, according to Barth: "We can substitute for revelation, Scripture, and proclamation the names of the divine persons Father, Son, and Holy Spirit and *vice versa*" (ibid., p. 121). As my argument below will show, I agree with Telford Work: "Barth's intuition that Scripture repeats and reflects—*participates* in—the work of the Trinity is fundamentally correct, even if we must develop it in a different way" (*Living and Active*, p. 92).

[73]Barth, *Church Dogmatics*, 1/1:312.

[74]Ibid., p. 304.

[75]Ibid., p. 530.

[76]John Godsey, recorder and editor, *Karl Barth's Table Talk* (Richmond, Va.: John Knox Press, [1963]), p. 26.

a divine event. Barth accuses conservative Protestants of holding a doctrine of Scripture that is "grounded upon itself apart from the mystery of Christ and the Holy Ghost."[77] In this context, Barth deploys the image of the Bible as a "paper Pope" delivered into the hands of its interpreters: "that the Bible is the Word of God was now transformed . . . from a statement about the free grace of God into a statement about the nature of the Bible as exposed to human inquiry brought under human control."[78] It is therefore for divine freedom that Barth sets God's Word free—free from objectification through inscripturation.

Is *this* the best an evangelical can do?[79] Barth rightly wants to uphold the unsurpassable dignity of Jesus Christ. One wonders, however, whether he is working with a biblical notion of God's freedom. God, the Lord of all, is free to speak or not to speak; yet if he *does* speak, is he free *not* to stand by his words? No, for he cannot deny himself. God is free, then, to make or not make a promise. Yet if God does make a promise, his own freedom binds him to keep it, for God reveals himself to be the one who determines to do what he says (i.e., to be faithful and true), and *this* is the ground of God's, and hence Scripture's, trustworthiness.

Nicholas Wolterstorff's analytic philosophy of divine discourse. Does God make promises? It is just here that Nicholas Wolterstorff weighs in, noting that, for Barth, the biblical witness is merely human speech. Yes, Barth uses the term *speech-act (Rede-Tat)*,[80] but Wolterstorff is not convinced. He finds three problems in Barth's view. In the first place, Barth restricts revelation to the life of Jesus Christ; the "speech" of God turns out to be not a stretch of language but history (i.e., the life of Jesus Christ).

---

[77]Barth, *Church Dogmatics*, 1/2:525.

[78]Ibid., p. 522.

[79]Some wonder whether Barth is christological enough: "Can his approach really account for Jesus' own stance towards the Scriptures of his day and the commissioned witness of his apostles?" (Mark Thompson, "Barth's Doctrine of Scripture," in *Engaging with Barth*, ed. David Gibson and Daniel Strange [Nottingham, U.K.: Apollos, 2008], p. 185). Telford Work makes a similar point: "If revelation is an event, why does Scripture cite Scripture?" (*Living and Active*, p. 79). Moreover, if the incarnation is no obstacle to God's freedom, why should inscripturation—where God binds himself to human speech rather than human flesh—be any different? To say that Scripture only becomes God's word when God in his freedom makes use of it is, to return to the christological heresies, what *adoptionists* said about the Logos taking on humanity.

[80]Barth, *Church Dogmatics*, 1/1:163.

Second, Barth views the Bible as human rather than divine speech for "the witness does not speak in the name of God."[81] Though God graciously employs the Bible's human words, they remain purely human speech: "God did not speak by way of the authoring of these books . . . [but] by way of a human being: . . . Jesus Christ."[82] Barth restricts what God speaks or authors to what he says in the person of Jesus Christ.

Third, what happens when the Bible becomes revelation has nothing to do with divine speech either. Barth connects the Bible to the event of revelation via a nonspeech-act in the life of the interpreter. The revelatory event is not a matter of God now speaking the words but of another kind of action altogether, effected by the Spirit: "God must so act on me that I am 'grabbed' by the content of what God has already said [in Jesus Christ]. I see no reason to call this action 'speech.'"[83]

There is no little irony in an analytic philosopher complaining that the preeminent twentieth-century theologian of God's Word has no room for God's *speech* in the dogmatic inn. "It's surprising. Barth is the great theologian of the Word of God."[84] So why does he shy away from identifying the Bible as God's speech? Wolterstorff has two explanations: First, he wants to honor the results of biblical criticism and acknowledge the full humanity of the Bible. Second, he does not want to compromise God's freedom by implying that, to use Warfield's rubric, "What Scripture says, God says,"[85] for such a statement would make God's Word captive to the words of the Bible.

Wolterstorff writes as an analytic philosopher for whom conceptual cleanliness is next to godliness. He wants to know precisely what we mean when we say "God speaks." For example, he spends considerable

---

[81]Nicholas Wolterstorff, *Divine Discourse: Philosophical Reflections on the Claim That God Speaks* (Cambridge: Cambridge University Press, 1995), p. 68.

[82]Ibid., p. 70. Wolterstorff distinguishes *authoring* a text from *presenting* a text to someone (pp. 55, 72).

[83]Ibid., p. 72.

[84]Ibid., p. 73. For an alternative and opposing view of Barth, see Stephen H. Webb, *The Divine Voice: Christian Proclamation and the Theology of Sound* (Grand Rapids: Brazos, 2004), pp. 171-76. According to Webb's reading of Barth, "God's voice is an event because it cannot become a property of any object in the world; . . . Barth's nuanced position is that God can cause the Bible to be God's word, but the Bible does not intrinsically represent God's voice" (p. 173).

[85]See B. B. Warfield, "'It Says:' 'Scripture Says:' 'God says,'" in *Inspiration and Authority of the Bible*, pp. 299-348, esp. p. 348.

energy in distinguishing between speaking and revealing. Revealing is a matter of dispelling ignorance.[86] Speaking, by contrast, "is a fundamentally different sort of action from communication [of information]."[87] I can make a promise by saying "I promise," but I cannot reveal something to you unless I transmit to you a piece of knowledge about which you were formerly ignorant.

On Wolterstorff's view, speaking is a matter of an agent taking up a certain normative stance with regard to one's speech-act. If I am driving on the tollway and signal a left turn, I acquire a normative standing: I ascribe to myself the obligation to turn left. Similarly, in speaking we acquire a whole host of rights and responsibilities. If I shout "Fire!" in a crowded theater, I am not merely transmitting information but also taking responsibility for my assertion and implying that you ought to trust me and flee the building. The implication for interpreters is that we need to determine what stance an author assumes vis-à-vis one's words. Such authorial discourse interpretation has nothing to do with plumbing the depths of an author's psyche, but with determining what assertings, promisings, warnings and so forth may be ascribed to an author who sets down just these words in just this order in the public domain of language.

God also acquires the rights and duties of a speaker. We can ascribe normative standing to God because God stands by his words (i.e., God does things with words that count as promising, warning, asserting, etc.). How can one who is immaterial spirit produce sounds so as to speak? Wolterstorff claims that God intervenes in history to cause events generative of divine discourse. In Genesis 9:9-17 the rainbow is the sign of God's covenant with the earth that the waters will never again become a flood to destroy all flesh. The rainbow is a sign; it has meaning. But what makes the rainbow count as a divine promise? Colors in a misty sky count as divine discourse only because there was an earlier instance of divine speech: the historical moment when God instituted the rainbow as a celestial promissory note. We cannot know what God intends by anything, however, unless somewhere and sometime there is an instance of literal divine speech.[88]

---

[86]Wolterstorff, *Divine Discourse*, p. 23.
[87]Ibid., p. 32.
[88]Of course, this simply pushes the question back a step: how did God speak to Noah? It is

Only speech disambiguates behavior, even—nay, especially!—when the behavior in question is divine.

With this thought we arrive at Wolterstorff's unique contribution to the discussion of God and Scripture. It trades on some fine conceptual tuning, such as the distinction between a person's reporting what somebody else has already said and a person's saying something by way of another's speaking.[89] The human authors of the Bible are not simply transcribing what they hear God saying in their heads. Divine inspiration is not yet divine discourse. Inspiration is a matter of causal generation, not communication: "The phenomenon of X inspiring Y to say such-and-such is not the same as X saying such-and-such."[90] How does X (God) say such and such? By appropriating human discourse: "To authorize a text is in effect to declare: let this text serve as medium of my discoursing."[91] Scripture is divinely appropriated discourse—discourse whereby one person (God) says/does something with words that another person (e.g., Isaiah, Paul) utters or inscribes.[92] When does God appropriate human words? Wolterstorff again appeals to a divine intervention in history, specifically, to Jesus' commissioning of the apostles to be his witnesses. The assumption is that God is acting by way of Jesus' acting. God appropriates the law and the prophets when Jesus co-opts them as his before-the-fact witnesses: "it is they [the Scriptures] that bear witness about me" (Jn 5:39 ESV; cf. Lk 24:27).

Wolterstorff's work has filled a longstanding lacuna between theologians who focus on God's Word without sufficient analytic precision and philosophers who analyze divine action without taking account of speaking as a form of divine action. His book—*Divine Discourse: Philosophical Reflections on the Claim that God Speaks*—is a landmark work that both recovers traditional wisdom and develops it in exciting new directions.

---

not entirely clear that what Wolterstorff says below about divinely appropriated discourse works in the case of Noah. Wolterstorff's main point nevertheless stands: God must *do* something—must make some kind of intervention in history—in order to author or authorize something as divine speech.

[89]Ibid., p. 282. Wolterstorff's conceptual elaboration of God's speaking conforms to the style of analytic philosophy. The responses have been in kind. See the criticisms of Paul Helm, Philip L. Quinn and Merold Westphal, together with Wolterstorff's response, in *Religious Studies* 37 (2001): 249-306.

[90]Wolterstorff, *Divine Discourse*, p. 283.

[91]Ibid., p. 41..

[92]Ibid., p. 38.

Wolterstorff approaches the topic of God as a philosopher, however, and it is telling that both of the operative terms in Barth's account—*triune* and *revelation*—are conspicuously absent from his own conceptual elaboration of divine discourse. The term "divine" in Wolterstorff's title is thus somewhat generic; presumably the analysis could work in Judaism or Islam as well as in Christianity. Moreover, because he does not make his case for divine speech on specifically christological or pneumatological grounds, divine discourse becomes a function of the divine nature rather than the divine persons. The one God "appropriates" discourse, we might say, yet this appropriating work is not "appropriated" to any one divine person in particular.[93] His model stops short of considering *triune* discourse.

CONCLUDING UNSCIENTIFIC CLIFFHANGER

It is time to sum up, at least provisionally. How far have we come, and what have we accomplished, besides putting question marks over some of the preferred ways of thinking theologically about the Bible?

1. We located the problem by examining the unevenly yoked doctrinal statements of the ETS.

2. We saw how the doctrines of the Trinity and Scripture have come apart in modernity.

3. We examined three doctrinal locations in which to house the doctrine of Scripture and say how it renders the Bible "of God."

4. We visited the first major attempt in church history to tie Scripture and the Trinity together via an analysis of the Word of God (Barth).

5. We discovered a problem with the above and the promise of a new approach (Wolterstorff), only to discover that it too is underdeveloped with regard to the Trinity.

It is not yet clear, therefore, where in the house of theology the doctrine of Scripture belongs. I take up the task of resolving the problem of Scripture's homelessness in the following chapter.

---

[93]I explain and develop this ancient doctrine of the divine appropriations in the next chapter.

2

Triune Discourse

Theological Reflections
on the Claim That God Speaks
(Part 2)

KEVIN J. VANHOOZER

INTRODUCTION: GOD TALKS!

"Garbo talks!" screamed *Variety* magazine in a 1929 headline marking Greta Garbo's transition from silent films to talkies. Five years earlier and with somewhat less fanfare, Karl Barth made history by announcing, *Deux dixit*, "God talks," and by identifying the central problem of dogmatics as "God's own speaking."[1]

As we saw in the previous chapter, Barth and Wolterstorff offer two contrasting conceptual elaborations of the claim that God speaks. Barth's account is richly trinitarian yet murky when it comes to language and semantics; Wolterstorff's account is philosophically rigorous but reticent when it comes to the Trinity.[2] One wonders whether either one, on his own, gives an account of God's relation to the Bible robust enough to capture

---

[1]Karl Barth, *Göttingen Dogmatics*, trans. Geoffrey W. Bromiley, vol. 1 (Grand Rapids: Eerdmans, 1991), p. 11.

[2]See Nicholas Wolterstorff, *Divine Discourse: Philosophical Reflections on the Claim that God Speaks* (Cambridge: Cambridge University Press, 1995). I am not at all implying that Wolterstorff rejects the doctrine of the Trinity, only that his account of divine speaking is only notionally trinitarian. Wolterstorff's account of divine speaking does not really need any categories or concepts drawn from the doctrine of the Trinity. The one important exception is his appeal to Christology, specifically to God's commissioning the prophets and apostles by way of Jesus' commissioning, on the grounds that Jesus speaks for God and as God.

both what Scripture says about itself and what the Westminster Confession of Faith affirms about the "Holy Spirit speaking in the Scripture."

The present chapter merges the best of Barth and Wolterstorff by attending to the biblical depiction of God's speech agency in order to set forth an evangelical, gospel-centered account of the Trinity and Scripture.[3] The gospel is the good news that God has freely chosen to communicate something of himself to us, the human creature. The gospel is part and parcel of what I shall call the economy of communication. Both the economic and the immanent Trinity are, I believe, best expressed in terms of "communicative action for communion," for God's outward work (his being *ad extra*) corresponds to or images God's inner life (his being *ad intra*): God is as God does. This economy of communication embraces both revelation and redemption—both divine speaking and divinely enabled human hearing—a crucial point to keep in mind as we continue to think about the right dogmatic location for a doctrine of Scripture. But we begin with a little biblical theology.

DIVINE DISCOURSE: GOD AND LANGUAGE

God's speaking is a clear and pervasive biblical theme: "Long ago, at many times and in many ways, God spoke to our fathers by the prophets" (Heb 1:1).[4] God both creates and covenants by speaking.[5] In Exodus 3, God calls to Moses out of the burning bush and names himself "I AM WHO I AM" (Ex 3:14 NASB). (Curiously, Wolterstorff passes over such biblical examples of direct divine discourse.) This act of *saying*, in which God audibly relates to Moses through the medium of Hebrew words, is arguably as important

---

[3]I agree with Wolterstorff that "revelation" may be too narrow a category to describe Scripture. Yet I also agree with Barth that no account of Scripture is sufficiently Christian when one keeps the doctrine of the Trinity in abeyance. For a description of Barth's position, see my preceding chapter.

[4]All Scripture references, unless otherwise noted, are from the English Standard Version of the Bible (ESV).

[5]The image of God is arguably a matter of communicative agent too; we speak because God first spoke to us. Humans are created to speak with God and others, created with the capacity to make and receive meaning through language and to name the world. See my "Human Being, Individual and Social," in *The Cambridge Companion to Christian Doctrine*, ed. Colin E. Gunton (Cambridge: Cambridge University Press, 1997); cf. Richard B. Gaffin, "Speech and the Image of God: Biblical Reflections on Language and Its Uses," in *The Pattern of Sound Doctrine: Systematic Theology at the Westminster Seminaries*, ed. David VanDrunen (Phillipsburg, N.J.: Presbyterian & Reformed, 2004), pp. 181-93.

as the name that God reveals.[6] Moses stands on holy ground because he is in the communicative presence of God, in a "speaking-with" relationship.[7] As Christians walk through the postmodern valley of the shadow of deconstruction, it is good to know that language is a God-ordained gift, a created good, a means of fellowship with God and others.

Consider what God does in, through and by speaking: He names (Gen 17:5), promises (Gen 15:5; Tit 1:2), commands (Ex 20:1-17), warns, exhorts, instructs, comforts and so forth. Consider, too, how many of these acts *require* the medium of language. That is because illocutions—what we do in saying—are performed by way of locutionary acts. The correspondence between revelatory word and redemptive deed is well known. What is less well known or appreciated is that much of what God does—including some of the key events in salvation history: making a covenant; giving the law; declaring righteous—takes place *by way of speaking*.

The paucity of systematic theological attention to the theme of divine speaking is surprising in light of its biblical prominence, especially in light of Scripture's own contrast between the speaking God of Israel and dumb pagan idols. False gods neither speak nor act; false gods tell no tales. But Yahweh talks! Divine discourse is simply God saying something to someone about something. It is a truth *not* universally acknowledged that much, if not most, of what God does vis-à-vis his human creatures consists in some kind of discourse. Thanks to the divine discourse, the people of God gain understanding of who God is, who they are, what God is doing in the world and what they can do in order rightly to participate in the action.

The episode of the burning bush is paradigmatic. God enters into a dialogue with Moses in order to make known his intentions toward Israel, just as he had done earlier with Adam and the patriarchs.[8] God uses language to tell Moses what he needs to know: "Communication between one mind

---

[6]Theologians and philosophers alike have expended enormous intellectual energy in thinking through the metaphysical implications of the declaration "I AM THAT I AM" (Ex 3:14 KJV).

[7]Oliver Davies, *The Creativity of God: World, Eucharist, Reason* (Cambridge: Cambridge University Press, 2004), p. 79 n. 10.

[8]Cf. Bernard Ramm's comment: "And this conversation springing from the readiness of this Person is special revelation" (*Special Revelation and the Word of God* [Grand Rapids: Eerdmans, 1961], p. 25).

and another is after all for Augustine the fundamental purpose of language."[9]
Here we may recall what I said in the previous chapter about the dual
meaning of *phatic*: language functions not only to convey information but
also to establish relationship.[10] Both functions are on display in Exodus 3,
where God freely speaks in love in order to establish a covenantal relationship. God's love and freedom—the two foci that Barth uses to order all the
divine perfections—are on full display in God's speech agency.[11]

If we attend to all that Scripture shows God doing with language, we see
that revealing proves too confining a category.[12] God does more in speaking (but not less!) than convey information about the unknown: "knowledge in the biblical sense is much more than cognition."[13] Indeed, God uses
language not merely to inform but also to form and transform, permit and
forbid, cajole and console. The point is far from incidental, for what is ultimately at stake is the dogmatic location of the doctrine of Scripture. Does
it really belong under *revelation*?

Modern philosophers and theologians are impressed by the capacity of
language to transmit information. It is tempting to think that this is all
words are good for: to serve as data or, in the case of Scripture, *revealed*
data. Yet this picture of language, and of God's word, is too small. I do not
disagree with what it says; I regret what it omits. Language is richer, more
subtle and more interesting than this picture of information processing suggests. We use language to do many other things besides stating how things
are. When your boss says, "You're fired," you are really unemployed. When

---

[9]Richard A. Norris Jr., "Augustine and the Close of the Ancient Period of Interpretation,"
in *A History of Biblical Interpretation*, vol. 1, *The Ancient Period*, ed. Alan J. Hauser and
Duane F. Watson (Grand Rapids: Eerdmans, 2003), p. 397.

[10]Language is the means by which speech agents perform other types of illocutionary acts as
well, as we shall see below.

[11]I set forth the "metaphysics," as it were, of this dialogical theism in my forthcoming book
Remythologizing Theology (Cambridge: Cambridge University Press, [2009]). Far from
imposing his will on human creatures as a puppeteer manipulates his marionettes, God
deals with his human creatures according to their communicative natures: "Come now, let
us reason together" (Is 1:18). Here we might appeal to Jürgen Habermas's contrast between
strategic action oriented toward instrumental control (i.e., success) and communicative action oriented toward rational consent (i.e., understanding).

[12]Nicholas Wolterstorff insists on making a distinction between illocutionary actions—i.e.,
commanding, promising—and revealing. Yet he concedes that "*by* speaking one invariably
reveals something about oneself" (see his "Response," *Religious Studies* 37 [2001]: 294).

[13]Telford Work, *Living and Active: Scripture in the Economy of Salvation* (Grand Rapids:
Eerdmans, 2002), p. 37.

God says, "You're forgiven," you are really justified.

There is a storm cloud that darkens our discussion of God and language, however, and it is expressed by the formula *finitum non capax infiniti* (the finite is not capable of the infinite). The worry is that mere human words can neither contain nor convey the thought of God. It is best to respond to this concern not speculatively but historically. By nature, the finite is indeed incapable of receiving the infinite. The incarnation is conclusive evidence that, by grace, the finite is made capable of receiving the infinite. Better: God is capable of "receiving" (assuming) human nature *(Deus capax humanitatis).*[14]

The incarnation thus serves as a check on our tendency to play divine transcendence off against human language. Furthermore, if the incarnate Son of God can speak our words, it follows that we have at least one instance of literal divine speech: "When Jesus opens his mouth and speaks Scripture, . . . Barth's distinction evaporates."[15] These words do not become but are the word of God. The line between divine and discourse is breached: the infinite intones.[16]

TRIUNE COMMUNICATION: IMMANENT AND ECONOMIC

We now turn from a consideration of discourse as generically divine to discourse that is specifically triune. True or false: "Has one of the Trinity spoken?" This simple question throws us into the deep end of the theological pool.

God's being in conversation: The immanent Trinity. Is God counted as one speech agent or three? Colin Gunton believes "that if we fail to identify three distinct agents, we are not being true to the biblical witness."[17] Thomas Aquinas concurs: "It is not true that the Father, Son, and Holy

---

[14]E. David Willis, "Finitum non capax infiniti," in *The Westminster Handbook to Reformed Theology*, ed. Donald K. McKim (Louisville, Ky.: Westminster John Knox Press, 2001), p. 84.

[15]Work, *Living and Active*, p. 85. Work moves from Christology to a doctrine of Scripture by rightly noting that much of what Jesus speaks is Scripture, in the form of direct quotations and allusions.

[16]Moreover, much of what Jesus says is Scripture. He cites and alludes to what is now our Old Testament, thus giving a divine seal of approval to the Law and Prophets. We here begin to see the advantages of formulating a doctrine of Scripture in a distinctly trinitarian way.

[17]Colin Gunton, *Act and Being: Towards a Theology of the Divine Attributes* (Grand Rapids: Eerdmans, 2002), p. 143.

Spirit are one speaker."[18] To deny that the divine persons are distinct agents is, for Thomas, to flout orthodoxy.[19]

Some trinitarian theologians are nevertheless uncomfortable with the word "person." They see a significant difference between what Nicaea means by *hypostasis* and what we mean by *person* today. Elizabeth Johnson says that the ancients never intended for us to take *person* literally, as if there were three distinct somebodies, three distinct centers of consciousness, three distinct agents, in the Godhead.[20] The $64,000 theological question is where to locate the center of divine subjectivity or communicative agency: in the oneness of the divine essence or the threeness of the divine persons? Since there is money at stake, I want to hedge my bets. I want to ascribe speaking both to the three persons and to the unitary being of God. My three-plus-one approach adds up to *triune* discourse.

"In the beginning was the Word, and the Word was with God, and the Word was God" (Jn 1:1 NIV). Is this primordial Word monological?[21] To the old chestnut "What was God doing before creation?" is the correct answer "giving a soliloquy"? "To be perfect being, or not to be"? On the

---

[18]Thomas Aquinas *Summa Theologica* I.q34.a.1.

[19]There certainly are other ways to flout orthodoxy. One of the more creative recent examples is an essay by the philosopher Richard Kortum, who argues that the very idea of a God who designs the universe is incoherent ("The Very Idea of Design: What God Couldn't Do," *Religious Studies* 40 [2004]: 81-96). His argument, though misguided, is instructive: (1) Without thought, one cannot intentionally create anything. (2) Without language, one cannot have higher-order thoughts. (3) Without others, one cannot have a language. (4) Before the physical universe existed, God was alone and without others. (5) Therefore, God could not have had either a language or the higher-order thoughts without which one can do nothing intelligent, much less design a universe. My colleague rightly spots the key equivocation in premise (4): "God was alone and without others" could mean either that there is at most one divine being, one God, or that there is at most one divine communicative agent, one divine person (see Thomas McCall, "Trinity and Creation: Why Kortum's Argument Fails," *The Heythrop Journal* 48 [2007]: 260-66).

[20]Elizabeth A. Johnson, *Quest for the Living God* (New York and London: Continuum, 2007), pp. 211-12; cf. Nicholas Lash, *Believing Three Ways in One God* (Notre Dame, Ind.: University of Notre Dame Press, 1993).

[21]Most biblical commentators focus on the question of the possible backgrounds for the Fourth Gospel's use of the term *Word*. See, e.g., Raymond E. Brown, *The Gospel According to John I-XII*, Anchor Bible 29 (Garden City, N.Y.: Doubleday, 1966), appendix 2, "The Word," pp. 519-24; Leon Morris, *The Gospel According to John*, New International Commentary on the New Testament (Grand Rapids: Eerdmans, 1971), pp. 115-26; Geerhardus Vos, "The Range of the Logos Title in the Prologue to the Fourth Gospel," in *Redemptive History and Biblical Interpretation* (Phillipsburg, N.J.: Presbyterian & Reformed, 1980), pp. 59-90.

contrary, as the incarnation makes clear, the Word *with* God in the beginning also speaks *to* God. I make this claim on the grounds that the way the Son and Father interact in the economy reflects the life of the immanent Trinity, and because one of the characteristic things Jesus does while on earth is communicate with the Father.

Indeed, each of the three persons in the Godhead has a speaking part. We have already mentioned Yahweh's self-naming out of the burning bush: "I am who I am." Interestingly, Jesus uses first this "I am" formula when he identifies himself to the Samaritan woman in John 4:26 with the theologically loaded phrase "I am, *the one who is speaking*" (NRSV; most English translations blunt the force of Jesus' *egō eimi*).[22] The Spirit, too, speaks on occasion,[23] and there is at least one other commentator in church history who, like me, detects a connection between the burning bush and the tongues of fire that descended on the apostles at Pentecost (Acts 2:4).[24]

The divine persons also dialogue with one another.[25] These dialogical occasions "come at crucial moments in the narrative of the unfolding drama of the Trinity, and they mark the nodal points of the inner relations of the Trinity, worked out in time and space."[26] One such occasion is the baptism of Jesus, where the Father's voice accompanies the descent of the Holy Spirit upon the Son as he ascends from the waters: "You are my beloved Son; with you I am well pleased" (Mk 1:11; cf. Mt 3:17; Lk 3:22).[27]

More often, we overhear the Son addressing the Father. Before raising Lazarus from the dead, Jesus says, "Father, I thank you that you have heard me" (Jn 11:41). When he realizes that the hour has come, he prays, "Father, glorify your name!" (Jn 12:28), only to be answered by a voice from heaven:

---

[22]George R. Beasley-Murray notes almost in passing that "the formula has the overtone of the absolute being of God" (*John*, Word Biblical Commentary 36 [Waco, Tex.: Word, 1987], p. 62). Cf. Ethelbert Stauffer, who gives six reasons in favor of understanding Jesus' words as the theophanic formula (*Jesus and His Story*, trans. Dorthea M. Barton [London: SCM Press, 1960], p. 152).

[23]See, e.g., Acts 8:29: "The Spirit said to Philip."

[24]See Cyprian *Treatises* 101.555.

[25]"Communication indicates the way the trinitarian persons relate to each in enacting their economy in history" (Hak Joon Lee, *Covenant and Communication: A Christian Moral Conversation with Jürgen Habermas* [Lanham, Md.: University Press of America, 2006], p. 109).

[26]Oliver Davies, *A Theology of Compassion* (London: SCM Press, 2001), pp. 199-200.

[27]We hear the Father's voice affirming Jesus' mission again in the account of the transfiguration (Mt 17:5-6; Mk 9:7; Lk 9:35).

"I have glorified it, and I will glorify it again." Glorification is the main topic of Jesus' longest prayer, the high-priestly prayer of John 17, which affords us a glimpse into the way in which Father and Son communicate not only words but also light—glory—to one another, for what is glorification but the communication of glory, the publication of God's excellence?[28]

The Spirit, too, plays a communicative role. Jesus says: "He [the Spirit] will glorify me, for he will take what is mine and declare it to you" (Jn 16:14). At the same time, "he will not speak on his own authority, but whatever he hears he will speak" (Jn 16:13). Though it is not explicitly stated that the Spirit speaks what he hears from the Father and the Son, one would not go too far wrong to hear a communicative variation on the *filioque* clause.[29] In communicating the mutual love of Father and Son, the Spirit glorifies them both. The Spirit makes public an inner-trinitarian communication.

The Spirit is more than a mere conversational go-between, however. He is a witness—an exhibit and extension—of the loving communication that exists between the Father and the Son.[30] Indeed, it is precisely as witness that the Spirit has a distinct personal identity: "A witness can be the bond of love between the Father and the Son *in Person* and not as an inanimate chain."[31]

The Spirit draws the church into the communicative action of Father and Son by pouring their love for one another into our hearts (Rom 5:5). What the Spirit ultimately communicates is eternal life: the gift of salvation. The Spirit is the gift of God, a gift that communicates not only meaning but also power. The term *communication* derives from the Latin *communicare* (to share). Communication has been defined as "social interaction through messages." It is the process of making common *(communis),* sharing something (e.g., beliefs, worries, memories, hopes, etc.) with someone by some symbolic means (e.g., language, gesture, pictures, etc.). The Spirit makes

---

[28]Words and deeds can glorify. Note too that glorification is a communicative act in which the church is to participate. Indeed, according to the Westminster Confession (and the catechisms based on it), humanity's "chief end" is to "glorify God."

[29]Raymond E. Brown in *The Gospel According to John XIII-XXI*, Anchor Bible 29A (Garden City, N.Y.: Doubleday, 1970), p. 704, translates Jn 16:14 as "because it is from me that he will receive what he will declare to you."

[30]So Eugene F. Rogers Jr., *After the Spirit: A Constructive Pneumatology from Resources Outside the Modern West* (Grand Rapids: Eerdmans, 2005), p. 141. For the connection between Spirit and witness, see Jn 15:26; Acts 15:8; Rom 8:16; Heb 2:4; 10:15.

[31]Ibid. Cf. Walter Kasper: "He [the Spirit] is in his very person the reciprocal love of the Father and the Son" (*The God of Jesus Christ* [New York: Crossroad, 2000], p. 226).

union common—and so brings about *communion*—by sharing God's love and life: the fellowship of Father and Son.[32] The Spirit communicates these things only because he has them in himself. The Spirit is himself the freedom of God's self-communicating life and love.[33]

What does this have to do with our theological reflections on the claim that God speaks? Just this: by examining the economy, we see that *God's being is in conversing,* and whatever we say the Bible is, it must, precisely as the word of this God, relate to this God's triune conversation. God communicates himself—his love, knowledge and life—through himself. This conversational analogy depicts God's being as essentially communicative and the three persons as a dialogue between communicative agents.[34]

"God" is the name for this common loving and glorifying activity of the three persons. The Father-Son communications we discover at key moments of Jesus' history are simply the communicative face of the perichoresis (the mutual indwelling) that characterizes God's eternal triune being. The things that constitute the identity of Father, Son and Spirit are not merely generative but also communicative relations: the eternal delight of the dialogical dance of call, response and acknowledgement. This inner-trinitarian conversation is perfect: there is complete union, and thus communion, between the communicants, in glorious contrast to the incomplete and broken nature of most human communicative ventures.

Divine appropriations and triune rhetoric: The economic Trinity. Do all three persons of the Trinity speak in Scripture, does one person in particular speak, or does the one God speak in three ways?[35] To do justice to

---

[32]"Communion means the state where unity is created without sacrificing the particularity of each person" (Lee, *Covenant and Communication,* p. 106).

[33]Kasper, *God of Jesus Christ,* p. 225.

[34]See my *Remythologizing Theology* for a fuller account of this "triune dialogical theism": three persons in communicative communion. Cf. Kasper: "The divine persons are not only in dialogue, they *are* dialogue" (*God of Jesus Christ,* p. 290); and Robert Jenson: "The one God is a conversation" (*Systematic Theology,* vol. 1, *The Triune God* [Oxford: Oxford University Press, 1997], p. 223). Oliver Davies says that the three persons can inhabit each other's voices: "There must be here some kind of *perichōrēsis* of utterance" (*Theology of Compassion,* p. 264). See also J. Scott Horrell, "The Eternal Son of God in the Social Trinity," in *Jesus in Trinitarian Perspective,* ed. Fred Sanders and Klaus Issler (Nashville: B & H Publishing Group, 2007), pp. 56-59.

[35]According to Nicholas Lash, "God is not an individual with a nature; nor is God an agent acting in three episodes; nor is God three people" (*Believing Three Ways in One God,* p. 33). Cf. Francesca Murphy's affirmation that what God does is the "single operation" of

the equal ultimacy of the threeness and oneness of God, we need both the social and the psychological analogies, or something like them. To confess God's being as conversational is to work a communicative variation on the social analogy. We turn now to work a communicative variation on the psychological analogy. Divine communication, I submit, is a unified action with three dimensions. Developing this idea will lead us to view Scripture not as divinely appropriated human discourse but as human discourse that from start to finish is caught up in the field of triune communicative action.

We begin with the patristic insight that everything God does is the work of the whole Trinity: *opera trinitatis ad extra indivisa sunt* (the external operations of the Trinity are undivided). It is nevertheless fitting to ascribe certain actions, or aspects of actions, to particular divine persons on the basis of what we see in the economy, that is, in light of the way Father, Son and Spirit actually operate in the history of redemption.

God's economic self-communication actually begins with creation. Paul declares in 1 Corinthians 8:6 that "there is one God, the Father, from whom are all things and for whom we exist, and one Lord, Jesus Christ, through whom are all things and through whom we exist." All things are created *through* the Word (Jn 1:3). Both the Father and Son are involved in creation, though in distinct fashion, signaled by the different prepositions "from" and "through," respectively. The Spirit was active in creation as well (Gen 1:2), as the psalmist declares: "When you send forth your Spirit, they are created" (Ps 104:30). Following Paul's lead in Romans 11:36, we may add a third preposition: "from him and through him and to him are all things." Gregory of Nyssa formulates it as follows: "Every operation which extends from God to the creation . . . has its origin from the Father, and proceeds through the Son, and is perfected in the Holy Spirit."[36] The Cappadocian parsing still makes good sense: all that God does the Father originates, the Son effectuates and the Spirit completes. "The three are engaged in *different* ways in *all* the activities of God."[37]

---

the three persons rather than the work of three distinct agents, each with his own agenda (*God Is Not a Story: Realism Revisited* [Oxford: Oxford University Press, 2007], p. 260).

[36]Gregory of Nyssa *To Ablabius, on "Not Three Gods,"* in *Nicene and Post-Nicene Fathers,* Series 2, 5:334.

[37]William Placher, *The Triune God* (Louisville, Ky.: Westminster John Knox Press, 2007), p. 147.

The technical term for this trinitarian phenomenon is *appropriation*, and it was developed by Hugh of St. Victor in the twelfth century. According to Hugh, God's power, knowledge and will are behind everything that he does: "The will moves, knowledge disposes, power operates."[38] None of the persons lacks perfection; each possesses the same power, knowledge and goodness, "and yet there was reason for distinguishing in the persons what in substance was the same."[39] The Son, for example, assumes human flesh, and the Father does not; yet Hugh insists that Father and Spirit are both active in the Son's assuming humanity: "There is one action on the part of two, rather one action on the part of three, . . . and in one action the three are not three agents but one agent."[40]

John Calvin makes a similar point: "Whenever the name of God is mentioned without particularization, there are designated no less the Son and the Spirit than the Father."[41] At the same time, "the peculiar qualities in the persons carry an order within them, e.g., in the Father is the beginning and the source."[42] Calvin goes on to give a classic statement of the divine appropriations: "To the Father is attributed the beginning of activity, . . . to the Son . . . the ordered disposition of all things; but to the Spirit is assigned the power and efficacy of that activity."[43]

John Owen brings the notion of divine appropriation even closer to our topic in his book *Communion with the Triune God*.[44] Owen emphasizes the saint's distinct communion with each person of the Trinity; the bulk of his book consists in setting forth "in what the peculiar *appropriation* of this distinct communion unto the several persons does consist."[45] Owen believes that each of the three divine persons bears distinct witness to salvation and that this giving and receiving of testimony is no small part of our commu-

---

[38]Hugh of St. Victor, *On the Sacraments of the Christian Faith*, trans. Roy J. Deferrari (Cambridge, Mass.: The Medieval Academy of America, 1951), 1.2.6.

[39]Ibid., 1.2.7. The "reason" Hugh gives for associating the Son with wisdom, for instance, is that some may be tempted to associate "youth" with one who is not wise (1.3.26).

[40]Ibid., 2.1.3.

[41]*Institutes* 1.13.20.

[42]Ibid.

[43]Ibid., 1.13.18.

[44]John Owen, *Communion with the Triune God*, ed. Kelly M. Kapic and Justin Taylor (Wheaton, Ill.: Crossway, 2007).

[45]Ibid., p. 95.

nion with God.[46] Sometimes the same thing (e.g., grace and peace) is ascribed jointly yet distinctly to the divine persons (e.g., Rev 1:4-5); at other times the same thing is attributed "severally and singly" to each person.[47]

There are gems of theological wisdom to be found in Owen's meticulous prose. First, "our communion with God is always communion with the divine persons, for *there is no God other than the persons.*"[48] Second, communion involves the "mutual communication" of good between persons; communion is communication's true end.[49] Third, the three persons act and communicate distinctly yet never independently. And last but not least, communication involves the addressee's response or, to use Owen's terms, "our return unto him,"[50] a point of the utmost hermeneutical importance, as we shall see. What is lacking in Owen's account, however, is anything like a doctrine of Scripture. Though he constantly appeals to the Bible throughout his work, there is nothing about Scripture as a mode of God's self-communication. Hence the present task: to apply the doctrine of divine appropriations to an understanding of Scripture as a medium of God's communicative action.

We begin with the Owenesque observation that God communicates himself in three ways: the Father is the locutor who utters the word; the Son is what is communicated, the content of the Father's speech; the Spirit is the "channel" (air) that carries the word. This formula preserves the patristic insight that God's works are indivisible (thus preserving the oneness of the divine nature) yet does justice to the biblical descriptions of the economy of communication, thus preserving the distinctness of the three persons' work. Note, too, how well this analogy of speech agency conforms to Calvin's account of the division of divine labor. The Father initiates communicative action, the Son executes it, and the Spirit carries it to completion.

---

[46]Ibid., p. 96. Owen bases this idea on a phrase in 1 Jn 5:7 (KJV) that is omitted from most modern translations because of scant textual evidence: "There are three that bear record in heaven, the Father, the Word, and the Holy Ghost" (p. 96).

[47]Owen's sole example of the latter phenomenon is teaching: the Father teaches by way of original authority, the Son by way of communicating from a purchased treasury (of grace), the Spirit by way of immediate efficacy (ibid., p. 104).

[48]Kapic, "Introduction" to Owen, ibid., p. 26, with his emphasis.

[49]Kelly Kapic, *Communion with God: The Divine and the Human in the Theology of John Owen* (Grand Rapids: Baker, 2007), p. 152.

[50]Owen, *Communion with the Triune God*, p. 94.

Although the conversational analogy highlights three distinct speech agents in the Godhead, this "rhetorical analogy" focuses on the distinct roles of the three persons in unified communicative action.[51] Why rhetoric? Because rhetoric deals with the pragmatics of speech, with language in action: "The classical world was fascinated by the power of speech, and its educational system was founded upon analysis of language and communication."[52] Augustine sanctified Aristotle's treatise on rhetoric by arguing that Christians must be concerned not merely with truth and not merely the "art of persuasion."[53] Aristotle's categories nevertheless give purchase on the way in which each person of the Trinity appropriates a certain rhetorical function to himself: the Father takes responsibility for the ethos of discourse, the Son for the logos of discourse and the Spirit for the pathos of discourse.[54]

Ethos pertains to a speaker's moral character. Something of a speaker's basic disposition is communicated over and above what the actual words say, which serves as a means of winning the audience's trust and assent (or not). This may explain the Bible's repeated insistence on God's faithfulness and unchanging character as holy love (e.g., Deut 7:9). There is none other than God to whom we should more diligently and believingly attend.

The logos of discourse pertains to the message itself, its form and content. Some traditions of rhetoric stress the importance of first establishing one's subject matter (res) before determining how best verbally to convey it. In the divine rhetoric, the Son is the basic thing God says, and the best means to convey this subject matter is through the narrative history of redemption. In his sermons on the Fourth Gospel, Luther observes that God has "from all eternity a Word, a speech, a thought"[55] that eventually gets expressed in and as Jesus.

---

[51]Mark Bowald appeals to divine rhetoric in the context of biblical hermeneutics rather than a doctrine of Scripture. See his *Rendering the Word in Theological Hermeneutics: Mapping Divine and Human Agency* (Aldershot, U.K.: Ashgate, 2007), pp. 174-81. In fact, the present chapter subsumes both the doctrine of Scripture and biblical hermeneutics under the broader rubric of the economy of communicative action.

[52]Frances Young, "Rhetoric," in *A Dictionary of Biblical Interpretation*, ed. E. J. Coggins and J. L. Houlden (Philadelphia: Trinity Press International, 1990), p. 548.

[53]See Augustine of Hippo *De doctrina christiana* 4.2.3.

[54]Cf. Work's alternative formulation: "Christian Scripture participates in the will of the Father, the *kenōsis* of the Son, the power of the Holy Spirit" (*Living and Active*, pp. 35-36).

[55]Martin Luther, *Luther's Works*, vol. 22, *Sermons on the Gospel of St. John, Chapters 1-4*, ed. Jaroslav Pelikan (St. Louis, Mo.: Concordia, 1957), p. 9.

Finally, the pathos of discourse pertains to the effect produced on a reader or listener. We typically associate pathos with the emotions, but I use it more broadly as a term for success in achieving one's communicative aims. As a new lecturer at Edinburgh University, I submitted to what I thought would be a routine visit from someone in the office of Teaching and Learning Assessment. After observing me lecture, he asked me how I thought I had done: "Pretty well," I replied. "I got through most of the material on my handout and managed to work in a few witty remarks." "But did you get through to the students?" Here the pedagogical scales fell from my eyes. Communication is a two-way street, involving giving and receiving. To put it in trinitarian terms of Word and Spirit, I was lecturing with one hand behind my back, relying solely on logos.

Divine communicative action, by contrast, is a two-handed affair: the triune God is the paradigm communicative agent, who ministers understanding via Word and Spirit alike. Understanding, the prime communicative result, is itself pathic: to understand is to "suffer" the effects of communicative action. This gives to pathos, and hence to the work of the Spirit, a broader range than mere emotionalism, encompassing the will and the imagination as well. The "pathos effect" is the Spirit's persuading the reader to embrace the point of view expressed in the logos.[56] The Spirit enables those who hear Paul's injunction "Have this mind among yourselves" (Phil 2:5) really to have Christ's mind.

In making these points, I am but standing on the shoulders of theological giants: "Calvin frequently uses the vocabulary of 'rhetoric' to describe God's relation to the world."[57] Augustine is even more specific: the Scriptures are for him "the external, verbal communication of the divine Rhetorician."[58] And both agree that the purpose of God's word is not only to instruct us in truth, but also to motivate us to do the good and to delight in the beauty of holiness: "God has something to say and he is very good at saying it."[59] Triune discourse is as pastoral as it is propositional.

---

[56]Note that both terms *ethos* and *pathos*, though rhetorical categories, apply to persons rather than texts.

[57]Serene Jones, *Calvin and the Rhetoric of Piety*, Columbia Series in Reformed Theology (Louisville, Ky.: Westminster John Knox Press, 1995), p. 132.

[58]Norris, "Augustine," p. 388.

[59]Mark D. Thompson, *A Clear and Present Word: The Clarity of Scripture* (Downers Grove,

SCRIPTURE IN THE ECONOMY OF COVENANTAL COMMUNICATION

Our theological reflections to this point have led us in two directions: first, toward a conversational analogy that highlights three divine speakers; second, toward a rhetorical analogy that, thanks to the notion of divine appropriations, highlights the one speaking of three persons (i.e., the ethos, logos and pathos of God's discourse). To the question What is the doctrinal home of the doctrine of Scripture? we can now answer, in the words James Carville made famous during Bill Clinton's successful 1992 presidential campaign: "It's the economy, stupid"—to be precise, the economy of communication. Scripture is triune discourse: something (covenantal) someone (Father, Son and Spirit) says to someone (the church) about something (life with God).

Scripture, like the church, requires both historical and theological description in order to do justice to its peculiar reality. Like the church, Scripture is a fully human phenomenon subject to the contingencies of language, culture and society. *Yet it is also God's communicative work, complete with divine ethos, logos and pathos: God-voiced, God-worded, God-breathed.* The triune God was active in producing this work and is active again whenever it is read and received with understanding. Thinking about Scripture in trinitarian perspective therefore obliges us to discuss both its composition and interpretation. We stop short of a full doctrinal account of what Scripture is when we speak in terms of its propositional revelation only. As a communicative act oriented to communion, the Bible is more than a compendium of need-to-know (for salvation) information: it is a divinely appointed medium for communion with the triune God.

The rhetorical analogy sheds light on the question of whether the Bible should be equated with revelation. *Logos* describes "God in the process of self-communication—not the communication of knowledge only, but in a self-communication which inevitably includes the imparting of true knowledge."[60] Logos in the Fourth Gospel is not only the source of light but also of life; remembering this "saves the Gospel from the charge of intellectualism."[61]

Ill.: InterVarsity Press, 2006), p. 170.

[60]C. K. Barrett, *The Gospel According to St John* (London: SPCK, 1955), p. 61.

[61]Vos, "The Range of the Logos Title in the Prologue to the Fourth Gospel," in *Redemptive*

The triune God as Voice, Word and Breath is the prime communicator, communication and communicatedness of Scripture. "Voice" signifies a living and active communicative presence—just what Moses encounters in the burning bush.[62] The voice identifies itself, initiates a covenantal relationship and declares the ground within the range of its hearing "holy." Scripture is the holy ground from whose midst the voice of God continues to address us.[63] The biblical text is not a substitute for the speaking God but the locus and medium of God's continued speaking.

The *ethos* of Scripture is ultimately a function of its being the discourse not only of prophets and apostles but also of the Creator of the universe, the Redeemer of Israel, the Father of Jesus Christ: "The question of biblical authority is ultimately a matter of Scripture's participation in God's character."[64] Or as Augustine puts it, "What is the Bible but a letter of God Almighty addressed to his creatures, in which letter we hear the voice of God, and behold the heart of our Heavenly Father?"[65] There is a real personal connection between agent and act, speaker and speech, writer and writing. *War and Peace* is not Leo Tolstoy, to be sure, but it is Tolstoy's work, a modality of his communicative action and an extension of sorts of his personal presence.

The *logos* of Scripture is thoroughly covenantal. The Bible is the God-ordained means of communicating the terms and the reality of the covenant whose content is Jesus Christ. The Son is both the promise of God and the obedient response of humanity. The prophets and apostles are commissioned literary executors whose texts set forth the terms of eternal life with God. The supreme covenant blessing—sharing in God's own triune love and fellowship—is thoroughly communicative. The Bible is the verbal me-

---

History and Biblical Interpretation, p. 66. Even when the Bible is not revealing, it continues to plays its appointed role in the economy of divine communication. We do well to remember that the knowledge of God is to some hearers of the gospel a fragrance of death but to others a fragrance of life (2 Cor 2:14-16).

[62]Stephen H. Webb suggests that Jesus Christ is the voice of God (*The Divine Voice: Christian Proclamation and the Theology of Sound* [Grand Rapids: Brazos, 2004], p. 196), yet the weight of the biblical evidence would seem to favor associating the incarnate Son with God's Word.

[63]See Oliver Davies, "Reading the Burning Bush," in *The Promise of Scriptural Reasoning*, ed. David F. Ford and C. C. Pecknold (Oxford: Blackwell, 2006), pp. 95-104.

[64]Work, *Living and Active*, p. 63.

[65]Augustine, cited in H. D. McDonald, "Word, Word of God, Words of the Lord," in *Evangelical Dictionary of Theology*, ed. Walter A. Elwell (Grand Rapids: Baker, 1984), p. 1187.

dium for communicative acts constitutive of the interpersonal relations that it both establishes and regulates. What God communicates in and through Scripture is not only information for the head but also vision for the imagination, direction for the will, shapes of hope for the heart—everything the community of interpreters needs.[66]

The *pathos* of Scripture reminds us that God's speech solicits our participation in the communicative economy.[67] Biblical inspiration refers to the Spirit's work in catching up the prophets and apostles into the triune communicative action.[68] My primary emphasis here, however, is on the Spirit's work of illumination that completes the process of communication. We who read the Bible in the church today are not commissioned witnesses as were the apostles. Our place in the economy of communication lies elsewhere; we do not author but hear the written logos.[69] Nor is it enough merely to hear or read the Bible; we must be doers—active responders—as well. After all, Scripture was written "so that you may believe that Jesus is the Christ" (Jn 20:31) and "for training in righteousness" (2 Tim 3:16). As the agent of divine communicative efficacy, the Spirit ministers understanding and obedience: faithful hearing is the pathos of the word. It is precisely by ministering the scriptural word that the Spirit draws the church into the economy of communication.[70]

---

[66]For further development of these ideas, see my work *The Drama of Doctrine* (Louisville, Ky.: Westminster John Knox, 2005), pp. 67-68.

[67]The triune discourse is a movement in language that calls forth an addressee, "one who participates, not only passively but also as a real agent, in the movement of the knowledge of God" (John Webster, *Confessing God: Essays in Christian Dogmatics II* [London and New York: T & T Clark, 2005], p. 60).

[68]"What the Father speaks the Son mediates, and what the Son mediates is actually spoken into the ear by the Holy Spirit" (Bernard Ramm, *The Witness of the Spirit* [Grand Rapids: Eerdmans, 1959], p. 31).

[69]Webb defends Barth's view that the Bible *becomes* the word of God when the Spirit enables us to hear it as such (*Divine Voice*, p. 174). His emphasis on theological "acoustemology" leads Webb to confuse sound and sense and then to associate God's speaking with the former rather than the latter. In my own view, God's triune communicative action involves Father, Son and Spirit alike: the divine speaking (locution), the divine word (illocution) and the divinely enabled hearing (perlocution).

[70]Bernard Ramm helpfully reminds us that Paul's contrast in Rom 7:6 and 2 Cor 3 is not between Scripture (*graphē*) and Spirit but between letter (*gramma*) and Spirit. The "letter" is written on tablets that cannot draw the reader into the economy of communication. Paul associates the *graphē*, by contrast, with the normative witness to Christ. Without the witness of the Spirit to human minds and hearts that results in faith in Christ, however, the *graphē* would dwindle into mere *gramma* (*Special Revelation and the Word of God*, pp. 183-84).

In sum: *Scripture is a work of triune rhetoric whose purpose is to shape the church's identity and solicit the church's participation in God's being-in-conversation.*[71] As to form, the Bible is divine communication, with its own ethos, logos and pathos; as to content, the Bible is covenantal discourse whose aim is communion, a becoming one (Jn 17:21).[72] The triune God ultimately deploys Scripture as a means of expanding the inner-trinitarian conversation and hence the circle of his friendly acquaintance.

To call the Bible God's word, then, is to identify it as a locus of divine speech: ongoing triune communicative action. Calvin believed that the highest proof of Scripture's authority is "the fact that God in person speaks in it."[73] Which person? Thanks to the doctrine of divine appropriations, we can now answer: the Holy Spirit—but only as the *porte-parole* (spokesperson; deputy) of the Father (and the Son). The Spirit is the Spirit of God and the Spirit of Christ (Rom 8:9), and he does not speak of himself but only what he sees and hears.[74] One of the Trinity has spoken in Scripture, then, on behalf of all three. As the Son is the communicative agent of the Father, so the Spirit is the communicative agent of Father and Son. The Spirit enables the human authors of Scripture to "suffer" the logos even as they were actively writing it. To confess the Spirit speaking in the Scripture is to acknowledge that the words of the human authors are ultimately *enhypophatic*: the voice or logos the church hears in and through the human words is the voice of the third person of the Trinity speaking from the Father through and about the Son.

The Spirit speaks. It therefore comes as no surprise to learn that some theologians house the doctrine of Scripture under pneumatology or, to be more precise, under sanctification, since we are dealing not with the Spirit's person but with his work. John Webster describes the human words of the

---

[71]See Matthew Levering, *Participatory Biblical Exegesis: A Theology of Biblical Interpretation* (Notre Dame, Ind.: University of Notre Dame Press, 2008).

[72]So Lee: "The divine action in history is primarily covenantal and communicative in nature" (*Covenant and Communication*, p. 109).

[73]Calvin *Institutes* 1.7.4.

[74]I say this in response to John Webster's recent claim that the one speaking in Scripture is the risen Christ: "The nature of Scripture is a function of its appointment as herald of the self-communicative presence of the risen one" ("Resurrection and Scripture," in *Christology and Scripture: Interdisciplinary Perspectives*, ed. Andrew Lincoln and Angus Paddison [New York: T & T Clark, 2007], p. 138).

Bible as creaturely media elected by the risen Christ and set apart by the Spirit for a divine purpose.[75] Webster, like Barth, resists ascribing divine properties to the Bible itself, preferring to keep our attention on the communicative activity of the divine agent.

Some evangelicals demur from Webster's locating Scripture under sanctification because they "cannot see [how he] ultimately avoids the charge of being adoptionist."[76] A broader concern is that sanctifying creaturely realities is not the same as authoring them. Webster seems to acknowledge this when, in the course of discussing verbal inspiration, he invokes the doctrine of providence, specifically, the Spirit's "concursive" action in moving the human authors to write.[77]

Is this not where we came in? In the previous chapter we saw that the standard evangelical account of inspiration typically appeals to providence. We now see providence itself in its proper dogmatic light, however, as a subset of something even bigger: the economy of communication. Indeed, *the mainspring of all Christian theology is nothing less than God—Father, Son and Spirit—in communicative and self-communicative action.* Thanks to this economic perspective, the doctrines of providence, revelation and sanctification, like Job's fortunes, are restored to their rightful places with regard to the doctrine of Scripture. We need all these doctrines to do full justice to Scripture as the voice of the Father articulated in the word of the Son as breathed by the Holy Spirit.

TRIUNE DISCOURSE: THE MOMENT OF TRUTH?

So much for the general connection between the Trinity and Scripture. The ETS statement of faith, however, focuses on inerrancy in particular, and the Bible's truth serves as an excellent test of my proposal. What is the place of truth in the economy of communication as concerns Scripture? Consider the options at either end of the spectrum: on one end, truth is a fixed textual property; on the other end, truth is a fleeting interpretative event. Is biblical truth a matter of its immaculate conception or its readerly recep-

---

[75]Webster, *Holy Scripture*, p. 27.
[76]Mark Thompson, *A Clear and Present Word*, p. 76 n.74.
[77]John Webster, *Holy Scripture: A Dogmatic Sketch* (Cambridge: Cambridge University Press, 2003), p. 38.

tion? Many prefer the latter option for, once the principle that God speaks is acknowledged, what is a poor theological liberal to do? The best way to postpone the moment of truth is furiously to begin interpreting and to spin off theories of interpretation.

The problem: No (fixed) scriptural place for truth? It is obvious to most evangelicals that one cannot preserve biblical authority by relativizing truth to the experience of the reader. By contrast, Barth's concern about the danger of absolutizing truth as a textual property of Scripture may be less obvious. For Barth, we may recall, God's Word is not an attribute inhering once for all in the text but rather in the event of God's use of Scripture here and now. The biblical text must be moved by the hand of God "just as the water was moved in the Pool of Bethesda that it might thereby become a means of healing."[78] Telford Work observes that "Barth makes the miracle of Scripture's truth an event in the present" when the living Word commandeers the written word.[79] This poses a problem for inerrancy, since "only for the duration of the event do the signs of the words of men truly point to the Word of God."[80]

For his part, Webster thinks that those on both the theological left and right fall prey to "disordered ontologies" of Scripture by isolating the text either from its place in God's revelatory activity (the liberal temptation) or from its reception in the community (the conservative temptation). He has written an excellent essay offering his own constructive take on the clarity of Scripture in the context of God's communicative action but has not yet attempted something similar with truth.[81] One reason for this reticence is his reluctance to endow the Bible with divine properties: "As sanctified creature, the text is not a quasi-divine artefact: sanctification is not transubstantiation."[82] Webster thinks that many so-called high views

---

[78]Karl Barth, *Church Dogmatics* 1/1 (Edinburgh: T & T Clark, 1975), p. 111.
[79]Work, *Living and Active*, p. 81.
[80]Ibid., p. 82. Compare Kenton L. Sparks's recent suggestion that God, in order to communicate effectively, "has intentionally adopted errant human viewpoints" (*God's Word in Human Words: An Evangelical Appropriation of Critical Biblical Scholarship* [Grand Rapids: Baker, 2008], p. 249). Sparks moves too fast, however, from human finitude to human fallenness; thus he fails to preserve the nuances of Calvin's own position on divine accommodation.
[81]Webster, *Confessing God*, pp. 33-68.
[82]Webster, *Holy Scripture*, p. 28.

of biblical authority turn the Bible into a self-standing object with super-natural powers rather than viewing Scripture as a servant of the gospel. Clarity and truth come to be seen as properties of the text as a finished product rather than as perfections of a communicative agent and his on-going action.[83]

Is it conceptual hairsplitting to insist that clarity pertains to an agent's activity rather than to the instrument of that activity? If this seems ab-struse, we can move from the field of divine communicative action to the baseball field. Is home-run power a property of the bat or of Derrek Lee's swing? The answer is both. To use Aquinas's categories, the bat is the in-strumental cause of the home run, and Derrek Lee is the efficient cause. The bat alone, however, lacks home-run power. Webster wants us to see that "God speaks truly in Scripture" and "The Bible is true" are not equiv-alent statements.

The queasiness that afflicts some evangelicals over the term *truth*, however, is nowhere to be found in Scripture. The gospel is the word of truth (Eph 1:13) put into written form. Written words *can* state truth: the one seated on the great white throne says, "Write this down, for these words are trustworthy and true" (Rev 21:5). A text is simply discourse fixed by writing; writing serves as a medium of communicative action every bit as much as speaking. This is why God commits his law to writing, why there are writing prophets, why we have Gospels, why Peter, Paul and John wrote letters to Christian communities. The New Testament uses some rather impressive terms with which to describe the Old Testament *graphē*: holy (Rom 1:2), sacred (2 Tim 3:15), reliable (Heb 2:2) and God-breathed (2 Tim 3:16). The thrust of my argument, however, is that we only fully understand the ontology of this product, Scripture, when we locate it in the economy of triune communication.

Truth in the Fourth Gospel: Divinely appropriated witness. We must learn to view the Bible's truth in light of the economy of communication in which Scripture lives, moves and has its being. This means returning, at least for a moment, to the Fourth Gospel. For it is here, in the depiction of the way in which the divine persons testify to one another, that we find the

---

[83]Webster, *Confessing God*, p. 35; and idem, *Holy Scripture*, p. 55.

missing link between the ETS confession of the Trinity and its affirmation of inerrancy, because it is here that we see how Father, Son and Spirit appropriate to themselves different aspects of the ministry of truth.

The Fourth Gospel features Jesus' trials before the Romans and the Jews. Indeed, the entire Gospel is structured like a courtroom trial. Everything that Jesus says or does is a "sign"—*evidence* that he is who he says he is. The Prologue asserts that Jesus the Word is full of "grace and truth" (1:14), an allusion to God's "steadfast love and faithfulness" of Exodus 34:6. All of Jesus' "I am" sayings are controversial to the extent that they implicitly make Jesus equal with God, but in John 14:6 Jesus explicitly says "I am . . . the truth." The Son, we might say, is the Father's truth claim. That Jesus is the truth—about who God is, about who we are, about the meaning of the Old Testament and so forth—is ultimately what is on trial in the Fourth Gospel; and the Father, Son and Spirit alike are witnesses.[84] To be precise: what is being tried in the Fourth Gospel is the claim that Jesus is the faithfulness and reliability of God.[85]

The truth of Jesus Christ has a redemptive as well as revelatory role to play in the economy of communication, as Jesus indicates in John 8:31-32: "If you abide in my word, you are truly my disciples, and you will know the truth, and the truth will set you free." Truth appears here less as a static property of a text than as a dynamic of discipleship, a quality of action—action that corresponds to the way things are "in Christ." What ultimately comes to be communicated in the economy is not only information, but also energy and life: *vital* truth.

The ties that bind Trinity, Scripture and truth together grow even tighter when we consider the ministry of the third divine person. Jesus says: "But when the Helper comes, . . . the Spirit of truth, who proceeds from the Father, he will bear witness about me" (Jn 15:26).[86] Jesus' disciples will

---

[84]See Andrew Lincoln's excellent study *Truth on Trial: The Lawsuit Motif in the Fourth Gospel* (Peabody, Mass.: Hendrickson, 2000).

[85]Cf. Andreas Köstenberger's remark that "the notion of truth is inextricably related to . . . Jesus' relationship with God" ("'What Is Truth?' Pilate's Question in Its Johannine and Larger Biblical Context," in *Whatever Happened to Truth?* ed. Andreas Köstenberger [Wheaton, Ill.: Crossway, 2005], p. 20).

[86]Clearly, the "truth witnessed to by the Fourth Gospel involves the triune God" (Andrew Lincoln, "Reading John: The Fourth Gospel under Modern and Postmodern Interrogation," in *Reading the Gospels Today*, ed. Stanley E. Porter [Grand Rapids: Eerdmans,

know what to say and be empowered to say it, thanks to the witness of the Spirit: "For it is not you who speak, but the Spirit of your Father speaking through you" (Mt 10:20). As Augustine rightly observes, the way the Spirit speaks is through Jesus' disciples: "Because he will speak, you will also speak—he in your hearts, you in words—he by inspiration, you by sounds."[87]

Jesus' high-priestly prayer thickens his description of the Spirit's role in this ministry of truth: "Sanctify them in the truth; your word is truth" (Jn 17:17). The Son prays to the Father that the Spirit will set apart disciples as his witnesses. The economy of communication co-opts and catches up both the Bible's authors and its readers, albeit in different fashion. Note well: the human witness given by the Bible's interpreters is part and parcel of the economy of communication. Stated differently, the Spirit's activity in communicating truth involves both inspiration and illumination. For the Bible's truth is not merely theoretical and historical but also practical, transformative and relational—a truth that sets free, gives life and promotes wisdom.

Truth, Scripture and divine rhetoric. Well and good. But I have not yet answered the original question: Is biblical truth a static textual property or a dynamic event? And does God's speaking occur only at the moment of the text's origin and/or in the moment of its interpretation? I reply: We must view the truth of Scripture in connection both to what the text is and to what we said earlier about how the divine persons appropriate it rhetorically in terms of ethos, logos and pathos. To anticipate, the truth of Scripture is that quality of the biblical text that, as God's communicative act, ensures that what is said corresponds to the way things are when interpreted rightly and read in faith.[88]

As to the ontology of the text, the biblical texts are divinely ordained elements in the economy of communication. Hence my thesis: *Scripture has its being-as-communication in this triune economy.* To view the Bible as a human and historical text is true so far as it goes, but it only goes so far. It

2004], pp. 147-48).

[87]Augustine, *In Jo.* (*Tractates on the Gospel of John*), cited in Brown, *The Gospel According to John XIII-XXI*, p. 700.

[88]Cf. Thompson's definition of Scripture's clarity: "*that quality of the biblical text that, as God's communicative act, ensures its meaning is accessible to all who come to it in faith*" (*A Clear and Present Word*, pp. 169-70, with his emphasis). Thompson implies but does not explicitly say that clarity is a textual property that only becomes effective when the Spirit, as catalyst of faith, is at work.

specializes in the Bible's "natural history," and that means only as far as Darwin goes. The Bible also has a "supernatural history" that involves the presence and agency of the triune God.[89] The way forward is to see biblical inspiration and illumination alike as components in the divine economy of communication, without abstracting them from it.[90]

Scripture, then, is a work of divine rhetoric. William Gouge, one of the Westminster Divines, unpacks Jesus' statement "Your word is truth" (Jn 17:17) in ways that correspond to what we have said about ethos, logos and pathos. Scripture is true, says Gouge, "1. In regard of the author, who is the God of truth. . . . 2. In regard of the matter. . . . 3. In regard of the effect. It persuades a man of the truth."[91] Let me briefly unpack these three rhetorical moments that comprise the economy of truth.

Ethos means that the character of God stands behind his promises and, indeed, all his covenantal discourse: "its character is his character."[92] This, rather than the incarnational analogy, is the proper ground on which to apply divine attributes to the biblical texts. Scripture's truth participates in triune discourse as an extension of the Father's character.[93] To take up and read the Bible is to take God at his word.

Logos reminds us that God binds himself to what he says in human words. God's communicative activity issues in textual deposits with both form and content. Surely it is relevant to discussions about inerrancy that the Bible contains not only the oracles (Warfield) but also the *orations* of God.[94] What is said *(res)* takes various literary shapes *(verbum)* so that the discourse can not only persuade the intellect, but also move the will,

---

[89]See Vern S. Poythress, "The Presence of God Qualifying Our Notions of Grammatical-Historical Interpretation: Genesis 3:14 as a Test Case," *Journal of the Evangelical Theological Society* 50 (2007): 87-104.

[90]"The *graphē* presupposes the continuing work of the Trinity in man's salvation, the reigning of Christ in heaven with authority which . . . reaches to earth, the indwelling of Christ in the heart of the believers" (Ramm, *Special Revelation*, p. 180).

[91]William Gouge, *A Commentary on the Whole Epistle to the Hebrews*, cited in John Woodbridge, *Biblical Authority* (Grand Rapids: Zondervan, 1982), p. 112.

[92]Work, *Living and Active*, p. 61.

[93]Ibid., p. 63.

[94]Reformers such as Calvin and Melanchthon were familiar with classical rhetoric and humanist learning and had a rich appreciation for Scripture's truth. See J. R. Schneider, "Melanchthon, Philip," in *Dictionary of Major Biblical Interpreters*, ed. Donald K. McKim (Downers Grove, Ill.: InterVarsity Press, 2007), pp. 716-21; and Serene Jones, *Calvin and the Rhetoric of Piety* (Louisville, Ky.: Westminster John Knox, 1995).

engage the emotions, fire the imagination.[95]

Pathos, we may recall, pertains to the Spirit's efficacious ministry of the word in the hearts and minds of interpreters. Some theologians equate this ministry with the moment of truth: truth is the event in which God's word hits home. This suits postmoderns just fine for, as Nietzsche said, truth is a matter of interpretation. Not so fast, Friedrich. The church does not author but *suffers* the truth—the objective truth—of God's word written.[96] Remember what Calvin said about divine appropriations: the Father initiates an activity, the Son orders it, but the Spirit oversees the efficacy of the activity. The Spirit is the telos of the word, the one who realizes the word's aim and objective and hence realizes its perfection. The outstanding question for evangelicals is whether the Spirit's work in illumining Scripture's truth is part and parcel of the communicative action.

There is, I submit, an *economy of truth*, a divinely supervised administration of truth that requires biblical interpreters not merely to push propositions around in theoretical arguments but also to embody them in concrete forms of practical reasoning. The economy of communication terminates not in the text but in us. We "realize" Scripture's truth the way a musician "realizes" a score. Let me quote from *Notes from the Pianist's Bench:* "The work of a performing musician is not a creative process (in the sense of actually producing something new) but a re-creative one. In other words, we are playing music written by somebody else. We are the medium through which this music becomes audible. The impression of a musical work that the listener receives depends on us. . . . 'The musical score is Sleeping Beauty, the performer is the Prince releasing her from the spell.'"[97]

The analogy is not exact, for what needs to be illumined in biblical interpretation is not the text but the reader. Illumination is the Spirit's kiss, the breath of life; by waking us, it wakens sleeping beauty, or rather, sleeping truth. The Spirit animates biblical truth by animating us to receive it and its transformative effects. If engineering rather than music (or fairy tales) is your thing, think of the Spirit as a hermeneutical catalytic

---

[95]See my "Lost in Interpretation? Truth, Scripture, and Hermeneutics," in Köstenberger, *Whatever Happened to Truth?* pp. 93-130.

[96]In the economy of truth, there is place for both an objective and a subjective component.

[97]Boris Berman, *Notes from the Pianist's Bench* (New Haven: Yale University Press, 2000), pp. 139-40.

converter:[98] the Spirit does not change the substance of the word but removes the noxious gases—the cloud of unknowing—that prevents unillumined readers from acknowledging the textual truth that is already there by virtue of the Spirit's inspiration.[99]

Illumination does not make Scripture true but renders its truth intelligible and efficacious for wide-awake interpreters. *We short-circuit the economy of communication if we simply affirm the objective truth of Scripture and then stop. In exaggerating biblical inerrancy, we risk abbreviating the economy.* Propositional truth exists, but not for its own sake; indeed, we deny the perfection of the word of truth to the extent that we neglect its rhetorical functions (e.g., persuasion, consolation). In sum, Scripture's truth does not eliminate the need for interpretation but rather calls for it.[100] For the purpose of Scripture's truth-telling is ultimately pastoral: to free us from the darkness of falsehood so that we can live and speak in the light and life of Jesus Christ.

What now may we say about the apparent incoherence of the ETS statement, the problem from which we embarked? At the very least, we may say that the Trinity and Scripture, despite looking initially like a doctrinal odd couple, actually fit together hand in glove. Wittingly or not, the ETS statement gestures in the direction of an evangelical "first theology" that juxtaposes God and God's word, the *principium essendi* (foundation of existence) and *principium cognoscendi* (foundation of knowing) of Christian dogmatics. Many of the great Protestant confessions of the sixteenth and seventeenth centuries did something similar; in this respect at least, the ETS statement is in good company.

CONCLUSION: THE TRINITY IS OUR SCRIPTURE PRINCIPLE

I conclude my theological reflections with the claim that God speaks in Scripture by offering a unifying theme, two benefits of the approach here

---

[98]My thanks to Armida Stephens for suggesting the metaphor of the Spirit as a catalyst for biblical interpretation.

[99]I have not specified the mode of the Spirit's inspiration beyond gesturing in the direction of providence (the Spirit's superintendence of the authors and the whole writing process). The economy of communication does not "explain" biblical inspiration but situates it.

[100]"Interpretation is necessary because Holy Scripture is an element in the economy of salvation" (Webster, *Holy Scripture*, p. 59).

commended and three summary theses.

One "big idea." To claim that the Trinity is our Scripture Principle is to confess that the supreme authority in the church is the triune God speaking in the Scriptures. The Father communicates the wisdom embodied in his Son to the authors of Scripture through the Holy Spirit and eventually to its readers as well. The doctrine of Scripture, therefore, has both its genesis and terminus in the doctrine of the Trinity.

That the Trinity is our Scripture Principle means that the doctrine of Scripture is "at home" in the economy of God's self-communication. Kevin's "big idea," in a nutshell, is that *we come to an adequate theological understanding of the nature, authority and interpretation of Scripture only when we view these things in light of the broader economy of triune communication.* Scripture lives and moves and has its very being in this economy of triune communication. J. I. Packer makes a similar point but with greater eloquence: Scripture is "God the Father preaching God the Son in the power of God the Holy Ghost. God the Father is the giver of Holy Scripture; God the Son is the theme of Holy Scripture; and God the Spirit, as the Father's appointed agent in witnessing to the Son, is the author, authenticator, and interpreter of Holy Scripture."[101]

Two benefits. One benefit of making the Trinity our Scripture Principle is that it helps us to avoid falling into what Ramm calls the "abbreviated Protestant principle" that focuses on the written word to the neglect of the Spirit's internal witness. The word of God is, after all, the "sword of the Spirit" (Eph 6:17): to wield the word without the Spirit is to short-circuit the economy. Interpretation without inspired text is empty, but inerrant text without illumined interpretation is blind.

A second benefit of viewing Scripture in trinitarian perspective is that it enables us to put our whole theological house in order: enables us rightly to order our love for Scripture among our other loves, including our first love, Jesus Christ. In recognizing Scripture's place in the economy—in welcoming Scripture home, as it were—we save it from endless disputes about words and historical-critical genealogies and restore its pedagogical function as a guide to the way of Jesus Christ. To paraphrase Peter, "Where else

---

[101]J. I. Packer, *God Has Spoken* (Grand Rapids: Baker, 1979), p. 97.

should we go? It has the words of eternal life" (cf. Jn 6:68). The economy of canonical truth funds the economy of covenantal life.

Three theses. The following three theses summarize our theological reflections on the claim that God speaks. They do not deny that Scripture is also human discourse but view the human discourse as an ingredient in what is ultimately divine communicative action: triune discourse.

The first thesis is with regard to the nature of Scripture. *The Bible is a gracious word, a self-communicating work of triune love.*

Why is there something rather than nothing? Because God graciously decided to communicate his goodness to us, creatures who are not God. Why is there something biblical rather than nothing? Because God graciously decided to expand the conversation that is his own being to include us human creatures. The Bible is triune discourse, something the Father initiates, the Son effects and the Spirit perfects. Scripture, the constitutional covenant document, lives and moves and has its being in this communicative economy, where what comes to be shared and transmitted is not only matter (true information) but also energy (life in the Spirit).

The second thesis is with regard to the authority of Scripture. *The Bible is a truthful word, a knowledge-giving work of triune light.*

Christ, the Father's light, commissions prophets and apostles to be his witnesses; the Spirit enables them to bear true witness. Christ is the true Word of the Father, the object of the Spirit's witness, the supreme content of the Scriptures. The Spirit who speaks only what he hears provides and preserves a normative written witness to Christ. The only Christ we have is the Christ of the Spirit speaking in the Scriptures.

The third thesis is with regard to the interpretation of Scripture. *The Bible is a sanctifying word, a freeing work of triune life.*

Our theological reflections may not have invented the wheel, but they may have discovered a new hermeneutical circle: our ability rightly to interpret Scripture is a function of our grasp of the economy of communication (and vice versa). We know the economy only in light of Scripture; we know what Scripture is (and is for) only in light of the economy. Hence arises the key hermeneutical question: *Are interpreters contributing to the economy or working against it?*

Interpretation works against the economy when it becomes something readers do to inert texts, as if hermeneutics were a kind of autopsy. On the contrary, to read Scripture in the church is not to operate on a dead text but rather to be caught up into a communicative movement of triune life. For what ultimately comes to be communicated is indeed the Word of life. What the Trinity and Scripture ultimately have in common is *life*. The Father has life in himself; the Son is the resurrection and the life; the Spirit gives new life. In the final analysis, the right doctrinal location of Scripture is the economy through which God—Father, Son and Spirit—shares his life with us. Interpreters will not go too far wrong as long as they remember that their aim is to read Scripture in order to further the cause of communicating God's life to the church. For Scripture exists to engraft and insert readers into the economy. Right interpretation means furthering the ends of God's communicative action: speaking the truth in love, proclaiming the reconciliation of all things in Christ, praising God for the gift of himself.

Perhaps the most radical part of my thesis is its implicit claim (now explicit!) that any future evangelical doctrine of Scripture ought to include an account of the reader's interpretative agency and action. Anything less is thin description only. The theological interpretation of Scripture is not an afterthought but lies at the heart of the action, for the interpreter is a co-worker in the field of triune communicative action. The field is ripe for harvest, but the laborers—willing and virtuous theological interpreters of Scripture—are few (Lk 10:2). Let us therefore pray earnestly to the Lord of the harvest to raise up God-approved laborers who know how rightly to handle the triune word of love, light and life.

3

The Gift of the Father

Looking at Salvation History Upside Down

EDITH M. HUMPHREY

> *From the heart of Jesus flowing,*
>
> *Cometh Heaven's peace to me,*
>
> *Ever deeper, richer growing*
>
> *Through the Cross of Calvary,*
>
> *Passing mortal understanding,*
>
> *Yet to seeking ones made known,*
>
> *And for all the race expanding,*
>
> *Gift of God unto his own.*
>
> CHARLES COLLER,
> "FROM THE HEART OF JESUS FLOWING"

The above hymn was written by an ordinary nineteenth-century Christian, not distinguished by any specialized education or position. A lay musician and clerk in the Salvation Army Trade Store for most of his life, Charles Coller also poured out his heart in memorable musical lyrics. When I was a teen, I remember being both enticed and irritated by this song. I understood the song to be true, but I also viewed it as a kind of sentimental hyperbole intended to warm our hearts with regard to the love of Jesus for us on the cross, to make us more and more aware of the peace that we ought to have within. I since have changed my mind.

It is that last line that did it for me: "Gift of God!" Think for a moment about the implication of those words. Perhaps most naturally our minds assume that the phrase refers to a "gift" or "grace" that belongs to God and that he gives to us—possessive or subjective genitive, for you grammar buffs. The *gift* of God. Frequently in the West, Christians have objectified "grace" as though it were a "something" separate from God himself, a substance that can be given in measure, parceled out and sent to us. But the incarnation astonishes us: God will not, in the end, allow us to divide "grace" from himself. God's greatest gift to us is *himself*. He *is* our salvation; he *is* our sanctification. And so we come to that other particularly Christian meaning of "Gift of God," the objective genitive—it is the Gift of *God*, that gift *who is God*, God-among-us, God-with-us, Immanuel!

The song also speaks about heaven's peace in an objective manner: this peace is something inexhaustible, something that grows richer and deeper and that is expansive beyond human sentiment or dreams. The moment we probe the mystery of peace, love and expansiveness, and the moment we meditate upon the words "gift of God unto his own," we are on the verge of another great mystery: "He came unto his own, and his own did not receive him; but to as many as received him, he gave the power to become the children of God, to those who believed upon his name" (Jn 1:11-12, my own translation). The gift of God is more than the gift of God incarnate among us—though, as our Jewish friends would put it on Passover night, "*Dayeinu*! That would have been enough!" It is also the gift of that one whom we now may dare to call God the Father, because he has given us the power to be his children in Christ Jesus, through the Holy Spirit. And so it is that meditation upon Jesus, upon the one who died for us, is inextricably connected with the mystery of the holy Trinity. As the seventeenth-century Anglican poet George Herbert put it:

> Thou hast but two rare cabinets full of treasure,
> The *Trinity*, and *Incarnation*:
> Thou hast unlockt them both,
> And made them jewels to betroth
> The work of thy creation
> Unto thy self in everlasting pleasure.
> ("Ungratefulness," *The Temple*, George Herbert)

How is it that these two rare cabinets, Trinity and Incarnation, are unlocked for us? Is this an incremental or wholly gradual unveiling, bound up with dispensations in time? Back in the twelfth century, this idea was advanced by the hopeful Joachim of Fiore: the Old Testament was the era of the Father, the New Testament was the era of the Son, and the era of the Holy Spirit was about to dawn. Though his teachings were declared heretical, many Christians today adopt a similar scheme: in the Old Testament, they suppose, a rather remote Father God was active in creation and in Israel; in the New Testament we come to know that there is a loving God the Son; and now, in the church age, we the blessed can appreciate and appropriate the ministrations of the Holy Spirit. Can I suggest to you that this is almost exactly backward?

A New Perspective?

We tend to think of the revelation and gift of the New Testament as focused upon the Son, God incarnate. It is meet and right so to do! However, the New Testament and patristic writers read the Old Testament in such a way that we must rethink this presupposition, not cleaving to it as an absolute. Indeed, attention to their witness suggests that we may approach the gifts and revelations of the new covenant in what might seem to us to be an upside-down fashion. What happens if we consider that the LORD of the Old Testament—the One who creates, acts, speaks and guides—is the Son incognito? What if the major actions of the New Testament are to reveal and indeed to *give* us a proper Father (as well as the Holy Spirit), in the sense that Christians become true children of God, now anointed in Christ Jesus? An early theologian of the church, Hilary of Poitiers (300?-368), declared that "the very center of a saving faith" is "not merely in God, but in God as Father, and not merely in Christ, but in Christ as the Son of God" (*De trinitate* 1.17).

Christians, then, are those who rightfully name God as Father, because of the Son, in the strength of the Holy Spirit. Irenaeus takes his cue from the words of Jesus himself: "*No one* knows the Father except the Son and *anyone to whom* the Son chooses to reveal him" (Mt 11:27; Lk 10:22, RSV). The Fourth Gospel takes Jesus at his word and rephrases his declaration, if possible, even more sharply: "*No one* has *ever* seen God; the only Son, who is in the bosom of the Father, *has 'exegeted'* him" (Jn 1:18, my own translation; the Greek word *exēgēsato* is commonly translated as "interpreted [him]," "made [him] known," cf. RSV). Here we see that true knowledge and intimate knowledge of God comes by way of our knowing the Son, who alone (with the Holy Spirit) is intimate with the Father: it is in the light of the Son that we come to know the ineffable light of the Father. The person and work of the Son, then, are both cognitive and effective: the Son reveals the Father to the faithful; the work of the Son makes us faithful children of God.

If this is the case, then it is wrong-headed to assume, without further reflection, that the voice of God speaking in the Old Testament texts is that of the Father. Certainly it is mistaken to assume that Hebrews, Israelites or early Jews, independent of the work of the Son, gave to God the proper name of Father (over against a metaphorical use, "father" alongside "fortress," "rock" or "tower"). That would be to give the lie to our Lord himself: "No one knows [or names!] the Father except the Son and anyone to whom the Son chooses to reveal him." There surely are several honorable traditions by which the LORD of the Old Testament may be understood. In the Hebrew Bible, do we find mysterious revelations of the Father or glimmerings of an abstract and undifferentiated deity who would later be recognized as the triune God? Perhaps. But a major and ancient stream in the church has considered the theophanies of the Old Testament to be revelations of the Son (albeit not yet named as such). This view, that the God who speaks and reveals himself in the Hebrew Bible is the Son, I remember hearing for the first time as a very young lecturer when I was teaching Old Testament at a Roman Catholic university in Ottawa. I had heard explanations of a few uncanny passages that placed the preincarnate Son back into the Old Testament—the fourth man in the fiery furnace in Daniel 3:25, for example. But I had always considered these readings to be fanciful. Moreover, my training in the historical-critical method had preconditioned me to react even against tracing the Trinity in the Hebrew Bible: that would be anachronistic. However, as one earnest young Eastern Christian ordinand sketched the difference that it made to see YHWH as the *Son* speaking from the bush to Moses, I remember doing something spontaneously that made the class titter. I tilted my head so that my forehead was facing the floor and said, "Things look very different upside down."

However, looking at things from a different vantage point is wholly biblical. John the visionary is told by the Lord, "Come up here, and I will show you" (Rev 4:1 NIV). Let us try, then, a new vantage point, putting the head the other way, to see how things look. In so doing, we follow a strong tradition of the church, a tradition that indeed extends back into the New Testament itself, understanding God as speaking always through the Son, the Word. We will begin by considering some key passages in the New Testament, showing their inner connection with the Old Testament in how they picture the Lord and doing this within the context of the theological and worshiping tradition of the church. After showing that the eternal Son speaks in the Old Testament, and that the same second Person reveals the Father to us in the New Testament and eternally, we will consider the importance of our own adoption as God's children and the thorny question of order within the Trinity.

JESUS AS YHWH

We begin with a deceptively pragmatic Pauline text: 1 Corinthians 8:1-13. Here Paul is giving practical instruction to the Corinthians regarding whether they may eat food that has been offered to idols. (This was a common practice in the ancient world, where much of the food for sale at the market had been previously "devoted" to a deity.) In the course of this contentious debate, Paul drops a theological bomb into the playground of any who might think that the one true God is a mere "monad"—a divine atom or simple unit. In a deft restatement of the beloved Jewish Shema, the Hebrew declaration of God's holiness and peculiarity, Paul sets us thinking about the relationship between Father and Son. "Hear, O Israel: the LORD our God, the LORD is one" (Deut 6:4 NIV) is now cast in this way:

> "*There is no God but one.*" For although there may be so-called gods in heaven or on earth—as indeed there are many "gods" and many "lords"— yet for us there is *one God, the Father,* from whom are all things and for whom we exist, and *one Lord, Jesus Christ,* through whom are all things and through whom we exist. (1 Cor 8:4-6 RSV, emphasis added)

What is most striking is how Paul recasts the Shema without any warning or defensiveness. Evidently, in the midst of clearing up a controversy regarding the existence of false gods and whether it is acceptable to eat food erroneously offered to these "nothings," he can draw upon a belief that he shares with the Corinthians. Here, amid practical teaching, we find a specifically Christian definition of monotheism, which gives us startling insight into how Paul and early Christians read the Old Testament: the One whom they know as Jesus Christ is KYRIOS (in the Greek translation of the Old Testament, the LXX), YHWH (in the Masoretic or authorized Hebrew text), the LORD whom the Hebrews proclaimed by means of their declaration, "Shema! Listen!" Through this One they have come to know the "one God, the Father," from whom are all things. Paul thus can declare: For Christians, there is one God, the Father, and one Lord, that same LORD of Israel, through whom all things exist and toward whom we are oriented. But all do not possess this knowledge, he laments. I submit that it is not simply ignorance of the Son in the Old Testament that he laments, but also ignorance of the Father, because the truths are intertwined. One plus one equals one: "Hear, O Israel: the LORD our God, the LORD is One."

This is not a haphazard and eccentric moment in Paul's writing: the apostle is not alone in this understanding of the LORD. This is confirmed by the luminous passage of Philippians 2:5-11, believed by many New Testament scholars to be representative of earliest Christian hymnody. Following the climax of that hymn—the Son empties himself to the point of death on the cross—the denouement swings up to glory, in a remarkable recasting of the words of the prophet Isaiah: "that at the name of Jesus every knee should bow, in heaven and on earth and under the earth, and every tongue confess that Jesus Christ is LORD, to the glory of God the Father" (Phil 2:11, my own translation). Recall the original location of this hymnic echo: the prophet is poking fun at the stupidity of Gentiles who worship lifeless idols, and he is assuring the scattered of Israel that the LORD alone is God.

Assemble yourselves and come, draw near together, you survivors of the nations! They have no knowledge *who carry about their wooden idols, and keep on praying to a god that cannot save.* Declare and present your case; let them take counsel together! Who told this long ago? Who declared it of old? *Was it not I, the* LORD? And there is no other god besides me, a righteous God and a Savior; there is none besides me. "Turn to me and be saved, all the ends of the earth! For I am God, and there is no other. By myself I have sworn, from my mouth has gone forth in righteousness a word that shall not return: '*To me every knee shall bow, every tongue shall swear.*' Only in the LORD, it shall be said of me, *are righteousness and strength*; to him shall come and be ashamed, all who were incensed against him. In the LORD all the offspring of Israel shall triumph and glory." (Is 45:20-25 RSV, emphasis added)

What cheek of the early Christians to borrow an oath from the one true God, spoken solemnly in the midst of a denunciation of idolatry, and to apply these words about knees and tongues to the Lord Jesus! This is truly audacious unless they identified Jesus as that one in the Hebrew Bible "who declared of old," who is the only "Savior," and who is the true Lord in whom "all the offspring of Israel [and the redeemed of the nations!] shall glory." Whenever this one is worshiped, when this one is confessed as Lord, then glory is not taken away from God. Rather, says Paul with the Philippian worshipers, it is given "to . . . the Father" (Phil 2:11).

BEGINNING THEOLOGY WITH THE SON

In his latest offering, *Jesus and the Father* (2006),[1] Kevin Giles poses the question, "Where should thinking about the Trinity begin?" He offers four possibilities, all practiced within systematics: we can start with the Father, we can start with the divine Three, we can start with the idea of a divine substance, or we can start with the notion of the Trinity. When we move from systematics to the story of our salvation and go back to the New Testament witness, it appears that we must rephrase the question: "Where *did* thinking about the Trinity begin?" Evidently, it began with the recognition that Jesus is Lord and that Jesus is the true Son of the true Father.

Indeed, the person of Jesus, identified with the LORD of the Scriptures, makes a good beginning! We see it everywhere in the New Testament—in the creedal statements, in the echoed hymns, in the narratives. So it is that the sequence of the apostolic benediction is impressed upon us: "The grace of the Lord Jesus Christ and the love of God and the fellowship of the Holy Spirit be with you all" (2 Cor 13:14). The grace of the Son, offered astonishingly in Jesus, opens to us the love of the Father and the shared life of the

---

[1]Kevin Giles, *Jesus and the Father: Modern Evangelicals Reinvent the Doctrine of the Trinity* (Grand Rapids: Zondervan, 2006), p. 77.

Holy Spirit. Thus, in brief confessional statements of the New Testament, Jesus is called eternal *Word* (Jn 1:1), wisdom and righteousness (1 Cor 1:30), and creator, eternal head, source and firstborn (Col 1:15-20). The paradox of this Word, Lord, *Archē* and Creator coming among us in the flesh is everywhere intimated and sometimes in the New Testament is remarked upon with shock: "The light shines in the darkness, but the darkness has not understood it" (Jn 1:5). The one who subdued chaos and contained the sea at the creation displays his authority by tracing his path upon the waters, and he quiets them with a word:

> Awake, awake, put on strength, O arm of the LORD; awake, as in days of old, the generations of long ago. Was it not thou that didst . . . pierce the dragon? Was it not thou that didst dry up the sea, the waters of the great deep; that didst make the depths of the sea a way for the redeemed to pass over? . . . "I, I am he that comforts you, . . . who stretched out the heavens and laid the foundations of the earth. . . . I am the LORD your God, who stirs up the sea so that its waves roar—the LORD of hosts is his name. And I have . . . hid you in the shadow of my hand, stretching out the heavens and laying the foundations of the earth, and saying to Zion, 'You are my people.'" (Is 51:9-16, RSV)

> Some went down to the sea in ships doing business on the great waters; they saw the deeds of the LORD. . . . For he commanded and raised the stormy wind, which lifted up the waves of the sea. . . . Their courage melted away in their evil plight; they . . . were at their wits' end. Then they cried to the LORD in their trouble, and he delivered them from their distress; he made the storm be still, and the waves of the sea were hushed. . . . Let them thank the LORD for his steadfast love, for his wonderful works to the sons of men! (Ps 107:23-31, RSV)

> "Teacher, do you not care if we perish?" And he awoke and rebuked the wind, and said to the sea, "Peace! Be still!" And the wind ceased, and there was a great calm. He said to them, "Why are you afraid? Have you no faith?" And they were filled with awe and said to one another, "Who then is this, that even wind and sea obey him?" (Mk 4:38-41, RSV)

This is only one of the descriptions of Jesus our Lord that rings bells, reminding us of the God who is Lord of the sea, who commands and it is created, who speaks and it is stilled. The most direct connection between Jesus the Son and what have been called the "Logophanies" of the Old

Testament is certainly seen in the event that is structurally central to the Synoptic Gospels and that underscores the entire presentation of Jesus in the Fourth Gospel—the transfiguration of Christ. There the voice from heaven directs the disciples, as they see Jesus illuminated and surrounded by the glory cloud, "This is my beloved Son; listen to him" (Mk 9:7 RSV).

The very same one who named Adam and who called Israel into being, the LORD, is in the New Testament pages doing battle on behalf of his people: casting out the enemy with the finger of God, healing even those associated with his enemies (think of the ear of the slave in the garden), restoring Israel by calling twelve and renaming them, hearing and responding to the cry of those who were like a flock without a shepherd. What the apostles see, and what we the believing community see through their stories and words, is the same One who walked with Adam and Eve in the garden, whom Moses glimpsed on Sinai and who strengthened Elijah on Carmel. The mighty acts of Jesus are not simply the style of a human prophet: they also correspond to the very acts of the LORD, to what the Lord has always done, as we are forcibly reminded by theologians, from the second century to the twenty-first.

Irenaeus declares: "It is he himself [the Logos] who says to Moses, 'I have surely seen the affliction of my people in Egypt, and I have come down to rescue them.' From the beginning he was accustomed, as the Word of God, to descend and ascend for the salvation of those who were in distress" (*Adversus haereses* 4.12.4). The one who made the plants grow and the animals flourish for the sake of humankind, who gave manna and quails in the wilderness for Israel, who empowered the prophets to feed the hungry—this LORD now empowers his disciples to feed the longing crowds with blessed bread. Thus, the twentieth-century C. S. Lewis, so imbued with the great tradition that he is recognized by Roman Catholic, Orthodox and evangelical alike, explains: "[In Jesus] God does suddenly and locally something that God has done or will do. . . . Each miracle writes for us in small letters something that God has already written, or will write, in letters almost too large to be noticed, across the whole canvass of nature"[2]—and, he would agree, not only of nature but also of history too.

---

[2]C. S. Lewis, *Miracles: A Preliminary Study* (1947; reprint, New York: HarperCollins 2001), p. 219.

In the New Testament, then, we perceive continuity between the style of YHWH and Jesus, coupled with an astonishment that the kingship of God is here and now, in Jesus, among those who see him speaking and acting. As Jesus declared to the Pharisees who had fixed ideas about the coming of God's rule, "The kingdom of God is *among you*" (*entos hymōn;* Lk 17:21, my translation). By this Jesus indicated that the kingdom, or reign, of God was there in his own very presence, words and actions. The surprise goes beyond this: Breathtakingly, this holy one also appears in glorious weakness, born of a woman though he is the source of the universe, wrapped in human clothing though he wrapped the Edenic couple with furs, baptized in the waters though he is the true baptizer, hungry in the wilderness though he can feed multitudes, judged by Gentiles though he is the king of the universe, scourged and pierced though he can call legions of angels at his command, giving up his spirit though he breathed life into all. We are so used to these stories that we perhaps do not recognize their implications. Moreover, our hymns have been bowdlerized so that we have miscarried that most wondrous of theological insights: among those who contemplate the one who is the Son, the real miracle is that he *died*, not even that he rose again. Many of our hymnbooks have altered the profundity of Charles Wesley, a theological concept that has a coherent line back to the second century, and back before that into the New Testament itself: "Amazing love! How can it be / That Thou, my God, shouldst die for me?" No, we assume, Wesley must have it wrong, so our present-day renditions change "God" to "King" or "Lord": "Amazing love! . . . / That thou, my Lord, should die." No! That is not what Wesley meant. For the very next line of the hymn, a verse often omitted, gasps: "'Tis mystery all: th'Immortal dies: / Who can explore His strange design?" We miss the paradox, through the efforts of well-meaning editors who are impoverishing our already non-imaginative era.

Yet, this great mystery, that the LORD of creation should be touched by human hands, has a persistent staying power. We trace it from Peter's sermon in Acts through to the "praise songs" of today:

If they had known this, they would not have "killed the Lord of glory."
(1 Cor 2:8, my translation)

Today, He who holds the whole creation in the hollow of His hand
is born of the Virgin.
He whom in essence none can touch
is wrapped in swaddling clothes as a mortal.
God who in the beginning founded the heavens
lies in a manger.
He who rained manna down on the people in the wilderness
is fed on milk from His Mother's breast.
(Byzantine hymn, "Ninth Hour of the Eve of Nativity: Glory Sticheron")[3]

A strange wonder it is to see the Maker of heaven and earth stand naked in
the river, and as a servant receive baptism from a servant, for our salvation.
("Eve of Theophany: Sticheron at the Ninth Hour")

How [demurs the Baptist] shall I stretch forth my hand
and touch the head of Him that rules all things? . . .
You, whose praises the seraphim sing,
walk upon the earth.
And I who am but a servant
know not how to baptize the Master.
("Matins of Theophany: Sticheron After the Gospel Reading")

The Wisdom of God that restrains the untamed fury of the waters
that are above the firmament,
that sets a bridle on the deep and keeps back the seas,
now pours water into a basin;
and the Master washes the feet of His servants.
("Holy Thursday Matins: Canticle 5, Sticheron 2")

He who hung the earth in space, is himself hanged;
He who fixed the heavens in place, is himself impaled;
He who firmly fixed all things, is himself firmly fixed to the tree. . . .
God has been murdered.
(Melito of Sardis, *Paschal Homily* 96)[4]

---

[3]For the stichera, I am indebted to the careful work of Bogdan G. Bucur, "Exegesis of
Biblical Theophanies in Byzantine Hymnography: Rewritten Bible?" *Theological Studies*
68 (2007): 92-112; idem, "The Feet That Eve Heard in Paradise and Was Afraid: Observations on the Christology of Byzantine Hymns," *Philosophy and Theology* 18, no. 1 (2006):
3-27.
[4]The translation is that of Gerald F. Hawthorne, "A New English Translation of Melito's

Though this hymnody of contrast is solemn and paradoxical, it is sometimes framed in utterly personal terms. The lovely lyrics of the ninth-century Cassiane are more ornate, but not very far in spirit from the resurrection scene in John's Gospel. There, Mary Magdalene is named "woman" and falls at the feet of Jesus, signaling the undoing of the cursed day when her mother Eve, reproached as woman by the Lord of creation, hid herself from the sound of those feet. The medieval hymn makes use of the same contrasts to picture, for the sake of penitent adoration, Mary's anointing of Jesus before his burial:

> O Lord, the woman who has fallen into many sins, perceiving Your divinity and taking upon herself the duty of a myrrh-bearer, with lamentations brings sweet-smelling oil of myrrh to You before Your burial. Woe is me, she says, for night surrounds me: a dark and moonless frenzy of unrestraint, the lust for sin. Accept the wells of my tears, for it is You that draws down from the clouds the waters of the sea. Incline to the groanings of my heart, for it is You that have bowed down the heavens in Your ineffable self-emptying. I shall tenderly kiss Your most pure feet and also wipe them with the locks of my hair—those feet whose sound Eve heard at dusk in Paradise and hid herself for fear. Who can search out the multitude of my sins and the abyss of Your judgments, O Savior of my soul? Despise me not, Your handmaiden, for You have mercy without measure. (Holy Wednesday)[5]

In case we think that such shocking juxtapositions have no place in our own context, let me remind you that they still slip through into today. Here they can still have the function of directing us to wonder and worship, when we think of them with sobriety and not merely with sentimentality:

> Come see His hands and His feet,
> The scars that speak of sacrifice;
> Hands that flung stars into space
> To cruel nails surrendered.
> (Graham Kendrick, "The Servant King")

Paschal Homily," in *Current Issues in Biblical and Patristic Interpretation,* ed. G. F. Hawthorne (Grand Rapids: Eerdmans, 1975) and partially reproduced in Bart D. Ehrman, *After the New Testament: A Reader in Early Christianity* (New York: Oxford University Press, 1999), p. 127. The historical concreteness of Melito, though striking, slides into anti-Semitism.

[5]Text from Bucur, "The Feet That Eve Heard," pp. 4-5.

This is the language that dares to call Mary the Theotokos—"Bearer of God"—and not simply Christotokos. This is the language that dares to say "God died" and not simply "Christ died." This is the language that takes seriously the ongoing refrain upon Jesus' lips in the Gospel of John: "I AM." It is the grammar that understands why it is that Jesus breathes upon his disciples after his resurrection, conferring now upon them the very Spirit of new life, a replacement for the common breath of life first breathed into the Adamic couple. This is an unapologetically incarnational grammar that finds its genesis in the stories, in the confessions and the hymns of the New Testament and indeed in the self-revelation of God the Son. It sees in the actions and person of Jesus of Nazareth the person, the character, the style (theologians say, "essence") of YHWH the LORD.

THE TRUE SON AND HUMAN SONSHIP

With a glance back to Herbert's two treasures, we see that the revelation of the incarnation and the Trinity, though hinted at for long ages, was not, in every sense, a gradual unveiling.[6] No sooner is the lock of the incarnation undone, than the lock on the treasure chest of the Trinity springs open. Granted, it took several centuries for all that treasure to be unpacked, to be taken into inventory, so to speak, but the doctrine of the Trinity was not dreamed in a vision, not framed as an utter novelty in the ecumenical creeds. Indeed, the truth about the triune God is implicit in the knowing confession that Jesus is LORD (as we think about his relation to us and the

---

[6]I am not here intending to critique the pastoral comments of Gregory of Nazianzus, who has been of enormous help to me in thinking through these issues. In *Orationes theologicae* 5.26, he speaks of the gradual realization of the church concerning the full doctrines of the Son and of the Spirit. With regard to his words in this passage, that the Father is seen clearly in the Old Testament, we may appeal to his context, which liturgically read the Father back into the Old Testament on a regular basis, as well as his reaction against the monotheistic (but not Christian) sect of Hypsistos (the Most High [God]) to which his own father belonged, a group that refused the name *Father* to God and steadfastly used philosophical terms. I think that if we were to question him, he would agree that one cannot know the full implications of God the Father until one understands truly that there is God the Son. Moreover, all the revelation about the Trinity is in the Son, waiting to be, so to speak, "unpacked." As Gregory would put it, "Again He said that all things should be taught us by the Spirit when He should come to dwell amongst us. Of these things one, I take it, was the Deity of the Spirit Himself, made clear later on when such knowledge should be seasonable and capable of being received after our Saviour's restoration, when it would no longer be received with incredulity because of its marvellous character. For what greater thing than this did either He promise, or the Spirit teach?" (*Orationes theologicae* 5.27).

world) and in our careful contemplation concerning his self-revealed and proper identity as Son to the Father, with the Holy Spirit. The Sonship, moreover, is intimated in a bizarre phenomenon of the New Testament that constantly has tripped up exegetes and theologians. Those very books and passages in our New Testament that have the "highest Christology"—clearly confessing Jesus as divine LORD—are infused, cheek-by-jowl, with so-called low christological language about the humility, submission and order of the Son in relation to the Father. In Hebrews, Jesus is greater than all that has come before; Jesus learns obedience as a Son. In the Fourth Gospel, Jesus is the great I AM; the Father is greater than the Son. In Paul we find the same paradox. Having declared Jesus to be YHWH the LORD in 1 Corinthians 8, the apostle goes on in 1 Corinthians 15 to imagine an ordering of the Son and the Father that is not simply time bound, but that goes as far as the human eye, aided by revelation, can reach: "When all things are subjected to him, then the Son himself will also be subjected to him who put all things under him, that God may be everything to every one" (1 Cor 15:28 RSV).

And there's the rub. With the incarnation, the willing humiliation of the Son, we catch a glimpse of the triune God that has dire implications for our twenty-first-century smugness. When he was Cardinal Ratzinger, the present pontiff of Rome wrote, in speaking of the common allergy to the doctrine of the incarnation, "We don't want any 'condescension.' We want equality."[7] Some would prefer to be called "friends of God," and this indeed is one of the pictures that Jesus uses in referring to his disciples as his very own friends. But the constant refrain of the New Testament is that, because of the person and work of Christ Jesus, the Son, we become the children or, more properly, "sons" of the Father. On that luminous Easter morning, Jesus tells Magdalene to go and tell the disciples, whom he now calls siblings, "I am ascending to my Father and your Father" (Jn 20:17): the implication is that those who are incorporated with Christ may also now call God "Father" because they are in the Son, who is Son to the Father.

All along in the Fourth Gospel, the Spirit is depicted as involved in the rebirth and marking out of those who are children of God. The word of the

---

[7]Joseph Cardinal Ratzinger, *The God of Jesus Christ: Meditations on God in the Trinity*, trans. R. J. Cunningham (Chicago: Franciscan Press, 1979), p. 52.

risen Lord to which Mary testifies is followed by the Son's own action of breathing the Spirit upon his disciples, reminiscent of God's life-giving animation in that first creation. There is a new creation, a new birth, and they are born from above as God's own children, because they belong to Jesus. So, too, with Paul's letters. Both Galatians 4 and Romans 8 speak about God having bestowed on us a gift of "sonship" *(huiothesia)*, made available to those who are "in Christ Jesus." In both letters, the Holy Spirit is called "the Spirit of sonship," who leads disciples as he led Jesus into the wilderness, who anoints them just as the Spirit lit upon the Son in the Jordan waters, who recognizes them and enables them to say "Abba! Father!" But the Son, Paul tells us in Romans 8, is the One who has fulfilled God's righteous requirements on our behalf, freeing us from sin and death, so that we may now walk according to the Spirit. It is in walking by the Spirit that we show ourselves to be children of God, coheirs with Christ. Again, in Galatians 4, Paul tells the story of salvation, how the Son, sent by the Father, was born of woman, born under the law, to redeem those who were under the law, so that we might receive the "sonship." All those who are in Christ Jesus are sons (Gal 3:26), because he is the Son par excellence.

In Paul, the language seems doubly offensive. Without any tip of the hat to egalitarianism, Paul speaks of slavery, from which we have been freed, and of sonship, as though this should relieve us. But our culture finds both distasteful, preferring the metaphor "friends" to the exclusively male and hierarchical language of sonship. Paul's intent surely is not to exclude women (and so he sometimes also uses the word *tekna*, children); rather, he uses language that aligns us in a most poignant way with the title for Jesus, the "Son of God." "Son of God" is the language of anointing, the language of messiahship. Paul describes us as following in the Messiah's shoes, anointed by the Spirit, led by the Spirit into the wilderness of godly suffering, crying out "Abba!" in our prayers. We are little "sons of God," little "christs," because our lives are now bound up with the one who is the true Son.

The sonship language is necessary in order to link us by name to the Son of God, the true Messiah. The sonship language also evokes our inheritance, since sons in the biblical world received the lion's share, the share that marked them as the child who would receive all that the father has. The particular kind of relationship that is indicated for us is far deeper and far more sober than the "friendship" imagery, which is sometimes used to describe one who is beloved of God. For we stand in need of receiving what the Father has to give us. Reciprocity is one of the wonders that we come to understand in the new creation. The Son surely does show us mysteries, so that in one sense we are, astonishingly, friends of God. God lovingly receives our affection, our worship, our gifts, our conversation. Be this as it may, the line is to be traced, for the most part, *from* him to us: he gives and we receive. All that we offer to him, our lives and hearts, come from him in the first place.

But we will not have it! Not yet content with muddling Wesley's words, liturgists have also flattened out the language of that ancient Celtic hymn "Be Thou My Vision," incorporated in altered form into many contemporary hymnals. One stanza of the original song reads as follows:

> Be Thou my Wisdom, and Thou my true Word;
> I ever with Thee and Thou with me, Lord;
> Thou my great Father, I Thy true son;
> Thou in me dwelling, and I with Thee one.[8]

Do we not sell short the imagination of twenty-first-century people by turning this into a banal wish, such as, "I thy true one"? Others have essayed a line that must be forced into scansion: "Thine own may I be." Or, more boldly going where no church ever dared to go before, some have penned: "Mother and Father, you are both to me / Now and forever, your child I will be" *(United Church of Christ Hymnal)*. These three strategies—omitting the stanza, changing it prosaically or audaciously revising—demonstrate how our age is uncomfortable with the ordered language of the Scriptures and the Celtic birthplace of this song.

ALLERGIC TO HIERARCHY

All this is not merely a matter of whether we prefer to use the language of children or friends. It is a thoroughgoing allergy to order or—God forbid!—to hierarchy. Indeed, the rational among us prefer a God who does not present us with paradox, a God who will be a model, even a mascot, of our

---

[8]"Rob tu mo bhoile, a Comdi cride," attributed to Dallan Forgaill, eighth century, translated by Mary Byrne as "Be Thou My Vision."

fond democratic ideologies. Consider the proliferation of newer, casual hymns that call us into the eternal and ineffable "dance" of the companionable Trinity. But *perichōrēsis* does not mean "a round dance," no matter how many would-be Greek specialists say so on the Internet![9] There is an ineffable movement toward the other and a mutual indwelling of the persons of the Trinity; however, this perichoresis does not negate the eternal order of Father begetting Son and "spirating" the Spirit. But many seem to think that the mutuality of the Godhead cancels out this basic relation, witnessed to in John's Gospel and elsewhere in the New Testament. Even evangelicals are so detached from the careful trinitarian debates of the past that some find plausible words such as these:

> One of the weirdest heresies that has been generated in the last century pertains to the postulation of a hierarchical order within the members of the Trinity—as if there ever could exist a threat of discord or of misconduct that would require the exercise of authority within the oneness of the Godhead.[10]

A "weird heresy"! Generated in the twentieth century? Because "order" must be a sign of "threatened discord"? The statement is astonishing, given the involved and longstanding discussions of the ancient church and the continued confessions of both East and West with regard to the relations of Father, Son and Spirit. A statement such as this relegates to the category of heretic the Roman Catholic Church, the Eastern Orthodox Church and much of the Reformed tradition, not to mention individuals of renown like C. S. Lewis, John Zizioulas, the current pontiff and myriad others.[11] There

---

[9]The etymology of *perichōrēsis* (verb *perichōreō*, *not* the verb *perichoreuō*) does not come from the root noun *choros* (meaning "chorus," as in Greek tragedy, or "dance") but *chōra* (meaning "place"). Though the preposition *peri* often has the connotation of "around," so that noun *can* mean "rotation," *peri* also means "about, near, by, above, beyond," and so *perichōrēsis* also takes on the meaning of "going beyond one's place" or "making room for." The ancient theologians used the word to refer to the reciprocity, alternation and interpenetration of the persons of the Trinity; in Latin, both the words *circumincessio* (interpenetration) and *circuminsessio* (mutual indwelling) were necessary to approximate the dynamic Greek. The point is that the term does not evoke anything so frivolous as a dance, but is used to describe the great mystery by which Persons of the holy Trinity occupy the same "space," yet are "near and toward" each other, in their distinctness. (By the way, in one ancient text, the cherubim *are* said to "dance"—*perichoreuō*—but *never* the Trinity.)

[10]The expostulation is that of Gilbert Bilezikian, printed in the front matter of Kevin Giles's book *Jesus and the Father*.

[11]As an example, consider the following statement, which insists that the debate over the filioque clause must not be construed from the Western side as an assault upon the monarchy

is, to be sure, a *heretical* subordinationism that pictures the Son as subordinate (and the Spirit with the Son) in being or essence to the Father. However, the tension between order and mutuality, in the inner life of the triune God, as well as in the external operations of the Godhead, is no heresy:[12] it is the only sense that we can make of the Scriptures and indeed safeguards the monotheism that we profess. Frequently folks lament that the creeds of the ancient church are complex and hard to follow. On the contrary, says Joseph Ratzinger, when the ancient theologians gathered for the Councils of Nicaea and of Chalcedon, they spoke *"piscatorie et non aristotelice* [like fishermen and not like philosophers]."[13] Despite their philosophical language, they responded simply to the basic questions of simple Christians. They declared that the profession of faith had a nucleus, and that nucleus was the "Son." The very heart of the Bible—its witness about Jesus Christ— is to be taken "literally."[14] The name "Son" implies "Father," and indeed the person and work of our LORD directs us to the Father of lights, from whom all good gifts come. Now, a whole spate of revising theologians and pastors have been spawned in our seminaries, who are teaching us that the metaphor "father" is expendable and indeed mere cultural baggage.

According to this approach, human beings are faced with the mystery that they believe to be God or the sacred or the divine. They cannot know it. So they project ideas and values onto a humanly constructed picture of the divine, always knowing that they are only grasping after this and can never be confident that the picture or the words or the ideas correspond to

---

of the Father: "Both traditions [the Orthodox Church and the Catholic Church] also clearly affirm that the Father is the primordial source *(archē)* and ultimate cause *(aitia)* of the divine being, and thus of all God's operations: the 'spring' from which both the Son and Spirit flow, the 'root' of their being and fruitfulness, the 'sun' from which their existence and their activity radiates." (*The Filioque: A Church-Dividing Issue? An Agreed Statement of the North American Orthodox-Catholic Theological Consultation,* October 25, 2003, United States Conference of Catholic Bishops http://www.usccb.org/seia/filioque.shtml).

[12]Bradford E. Hinze, "Dialogical Traditions and a Trinitarian Hermeneutic" (in *Theology and Conversation: Towards a Relational Theology,* ed. J. Haers and P. De Mey [Leuven: Leuven University Press, 2003]), insists that "the trinitarian mystery is one of mutual obedience!" and speaks of this as "the simple truth of the matter, abundantly testified to in Scriptures" (p. 302). The scriptural evidence adduced for the "obedience" of Father to Son or Spirit is stretched, to say the least. Certainly the persons are in a mutual relation and respond to each other—but to give glory to another or to answer prayer is not to "obey." Mutuality seemingly coheres with asymmetry in the trinitarian mystery.

[13]Ratzinger, *The God of Jesus Christ,* p. 79.

[14]Ibid., p. 82.

this mysterious essence. As Canadian theologian and liturgist Paul Gibson puts it, "We cannot speak of God without images, for to do so would be to claim to have seen God's face and survived. . . . To confuse our images with the reality of God is idolatry. The Old Testament employs many images to speak of God. . . . None of these images say what God is; they each say something of what God is like. . . . The images of mother and father suggest that in the best of responsible, caring, compassionate, loving fatherhood and motherhood we see something of the true nature of God."[15]

What is wrong with this perspective? Gibson is certainly right that God is all mystery, totally other, beyond our frame of reference. Since we do see through a veil darkly, since we use these fallen minds and wounded hearts and blinkered eyes to see and to understand, it is true that our talk about God will be, for now, always human talk. So it is true that our talk about God must use images, or metaphors. Yet, as Christian people, we claim that something new has happened in the human understanding about God. We have been told and have come to believe that God himself came to dwell among us in Jesus; or to put it in Paul's terms, we have now been given "the light of the knowledge of the glory of God in the face of Christ" (2 Cor 4:6 RSV). How did that mouth of Jesus speak about God? "Abba, Father" (Mk 14:36 RSV).

But one of the hymns in the most current Canadian Anglican Hymnbook neutralizes Jesus' characteristic prayer nicely:

All praise, O God, for Joseph, the guardian of your Son,
Who saved him from King Herod when safety there was none.
He taught the trade of builder when they to Nazareth came,
And Joseph's love made "Father" to be, for Christ, God's name.[16]

What impudence, that we could pretend to know that it was only Jesus' human experience of a nice foster-daddy that led him to address the Father! Presumption like this comes, I think, rather close to blasphemy against the Holy Spirit. Jesus, in speaking the name "Father," surely did not tell his disciples everything that there was to know. But God has taught us truly, if

---

[15]Paul Gibson, Liturgical Officer of the Anglican Church of Canada, "A Response to Mr. Warren's Critique," pp. 1-2. I personally saw this document concerning the 1998 Canadian hymnal *Common Praise*; it is a piece of correspondence between Paul Gibson and Wesley Warren, organist at a prominent Anglican Church in Ottawa.

[16]*Common Praise* (Toronto: ABC Press, 1998), no. 283, option for March 19.

not exhaustively, about his own nature and about how we should name him. Our knowledge about the Father does not come by what we know about human fathers, projected onto God. Rather, God himself takes up our human language and teaches us the best way to use it. As the Reformers put it, "God 'lisps' his word to us like the parent to an infant." And so, God gives us back our words about him, shows us how this name is best suited to his nature and even fills in what that name means. By the Holy Spirit, the author to the Ephesians tells us that it is God "the Father, from whom his whole family [or even, from whom all *fatherhood*] in heaven and on earth derives its name" (Eph 3:14-15 NIV). This profound theology, a reversal of our instincts, has proved itself to be strong medicine even for those who have had absentee or abusive fathers—for such pitiful men are not the mold; God himself is!

The great heavenly Father, the One whom we should be astonished to address as Jesus taught us in the "Our Father," is the One who shows every earthly father the measure of his calling; this is the one who shows the church family what our name and our identity is. God has called us by name and plans to strengthen us from within, so that Christ dwells in our hearts. There are more and more mysteries to know because God's riches are inexhaustible. We may look forward to learning, in the company of all God's people, the width, height, depth and length of Christ's love; we may look forward to being filled with God's fullness, because of what Jesus, God-with-us, has done and because of what we are taught by the ministry of the Holy Spirit.

It was a while before the entire church understood the full mystery of the Trinity and agreed to call the Son "of one essence with the Father." But the ancient theologians never left behind the clear implications of the name "Father," nor did they ignore the intimations of Scripture that the Son is eternally obedient to the Father. God's being remains beyond our imagination. The Son and Spirit "go out" from the Father eternally, even as each person of the Godhead goes out to and indwells the others of the Godhead, in abandon and intimacy. Only in the Godhead do we see the answer to the dichotomy that we tend to make, both intellectually and in our lives, between mutuality and order. From the Father the Son is begotten, and from the Father the Spirit proceeds (through the Son, say some); there is a certain order, yet it is eternal. The Father would not be the Father and source without the Son and Spirit; nor would the Son be the Son without the Father and the Spirit; nor would the Spirit be the Spirit without the other two: they are *toward* each other, as John puts it in the first verse of his Gospel ("And the Word was toward God *[pros ton theon]*"; Jn 1:1, my translation). Here is God's own answer to our faltering and power-hungry relationships. We need God's own pattern in our day, which is experiencing both a crisis of authority and a disregard for the dignity of each person.

In the wisdom of the Holy Spirit, we have come to understand that hierarchy and mutuality are not at odds in the triune God, but an ineffable mystery. The great Gregory of Nazianzus, to whom some have lately appealed[17] in order to remove order from the midst of our holy Godhead, would scratch his head in wonder at our worry over the monarchy of the

---

[17]For various examples of this appeal to Gregory, see T. F. Torrance, Robert Letham and most adamantly Kevin Giles. The work of Giles (in *The Trinity and Subordinationism: The Doctrine of God and the Contemporary Gender Debate* [Downers Grove, Ill.: InterVarsity Press, 2002] and in *Jesus and the Father*) seems fundamentally directed by theological anthropology and social egalitarian concerns; Giles appears to read Gregory in a particularly tendentious manner. Robert Letham (*The Holy Trinity: In Scripture, History, Theology, and Worship* [Phillipsburg, N.J.: Presbyterian & Reformed, 2004]) is far more measured, urging the use of the term *taxis* (order) rather than hierarchy. We are also well served by Letham's helpful caution: "There is very little in the Bible that allows us to peer into the life of the immanent Trinity" (p. 403). Thomas F. Torrance's work in *The Trinitarian Faith: The Evangelical Theology of the Ancient Catholic Church* (Edinburgh: T & T Clark, 1995) and "The Doctrine of the Holy Trinity—Gregory Nazianzen and John Calvin" (in *Calvin Studies V*, ed. John H. Leith and W. Stacy Johnson [Richmond, Va.: Union Theological Seminary, 1990], pp. 7-19) is rightly celebrated for its sanity and vigor. I am particularly grateful to Torrance for his careful examination of *perichōrēsis* and the insistence that this term refers to something far more profound than a "circular dance." (On this see also my *Ecstasy and Intimacy: When the Holy Spirit Meets the Human Spirit* [Grand Rapids: Eerdmans, 2006], pp. 92-93). His objection to an orthodox form of subordination in the Trinity, however, does not seem to cohere with this understanding of *perichōrēsis;* moreover, his use of Gregory of Nazianzus to push against the other Cappadocians ignores the places where the second Gregory speaks of the monarchy of the Father and of the sense in which he is "greater" than the Son. See also the debate in Alan Torrance, *Persons in Communion: Trinitarian Description and Human Participation* (Edinburgh: T & T Clark, 1996), pp. 288-91; and John Zizioulas, *Communion and Otherness: Further Studies in Personhood and the Church* (New York: T & T Clark, 2006), chap. 3. In considering this debate, it is helpful to recall that Father as both *aitia* and *archē* is common to both the Roman Catholic and the Orthodox communions. In dissent from this view, the burden of proof would lie with the Protestants who urge a qualification or even denial of *taxis* in the Godhead. It is hardly a matter of "evangelicals reinventing the doctrine of the Trinity" (cf. Giles, in his subtitle of *Jesus and the Father*). Is such a move truly reformed, or is it fueled by modern and postmodern egalitarian ideals?

Father. Indeed, in the course of one discourse, he said that he was "fearful" of using the word *archē* to refer to the Father—in case the neo-Arians of his day would grasp hold of the idea and run. At the same time, he understands that the Father gives everything to the Son and the Spirit, including "monarchy": the sole origin and headship of the one God over the cosmos. However, in responding to our egalitarian context, I believe that Gregory would repeat himself, exclaiming with characteristic fervor:

> The three most ancient opinions concerning the doctrine of God are Anarchia, Polyarchia, and Monarchia. The first two are the playground of the children of Hellas, and they can keep them! For Anarchy is a thing without order; and the Rule of Many is divisive, thus anarchical, and thus disorderly. . . . [But the Three are] One because of the Monarchy![18]

The Son, in plunging into our world and assuming our flesh, revealed the Father and accomplished all things so that we could, in reality, join him in his prayer, "Abba! Father!" (Rom 8:15). We need not fear the nightmare of anarchy. The Spirit, who proceeds from the Father and is sent to us by Father and Son, binds us together so that we are one people of the one God. Thus we know that there are not three gods to please, for One is holy. I have asked us to consider our understanding of the triune God beginning with the revealed Son, who gives us the gift of a heavenly Father, through the power of the Holy Spirit. There certainly are other ways of understanding how God deals with us: unless the Holy Spirit is at work secretly within us, we will never recognize the Son. (The Spirit leads to the Son, who leads to the Father.) The poor Spirit has received rather short shrift here, but he is used to that: for just as the Son was incognito in the Old Testament, so is the Spirit rather incognito in Jesus, and he comes to be known in the unity of the body of Christ, the church. Indeed, we could have begun this discussion, as would the early theologians Hilary of Poitiers (*De trinitate* 8) and Irenaeus (*Adversus Haereses* 5.36.2), with the work of the Spirit: but that would illumine

---

[18]The phrases, in my own playful translation, are a pastiche of Gregory of Nazianzus's *Third Theological Oration (Oration 29)* 2 and *In sanctum baptisma* 36.417.26. For further examination of Gregory's ability to hold together the *monarchia* of the Father with the mutual *monarchia* over the cosmos and with the ineffable *perichōrēsis* of the persons, see the careful works of J. A. McGuckin (see n. 19 below) and Christopher A. Beeley (*Gregory of Nazianzus on the Trinity and the Knowledge of God: In Your Light We Shall See Light* [New York: Oxford University Press, 2008]).

other wonderful things than the place where we have started: with the Son incarnate. As for Jesus, it is his very delight to direct us to the Father, so that we are forcibly reminded us that "no one can come to the Son unless the Father draws him" (cf. Jn 6:44; Father sends Spirit, who sends the Son; from the Father both Son and Spirit come, eternally and forever).

My purpose in starting with God the Son, our Lord Jesus, has been heuristic, to be of help. I hope that it has at least sketched two important facets of our faith: (1) the importance of tying together the two Testaments, for the Son shines in the Old Testament too! and (2) the imperative of honoring the Father as his children, because of the Son, by the power of the Holy Spirit.

A single-minded quest for the mind of Christ, to understand God as he has revealed himself, will convince us of a mystery that we can barely imagine: the Father's hierarchy, holy headship or monarchy does not drive out, but is the condition for mutual honor, responsive love and fruitfulness beyond measure! In rediscovering this foundational truth of the Father, it may well be that people of our generation will find themselves joining with those who pray the traditional Eastern prayer of contrition: "Most holy One, we have recklessly thrown aside your fatherly glory, and we have squandered the wealth and graces that you gave to us. So we cry to you with the Prodigal, 'We have sinned, O Merciful Father: Receive us again, and make us your servants, in your house, forever!'" In the end, the beckoning treasure of the Trinity opens more and more to us as we contemplate Scripture, as we partake of Eucharist, as we pray in closet and in community and as we "marvel at the mercy of it all!"[19]

> I sought the Lord, and afterward I knew
> he moved my soul to seek him, seeking me.
> It was not I that found, O Savior true;
> no, I was found of thee.
>
> Thou didst reach forth thy hand and mine enfold;
> I walked and sank not on the storm-vexed sea.
> 'Twas not so much that I on thee took hold,
> as thou, dear Lord, on me.

---

[19]I borrow this happy phrase from John A. McGuckin's poetic description of the stance of St. Gregory of Nazianzus, which stands as a proem to his spiritual biography: *St. Gregory of Nazianzus: An Intellectual Biography* (Crestwood, N.Y.: St. Vladimir's Press, 2001).

I find, I walk, I love, but oh, the whole
of love is but my answer, Lord, to thee!
For thou wert long beforehand with my soul,
always thou lovedst me.

(anon., nineteenth century)

PART TWO

COMMUNITY

The Trinity and Society?

4

God Is Love

The Social Trinity and the Mission of God

JOHN R. FRANKE

Perhaps the single most significant development in twentieth-century trinitarian theology has been the broad consensus among interpreters of the significance of relationality as the most fruitful model for understanding the doctrine of the Trinity. This so-called relational turn is viewed as an alternative to the ontology of substance that dominated theological reflection on the Trinity throughout much of church history. Although the debate continues on the degree to which the technical theological category of substance ought to be abandoned in the formulation, construction and articulation of the doctrine of the Trinity, contemporary theologians voice considerable agreement that the primary accent should be placed on the relational aspect of the divine life.

In this chapter I will consider the nature of the relational turn and the social conception of the Trinity that it produced. In keeping with the focus of the book on the relationship of the Trinity to the life and witness of the church, I will also consider the potential significance of these developments for our understanding of the mission of God in sending the church into the world as a participant in this mission and as a provisional demonstration of the will of God for all people. However, before doing so, it is important to be clear about the nature of the theological formulations and constructions concerning the doctrine of the Trinity.

THE CHARACTER OF THEOLOGY

Theology is an ongoing, second-order, contextual discipline that engages in critical and constructive reflection on the beliefs and practices of the church.

In the words of Karl Barth, it is "the science in which the Church, in accordance with the state of its knowledge at different times, takes account of the content of its proclamation critically, that is, by the standard of Holy Scripture and under the guidance of its Confessions."[1] Theology is a human enterprise and as such must not be viewed as "a matter of stating certain old or even new propositions that one can take home in black and white."[2] In keeping with the calling to bear witness to the God revealed in Jesus Christ, it is the perpetual task of theology to continually start again at the beginning in accordance with the nature of its subject.

This task calls forth the production of theological models that are faithful to the biblical narratives and teachings, relevant to the contemporary setting and informed by and in continuity with the historic position of the church. Therefore, the sources for these models are the canonical Scriptures, the thought forms of the contemporary setting and the tradition of the church. The goal in this process is to envision all of life in relationship to the triune God revealed in Jesus Christ through the articulation and practice of biblically normed, culturally relevant and historically informed models of the Christian faith. These models should express and communicate the biblical story in terms that make sense of it through the use of contemporary cultural tools and concepts, without being controlled by them.

Models are constructions and not exact representations of particular phenomena. For example, the doctrine of the Trinity serves as a model of God and the relationship between Father, Son and Holy Spirit. It does not provide a precise and literal picture of God, but based on God's self-revelation, it does disclose actual features of God's character and the divine life. It is a second-order linguistic construction that, while not an exact replica of God, does provide genuine comprehension concerning the nature and character of God. As Stephen Bevans puts it, models function like images and symbols and "provide ways through which one knows reality in all its richness and complexity. Models provide knowledge that is always partial and inadequate but never false or merely subjective."[3]

---

[1]Karl Barth, *Dogmatics in Outline* (New York: Harper & Row, 1959), p. 9.
[2]Ibid., p. 12.
[3]Stephen B. Bevans, *Models of Contextual Theology* (Maryknoll, N.Y.: Orbis Books, 1992), p. 30.

As analogues and as heuristic conceptions of God and the relationship of God to the created order, models facilitate engagement and provide insight and understanding without the claim that they provide an exact and referential representation of God. God is transcendent and unique, categorically different from anything in creation. As the early-church theologian Irenaeus once remarked, "God is light and yet unlike any light that we know."[4] In reflecting on this statement, George Hunsinger remarks that "God's cognitive availability through divine revelation allows us, Irenaeus believed, to predicate descriptions of God that are as true as we can make them, while God's irreducible ineffability nonetheless renders even our best predications profoundly inadequate."[5]

This observation points to the importance of maintaining a pluralist and inclusive understanding of the theological models we construct. Inclusive models suggest the importance of multiple perspectives and angles of vision in the exploration and interpretation of theological truth. Bevans comments that due to "the complexity of the reality one is trying to express in terms of models, such a variety of models might even be imperative" and goes on to suggest that "an exclusive use of one model might distort the very reality one is trying to understand."[6] The situated character of human knowledge and the divine subject matter of theology lead to the conclusion that faithful witness to the infinite God requires a diversity of perspectives. All constructions are inadequate on their own and need to be supplemented by other models. This does not preclude the possibility of adopting one particular model as the most helpful from a particular vantage point; but as Avery Dulles comments, even this procedure does not require one to "deny the validity of what other theologians may affirm with the help of other models. A good theological system will generally recognize the limitations of its own root metaphors and will therefore be open to criticism from other points of view."[7] No one model is able to account for all the diversity of the biblical witness, the diversity of perspectives on it and the complexity in the interaction between gospel and culture, which gives rise to theology.

---

[4]Irenaeus *Against Heresies* 2.13.4.
[5]George Hunsinger, "Postliberal Theology," in *The Cambridge Companion to Postmodern Theology*, ed. Kevin J. Vanhoozer (Cambridge: Cambridge University Press, 2003), p. 47.
[6]Bevans, *Models of Contextual Theology*, p. 30.
[7]Avery Dulles, *Models of Revelation* (Garden City, N.Y.: Doubleday, 1983), pp. 34-35.

It is from this perspective that we turn our attention to the doctrine of the Trinity.

THE CLASSICAL TRADITION

The decisions of the ecumenical councils at Nicaea and Constantinople provided the framework for the development of trinitarian theology in Christian history. While the councils affirmed the full deity of the Son and the Spirit along with the Father, the creeds that articulated the results of the conciliar deliberations did not address the question as to how the three comprise one God or the implications of this doctrine for the Christian message. In developing their conception of the triune God, the Cappadocian fathers—Basil the Great, Gregory of Nyssa and Gregory of Nazianzus—appropriated two Greek terms, *ousia* and *hypostasis*, theorizing that God is one *ousia* (essence) but three *hypostases* (independent realities) who share the one essence. The Cappadocian formulation of the Trinity provided the church with a fixed reference point, but it did not bring the discussions of the doctrine to an end. On the contrary, it opened the door for an ensuing debate as to the exact way of construing the threeness and oneness of God, a debate that eventually led to a theological parting of ways between the Eastern and Western churches.

The theologians of the East sought to draw out the implications of the distinction posited by the Cappadocians between the words *ousia* and *hypostasis*. Colin Gunton notes that by the time of the Cappadocians, the Greek term *hypostasis* had come to be used in distinction from the term *ousia* in order to refer to the concrete particularity of Father, Son and Spirit. In this rendering the three are not to be viewed simply as individuals but rather also as persons whose reality can only be understood in terms of their relations to each other. By the virtue of these relations, they together constitute the being or *ousia* of the one God. The persons are therefore not relations, but concrete particulars who are in relation to one another. Gunton notes that this conceptual development not only provided a way to understand the threeness of the Christian God without loss to the divine unity; it also established a new relational ontology: for God to be means that God is in communion.[8]

---

[8]Colin Gunton, *The Promise of Trinitarian Theology*, 2nd ed. (Edinburgh: T & T Clark, 1997), p. 39.

This theological conclusion arose out of the linguistic connection between the terms *hypostasis* and *ousia*; although being conceptually distinct because of their mutual involvement with one another, they are inseparable in thought. The Eastern understanding was also characterized by the tendency to focus on the three individual members of the Trinity rather than on the divine unity. Although not denying that Father, Son and Spirit possess the one divine essence, the Eastern thinkers tended to highlight the specific operations of the Father, the Son and the Spirit in the divine acts of creation, reconciliation and consummation.

The linguistic differences between Latin and Greek as well as the differing cultural and theological temperaments of East and West led the Western theologians to travel a somewhat different pathway. Their use of Latin meant that Western theologians were not fully cognizant of the nuances of the linguistic formulations emerging from the East. Instead, they drew on the work of Tertullian, whose formula *tres personae, una substantia* (three persons, one substance) became a staple of the Latin conception. Tertullian's formula served to complicate the discussion with Eastern thinkers, however, in that the term *substantia* was the usual Latin translation of *hypostasis*, not *ousia*. The linguistic difficulties were compounded by the continuing influence of Athanasius, who had understood *ousia* and *hypostasis* as synonyms.[9] Use of the formula *tres personae, una substantia* led Western theologians to emphasize the one divine essence or substance rather than the plurality or threeness of divine persons, characteristic of the East.

The classic statement of the Western understanding of the Trinity came in Augustine's influential work *De trinitate*. Augustine appeals to the nature of human beings who, because they are created in the image of God, display "vestiges" of the Trinity, an approach that leads him to look for analogies of the Trinity in the human person's nature.[10] Augustine offered a long series of analogies based on humans as the *imago Dei* (image of God), the most central of which is the triad of *being, knowing* and *willing*.

---

[9]Edmund Fortman, *The Triune God: A Historical Study of the Doctrine of the Trinity* (Philadelphia: Westminster Press, 1972), pp. 72-83.
[10]Cyril C. Richardson, "The Enigma of the Trinity," in *A Companion to the Study of St. Augustine*, ed. Roy Battenhouse (Oxford: Oxford University Press, 1955), pp. 248-55.

Augustine's psychological analogy of the Trinity, with its focus on the oneness of God in contrast to the Eastern emphasis on the divine threeness and with its starting point in the divine essence rather than the saving act of God in Christ, set the stage for the trinitarian theologizing prominent in the West.[11]

Perhaps the most significant alternative to Augustine in the West was that of Richard of St. Victor. Of particular interest is Richard's discussion of the necessary plurality of persons in the Godhead. To develop this point, he turns to the concept of divine goodness and observes that supreme goodness must involve love. Richard argues that because self-love cannot be true charity, supreme love requires another, equal to the lover, who is the recipient of that love. In addition, because supreme love is received as well as given, such love must be a shared love, one in which each person loves and is loved by the other. Cognizant that the witness of Christian faith declares that the one God is three persons, not merely two, Richard claims that further analysis of supreme love demonstrates that indeed three persons are required. He argues that for love to be supreme, it must desire that the love it experiences through giving and receiving be one that is shared with another.[12] Consequently, perfect love is not merely mutual love between two but is fully shared only among three.[13]

Richard's work is significant in that it provides a relationally based alternative to Augustine's psychological approach to the Trinity. As Gunton notes regarding Richard, "Unlike Augustine, the fountainhead of most Western theology of the Trinity, he looks not at the inner soul for his clues to the nature of God, but at persons in relation."[14] Moreover, Richard's conception of the interior life of God demands a fully personal Trinity. By extension, the relationality within the divine life captured in Richard's theological model carries implications for a theological understanding of humans as the *imago Dei* as well. As Grover Zinn explains, "The reflection of this life should lead to a renewed appreciation of charity as a love lived in community with others, involving interpersonal sharing of the deepest

---

[11]Fortman, *The Triune God*, p. 141.
[12]For an English translation of Richard of St. Victor's *De trinitate*, book 3, see Grover Zinn, ed., *Richard of St. Victor* (New York: Paulist Press, 1979), pp. 373-97.
[13]Fortman, *The Triune God*, p. 194.
[14]Gunton, *The Promise of Trinitarian Theology*, p. 89.

kind."[15] In short, whereas Augustine's conception of the individual soul as an image of the Trinity provided the basis for an interior approach to spirituality that emphasizes the ascent of the individual to union with God, Richard's approach suggests the possibility of spirituality based on interpersonal community.[16]

Although it would be misleading to say that Richard developed a fully relational view of the person in his thought, Gunton points out that he provided "an approach to the doctrine of the Trinity that contains possibilities for the development of a relational view of the person."[17] Commenting on the significance of Richard's theological program, Edmund Fortman declares that henceforth "there will be two great trinitarian theories in the medieval theological world, the Augustinian that St. Thomas will systematize, and the theory of Richard of St. Victor, whose principal representative will be St. Bonaventure."[18]

THE RELATIONAL TURN

The traditional emphasis on an abstract property of substance, or a divine essence, standing under God has come under scrutiny in recent trinitarian studies. Theologians today routinely critique the concept as implying that God is an isolated, solitary individual. The question of the nature of a substance was initially placed on the theological table by Tertullian through his famous formula *tres personae, una substantia*. Theologians, especially in the West, subsequently took up the challenge of devising an understanding of the nature of a substance when used with reference to God. Hence, Augustine spoke of God as a substance that was eternal and unchangeable. Later, Thomas Aquinas defined God as pure act, thereby excluding such ideas as *becoming* or *potency* as inapplicable to God, insofar as these would imply change in the immutable God in the act of becoming or in the transition from potency to act. The definitional link these theologians forged between substance and unchangeability meant that they viewed God as eternal and unchanging, in contrast to creation, which is temporal and in a

---

[15]Zinn, *Richard of St. Victor*, p. 46.
[16]Ewert Cousins, "A Theology of Interpersonal Relations," *Thought* 45 (1970): 59.
[17]Gunton, *The Promise of Trinitarian Theology*, p. 91.
[18]Fortman, *The Triune God*, p. 191.

constant state of change in its relation to God.

The substantialist conception carried within itself the distinction be-tween absolute essence and relational attributes. According to this under-standing, essence is absolute and therefore must remain unchanged in or-der to preserve its identity. If change occurs in the essence of an entity, its identity is lost. Relationality, in turn, was deemed to belong to the dimen-sion of attributes, not substance. Consequently, substantialist theologians suggested that God is absolute and immutable in his essential nature, whereas he maintains relationality to creation through the divine at-tributes. As Ted Peters notes regarding the classical position, "What could not be countenanced is the notion that the divine essence is contingent upon the relational dimensions of its being."[19] The result, however, has been the obscuring of God's internal relationality and of God's loving re-lationship to creation in much of the classical literature on the nature of God. In recent years, the classical commitment to a substantialist concep-tion of God's nature has been critiqued. At the heart of this critique is the apparent incompatibility of an eternal, essentially immutable God with the portrait in the biblical narratives of a God who has entered into loving relationship with creation. Although the debate continues as to the degree to which the category of substance ought to be abandoned, theologians voice considerable agreement that the primary accent should be placed on the category of relationality.

Catherine LaCugna, to cite one example, asserts that *person* rather than *substance* is the primary ontological category, noting that the ultimate source of reality is not a "by-itself" or an "in-itself" but a person, a "toward-another." She concludes that the triune God is "self-communicating" and exists from all eternity "in relation to another."[20] Likewise, Robert Jenson writes, "The original point of trinitarian dogma and analysis was that God's relations to us are internal to him, and it is in carrying out this insight that the 'relation' concept was introduced to define the distinction of identities."[21]

---

[19]Ted Peters, *God as Trinity: Relationality and Temporality in Divine Life* (Louisville, Ky.: Westminster John Knox, 1993), p. 31.
[20]Catherine Mowry LaCugna, *God for Us: The Trinity and Christian Life* (San Francisco: Harper/Collins, 1991), pp. 14-15.
[21]Robert W. Jenson, *The Triune Identity: God According to the Gospel* (Philadelphia: For-tress, 1982), p. 120.

In a similar manner, Elizabeth Johnson claims that the priority of relation in the triune God challenges and critiques the concentration of classical theism on "singleness" in God. Because the persons are "constituted by their relationships to each other, each is unintelligible except as connected with the others."[22] The assertion that each of the persons in the triune life is constituted only in relationship to the others leads Johnson to the conclusion that the "very principle of their being" is to be found in the category of relation.[23]

David Cunningham notes that the breadth of the current consensus about the priority of relationality in trinitarian discourse is evidenced by the fact that both Jenson and Johnson may be cited in support of it, even though the two thinkers "are not usually noted for being in close agreement with one another."[24] This theological consensus encompasses a variety of thinkers, including John Zizioulas, Jürgen Moltmann, Wolfhart Pannenberg, Leonardo Boff, Colin Gunton, Alan Torrance, Millard Erickson and Stanley Grenz.[25] While these theologians may differ from each other on the precise construction of relationality within the life of God, they have all followed the relational turn.

In addition to the consensus among contemporary theologians, Veli-Matti Kärkkäinen states that the "move to relationality is also in keeping with the dynamic understanding of reality and the human being as well as human community in late modernity." He notes that the ideas and conceptions of isolation, individualism and independence are the prod-

---

[22]Elizabeth A. Johnson, *She Who Is: The Mystery of God in Feminist Theological Discourse* (New York: Crossroad, 1992), p. 216.

[23]Ibid., p. 216.

[24]David S. Cunningham, *These Three Are One: The Practice of Trinitarian Theology* (Malden, Mass.: Blackwell, 1998), p. 26.

[25]John Zizioulas, *Being as Communion: Studies in Personhood and Communion* (Crestwood, N.Y.: St. Vladimir's Seminary Press, 1985); Jürgen Moltmann, *The Trinity and the Kingdom: The Doctrine of God* (Minneapolis: Fortress, 1993); Wolfhart Pannenberg, *Systematic Theology*, vol. 1 (Grand Rapids: Eerdmans, 1988); Leonardo Boff, *Trinity and Society*, trans. Paul Burns (Maryknoll, N.Y.: Orbis Books, 1988); Colin Gunton, *The One, the Three and the Many: God, Creation and the Culture of Modernity* (Cambridge: Cambridge University Press, 1993); Alan J. Torrance, *Persons in Communion: Trinitarian Description and Human Participation* (Edinburgh: T & T Clark, 1995); Millard J. Erickson, *God in Three Persons: A Contemporary Interpretation of the Trinity* (Grand Rapids: Baker, 1995); Stanley J. Grenz, *The Social God and the Relational Self: A Trinitarian Theology of the Imago Dei* (Louisville, Ky.: Westminster John Knox, 2001).

ucts of modernist thought forms. "Over against the typical modernist bias to classify and categorize everything into distinct units [only think of the methods of the natural sciences], postmodernity speaks of relationality, interdependence, becoming, emerging, and so on. In this changing intellectual atmosphere, the value of communion theology is being appreciated in a new way."[26] With respect to our understanding of God, Stanley Grenz speaks of this relational turn as envisioning a move "from the one subject to the three persons."[27] In other words, God is social, not solitary.

THE SOCIAL TRINITY

The biblical narration of the experience of the Christian community with God points beyond this encounter to the eternal life of God. In other words, in addition to acting in the history of the world, the Bible pictures God as having a history in which creation is not the beginning point, but a particular event in the continuing story of the divine life that stretches from the eternal past into the eternal future. Hence, while the acts of God in history provide the basis for speaking of the doctrine of the Trinity, they are also indicative of God's ongoing internal life, and Scripture invites us to think through the implications of this history with respect to the character of God.

This suggests a theological principle: God is as God acts. The identity of God is known through the actions of God. The self-revelation of God is reflective of the character of God. The character and being of God are made known by the actions of God in history. Following this principle, we can say that God is a being in act.

The revelation of God in Jesus Christ as Father, Son and Holy Spirit and the actions of Jesus of Nazareth allow us to say that God is as God does, and what God does is love. Through the revelation of God in Jesus Christ, we encounter the living embodiment and exposition of God's gracious character in relation to humanity as the One who loves. In this focus on the

---

[26]Veli-Matti Kärkkäinen, *The Trinity: Global Perspectives* (Louisville, Ky.: Westminster John Knox, 2007), p. 387.
[27]Stanley J. Grenz, *Rediscovering the Triune God: The Trinity in Contemporary Theology* (Minneapolis: Fortress, 2004), pp. 23-57.

actions of God as indicative of the being of God, we must set aside all of our assumptions and preconceptions concerning what we already believe to be true of God and instead seek to learn from the God who is through the actions of God. God is known through what God has done, and what God has done emerges from the person Jesus Christ and the witness of Scripture. What we see in the life of Jesus and narratives of Scripture is that God is the One who loves.

Therefore, in seeking to know the character of God in response to the action of divine self-revelation, we must seek to understand the fundamental biblical assertion: "God is love." However, we must not presume that we know in advance the character of love based on particular individual or generally accepted cultural assumptions and then impose that understanding on the love of God. Rather, our knowledge of the love of God should be shaped by the particular way in which God loves through the ongoing establishment of communion between God and God's creatures in and through Jesus.

God's love for the world is not that of an uninvolved, unmoved, passionless Deity, but rather that of one who is actively and passionately involved in the ongoing drama of life in the world, one who lavishly pours out this love in Jesus Christ. This lavish expression of love for humanity and creation is revealed in Jesus Christ and points us to the internal life of God as an eternal trinitarian fellowship of love shared between Father, Son and Holy Spirit. In other words, explication of the triune God in God's self-disclosure in and to creation is at the same time the explication of the triune God in the divine reality.

When we affirm with Scripture that "God is love" (1 Jn 4:8 NIV), this points not simply to the feelings of God but also to the eternal life of God lived in a set of ongoing and active relationships of love that constitute God's being in and for Godself. These are the active relationships of God's eternal trinitarian fellowship in which Father, Son and Holy Spirit participate in the giving, receiving and sharing of love that includes both difference and unity. Technically, we might say that God gives, receives and shares love from all eternity in self-differentiated unity and unified self-differentiation. In other words, this eternal fellowship of divine love is characterized by both unity-in-plurality and plurality-in-unity, in which we affirm that the one God exists in three distinct persons, Father, Son and

Holy Spirit; and we affirm that the three together, Father, Son and Holy Spirit, are the one God. In these active relations, God freely constitutes the divine being in this distinctively trinitarian fashion.

In understanding God as social plurality rather than a solitary being, the question is therefore raised, What does it mean to affirm that God is one? In John's Gospel, Jesus says, "I and the Father are one" (Jn 10:30 NIV) and explains that his works were done so that those who saw them might "know and understand that the Father is in me and I am in the Father" (Jn 10:38 RSV). In seeking to explain this, thinkers in the early church turned to an idea known as *perichōrēsis*. This refers to the mutual interdependence, even mutual interpenetration of Father, Son and Holy Spirit in their trinitarian relation with one another. It seeks to explain the nature of the divine life with the assertion that while the three members of the Trinity remain wholly distinct from each other, they are also bound together, wholly interior to each other in such a way that the Father, Son and Spirit are dependent on each other for their very identities as Father, Son and Spirit. In other words, the Father, Son and Spirit would not be who they are, would not be God, apart from the interdependent relationality they share with each other.

This relational interdependence is manifested in the earthly life of Jesus, who did not function as an autonomous, independent individual. Rather, Jesus says that he constantly seeks the will of the Father and that he can do nothing by himself "but only what he sees the Father doing" (Jn 5:19 RSV). At the same time, he also says that the Father judges no one, but has entrusted all judgment to the Son (Jn 5:22). Nevertheless, in rendering these judgments he says, "By myself I can do nothing; I judge only as I hear, and my judgment is just, for I seek not to please myself but him who sent me" (Jn 5:30 NIV). This understanding of perichoresis leads us to conclude that the persons of the Trinity—Father, Son and Holy Spirit—are one by virtue of their interdependent relationality. The contemporary consensus concerning the relationality of the life of God brings us back to the affirmation that God is love.

Articulating the doctrine of the Trinity in accordance with the category of relationality gives us an indication as to how this biblical and classical assertion is to be comprehended. From the beginning and throughout all of eternity, the life of the triune God has been and continues to be character-ized by love. This divine love is found in the reciprocal interdependence and self-dedication of the trinitarian members to each other. Indeed, there is no God other than the Father, Son and Spirit bound together in the active rela-tions of love throughout eternity. This love provides a profound conception of the reality of God as understood by the Christian tradition. Love ex-pressed and received by the trinitarian persons among themselves provides a description of the inner life of God throughout eternity apart from any reference to creation.

In addition to enjoying the support of the biblical witness and the tradi-tion of the church, love is an especially fruitful term for comprehending the life of God since it is an inherently relational concept. Love requires both subject and object. Because God is a triune plurality-in-unity and unity-in-plurality, God comprehends both love's subject and love's object. For this reason, when viewed theologically, the statement "God is love" refers pri-marily to the eternal, relational intratrinitarian fellowship among Father, Son and Holy Spirit, who together are the one God. The life of God, who is the truth, is characterized by difference and plurality expressed in unity through interdependent relationality—in other words, the plurality of truth itself. These three, Father, Son and Holy Spirit, are one throughout eternity by virtue of their interdependent relationality. In this way, God is love within the divine reality; and in this sense, through all eternity God is the social Trinity, the community of love.

THE MISSION OF GOD

The relational and social character of the triune God as an eternal commu-nity characterized by the giving, receiving and sharing of love is further de-veloped by the concept of mission. The Christian tradition has maintained that God has a mission in the world and therefore speaks of the mission of God. However, in addition to the affirmation that God *has* a mission, let us also assert that God's very character as the one who loves from all eternity is missional. Love characterizes the mission of God from all eternity, and therefore God loves the world lavishly in Jesus Christ.

Creation itself may be viewed as a missional act, a reflection of the ex-pansive love of God, whereby the triune God brings into being another re-

ality, that which is not God, and establishes a covenantal relationship of
love, grace and blessing for the purpose of drawing that reality into participation in the divine fellowship of love. Creation forms the external basis
and context of God's covenant with humanity in that God's act of creation
always has in view the institution, preservation and execution of the covenant of grace, into which God has called human beings for participation
and partnership. The covenant of grace is the internal basis of the act of
creation in that God's covenant with humanity constitutes the fulfillment
of the very intentions of God in the work of creation.

The missional character of God's eternal life is reflected in the relation
of God to the world and the biblical witness of God's concern for engagement with the world. Indeed, mission is at the heart of the biblical narratives concerning the work of God in human history. It begins with the call
to Israel to be God's covenant people and the recipient of God's covenant
blessings for the purpose of blessing the nations. Hence, the mission of God
is at the heart of the covenant with Israel and is continuously unfolded over
the course of the centuries in the life of God's people as recorded in the narratives of canonical Scripture.

This missional covenant reaches its revelatory climax in the life, death
and resurrection of Jesus Christ. It continues through the sending of the
Spirit as the one who calls, guides and empowers the community of Christ's
followers, the church, as the socially, historically and culturally embodied
witness to the gospel of Jesus Christ and the tangible expression of the mission of God.

In every culture around the world, this mission is carried out in the
churches' global ministry and witness to the gospel; guided by the Spirit,
this mission moves toward the promised consummation of reconciliation
and redemption in the eschaton. This missional pattern is communicated in
the words of Jesus recorded in the Gospel of John, "As the Father has sent
me, even so I send you" (Jn 20:21 RSV). With respect to Jesus, this suggests
not simply that the Son of God sends the church into the world, but also
that the Son has been sent. God is both sender and sent; in turn, God
through Jesus Christ sends the church into the world after the pattern by
which Jesus had been sent by the Father. The love of God lived out and
expressed in the context of the eternal community of love gives rise to the

missional character of God, who seeks to extend the love shared by Father, Son and Holy Spirit into the created order.

God is missional by nature. The love of God lived out and expressed in the context of the eternal community of love gives rise to the missional character of God, who seeks to extend the love shared by Father, Son and Holy Spirit into the created order. According to David Bosch, mission is derived from the very nature of God and must be situated in the context of the doctrine of the Trinity rather than in the context of ecclesiology or soteriology. In this context the logic of the classical doctrine of the *missio Dei* expressed as God the Father sending the Son, and the Father and the Son sending the Spirit, may be expanded to include yet anther movement: "Father, Son, and Spirit sending the church into the world."[28] In this context, the church is seen as the instrument of God's mission and its various historical, global and contemporary embodiments may be viewed as a series of local iterations of God's universal mission to all of creation.

[28]David Bosch, *Transforming Mission: Paradigm Shifts in Theology of Mission* (Maryknoll, N.Y.: Orbis Books, 1991), p. 390.

5

The Trinity Is *Not* Our Social Program

Volf, Gregory of Nyssa and Barth

MARK HUSBANDS

INTRODUCTION

This chapter is an instance of negative theology that shows the problematic nature of the social analogy of the Trinity. Its principal aim is to show that social trinitarians such as Miroslav Volf are misguided in believing the Trinity to be *our* social program. When, for instance, Cornelius Plantinga Jr. speaks of the holy Trinity as "a divine transcendent society or community of three fully personal and fully divine entities,"[1] significant features of the Nicene Creed risk being summarily dismissed with a stroke of a pen. As a dogmatic and historical argument, it demonstrates the degree to which social trinitarians are mistaken in their reading of the Cappadocian fathers. Our close reading of Gregory of Nyssa's treatise *Ad Ablabium* provides us with a clear line of sight upon the tradition and demonstrates how it is injudicious for contemporary theologians to claim that the Cappadocians employ a social analogy of the Trinity. While social trinitarians tend to accuse Karl Barth of being a modalist—thereby implying that he remains at a profound distance from the trinitarian riches of the East—we argue the counterintuitive claim that it is Barth, not social trinitarians, who shares a strong family resemblance to the trinitarian theology of the Cappadocians.

Before considering Miroslav Volf's social trinitarianism, I offer the fol-

---

[1]Cornelius Plantinga Jr., "Social Trinity and Tritheism," in *Trinity, Incarnation, and Atonement: Philosophical and Theological Essays*, ed. Ronald Jay Feenstra and Cornelius Plantinga Jr. (Notre Dame, Ind.: University of Notre Dame Press, 1989), p. 27.

lowing basic rule by which to measure the relative value of a given proposal regarding the doctrine of the Trinity: a theology that purports to be properly "trinitarian"—and by this I mean consistent with both the biblical witness and Nicene Christianity—must preserve an ontological distinction between God and humanity in order to maintain an order consistent with their distinct natures. The inherent danger in failing to maintain this ontological distinction is the possibility that one's doctrine of God will be eclipsed by any number of contemporary social, cultural or political concerns. Moreover, it is here where the importance of the question "What difference does it make if one adopts social trinitarianism?" comes into view.

An illuminating example of what happens when this dogmatic rule is broken is found in Catherine LaCugna's work *God for Us: The Trinity and Christian Life,* in which she states: "The life of God is not something that belongs to God alone. *Trinitarian life is also our life.* . . . To conceive trinitarian life as something belonging *only* to God, or belonging to God apart from the creature, is to miss the point entirely."[2] When the triune God is so closely tied to the social existence and well-being of the community, as is this case in LaCugna's work, it becomes difficult to conceive of the way in which God remains Lord, in the sense of the one who may bring both judgment and life. In the course of developing her argument, LaCugna asserts that "the doctrine of the Trinity is not ultimately a teaching about 'God' but a teaching about *God's life with us and our life with each other,*" to which she adds, "It is the life of communion and indwelling, God in us, we in God, all of us in each other."[3] The sheer boldness of LaCugna's position leads Paul Molnar to offer a characteristically trenchant critique: "Unwilling and unable to distinguish God *in se* [in himself] from God acting *ad extra* [in relation to the world], this thinking invites pantheism and dualism. God is no longer the subject acting toward us and for us from within history but becomes little more than our experiences of love and communion."[4] As you can see from this, theological commitments associated with an appeal to the social analogy of the Trinity are by no means

---

[2] Catherine Mowry LaCugna, *God for Us: The Trinity and Christian Life* (San Francisco: HarperSanFrancisco, 1991), p. 228.
[3] Ibid.
[4] Paul D. Molnar, *Divine Freedom and the Doctrine of the Immanent Trinity: In Dialogue with Karl Barth and Contemporary Theology* (New York: T & T Clark, 2002), p. 128.

benign. Scholars on both sides of this debate readily admit that there is much at stake in deciding for or against social trinitarianism. With all of this in view, let us turn our attention to the work of Miroslav Volf, one for whom the social analogy of the Trinity has proved to be an effective organizing and moral theme.[5]

MIROSLAV VOLF AND THE TRINITY AS "OUR SOCIAL PROGRAM"

Early on in the celebrated monograph *Exclusion and Embrace*, Miroslav Volf turns to the Orthodox theologian Dumitru Stăniloae in order to secure one of the leading themes of his own work: the use of the social analogy of the Trinity. Volf enthusiastically declares that "Dumitru Stăniloae speaks for the whole Christian tradition when he highlights 'two truths beside which there is no other truth'—'the holy Trinity is the model of supreme love and interpersonal communion, and the Son of God who comes, becomes a man, and goes to sacrifice.'"[6] The substantial shape of Volf's theological program is one of bringing the first of these two claims to full term. He carries out this project perhaps unaware of the degree to which it risks a nominalist reduction of the doctrine of God to ecclesiology and, in turn, of ecclesiology to social practices.

In an essay titled "'The Trinity Is Our Social Program': The Doctrine of the Trinity and the Shape of Social Engagement," Volf wisely sets aside Nicholas Fedorov's claim that participation in the triune life of God is a present realization for all people. Yet Volf maintains that the Trinity is *our* social program, or at least a social program for the church. Seeking to find the golden mean between Fedorov's trinitarian divinization of humanity and the sheer alterity of the holy Trinity,[7] he conceives of the Trinity as a personal center of communal life and sharing whose dynamic gratuity elicits a corresponding human "social vision" for justice.

Although Volf seeks to qualify the way in which trinitarian categories such as *divine* "persons," "relation," or "perichoresis" are too quickly

---

[5]The following critique of Volf's social trinitarianism bears directly upon John Franke's contribution to this volume, "God Is Love: The Social Trinity and the Mission of God."

[6]Miroslav Volf, *Exclusion and Embrace: A Theological Exploration of Identity, Otherness, and Reconciliation* (Nashville: Abingdon, 1996), p. 25.

[7]Miroslav Volf, "'The Trinity Is Our Social Program': The Doctrine of the Trinity and the Shape of Social Engagement," *Modern Theology* 14 (1998): 405.

transferred to human persons, his vigilance remains in place only for a moment. Reminding us that "human beings can correspond to the uncreated God only in a *creaturely* way,"[8] he quickly proceeds to depict the goal of salvation as restored *human* community corresponding to the mutual self-offering of the triune God.

Failing to set aside any and all efforts to extend trinitarian language of *divine* "persons," "relation," or "perichoresis" to human persons and community, Volf connotes that the Trinity is an exemplarist model for the social life and moral witness of the church. This is evident in his declaration that we are to "live with one another and with God in the kind of communion in which divine persons live with one another."[9] Far from maintaining the categorical distinction between the triune God and human persons ingredient to our rule for the evaluation of trinitarian doctrine, Volf draws a similarity between God and humanity at the level of moral action, presumably on the grounds of there being an ontological likeness between divine and human "persons" and "relations."

One of the most helpful ways of making sense of Volf's trinitarian theology is to discern the echoes of the reading of the Cappadocians offered by Volf's *Doktorvater*, Jürgen Moltmann. For instance, Moltmann fears that belief in the unity or oneness of God inevitably leads to the adoption of putatively static categories of substance, as found within classical theism. Believing that Western Christianity is thoroughly tainted by the ontotheology of Hellenized metaphysics, Moltmann (and subsequently Volf) opts for a reading of the Eastern tradition in which *being* is predicated of the persons. Both Moltmann and Volf maintain that we ought not speak of divine unity in terms of the mutual coinherence of three persons in one *ousia* (being). Rather, the correct grammar of divine unity is determined by the degree to which one's account of the Trinity is consonant with the social phenomenon or principle of relationality. This is captured well in Moltmann's claim:

> The fact that God *is* the Father . . . adds to the mode of being, being itself.
> Person and relation therefore have to be understood in a reciprocal relation-

---

[8]Ibid.
[9]Miroslav Volf, *Exclusion and Embrace*, p. 181.

ship. Hence there are no persons without relations; but there are no relations without persons either.[10]

As such, "persons" and "relation" are not only irreducible but also constitutive of the very identity of God.[11]

Following the lead of Moltmann, Volf maintains that perichoresis denotes a mutual self-giving in such a way that divine unity is determined by mutuality or the relation of persons. Volf writes:

> In every divine person as a subject, the other persons also indwell; all mutually permeate one another, though in so doing they do not cease to be distinct persons. . . . The unity of the triune God is grounded neither in numerically identical substance nor in the accidental intentions of the persons, but rather in their *mutually interior being*.[12]

The difficulty in moving from the triune God to human social existence or fellowship is not entirely lost on Volf. He writes: "In a strict sense, there can be no correspondence to the interiority of divine persons at the human level. Another human self cannot be internal to my own self as subject of action."[13] Yet this cautionary note fails to inhibit his movement toward what he terms "perichoretic personhood."

The belief that there is a likeness between the being of God and the possibility of social relations marked by a commitment to forgiveness and reconciliation lies very close to the heart of Volf's work. For instance, he rightly claims that "the nature of God . . . fundamentally determines the character of the Christian life"[14] yet fails to show how the being of God is of a fundamentally different *order* than is human being or creaturely existence. Look simply at the *promeity* of God. Appeals to the *imago Dei*, or the so-called *imago Trinitas,* apart from the disturbing, free and constitutive movement of God in Christ and the Spirit, suggest that this "image" is a natural predi-

---

[10]Jürgen Moltmann, *The Trinity and the Kingdom: The Doctrine of God* (Minneapolis: Fortress, 1993), pp. 172-73.

[11]Moltmann, "Die einladende Einheit des dreieinigen Gotte," p. 124, cited in Miroslav Volf, *After Our Likeness: The Church as the Image of the Trinity*, Sacra Doctrina (Grand Rapids: Eerdmans, 1997), p. 210.

[12]Volf, *After Our Likeness*, pp. 209-10.

[13]Ibid., p. 210.

[14]Miroslav Volf, "Being as God Is: Trinity and Generosity," in *God's Life in Trinity*, ed. Miroslav Volf and Michael Welker (Minneapolis: Fortress, 2006), p. 4.

cate of human existence. When this appeal is then offered as the basis for creaturely moral action, one is immediately set up for disappointment, as is the case in all creaturely imitations of Christ. To put the matter even more pointedly: one might just as easily ask of Volf and others, "Where is this concrete human community of dynamic self-giving and love of which you speak so positively?" Is it not in fact the case that social trinitarians offer an inordinately idealist account of social relations? Nonetheless, Volf continues to hold out the prospect of a creaturely imitation of God:

> So when I speak about human *imaging* of the Trinity, I mean that human beings receive themselves as created in the image of the Trinity by the power of the Spirit. Their *imaging* of the Trinity is the gift of God's movement out of the circumference of the trinitarian life to create human beings and, after they have sinned, to restore them by dwelling within them and taking them into the perfect communion of love, which God is. . . . Because God has made us to reflect God's own triune being, our human tasks are not first of all to *do* as God does—and certainly not to make ourselves as God *is*—but to let ourselves be indwelled by God and to celebrate and proclaim what God has done, is doing and will do.[15]

While there may be quite reasonable ways of handling much of this material, it is crucial for us to see that Volf is working with an eschatological vision of communal life. The implied claim in all of this is that we can pass from a disparate gathering of perhaps broken and alienated selves into a perichoretic community of love that "bears all things, believes all things" (1 Cor 13:7 RSV). This depiction of human fellowship and transformation takes shape here much too quickly for this to be regarded as a concrete, historical creaturely fellowship. I am reminded of Oliver O'Donovan's injunction: "To invoke *that* love prematurely has often been a temptation in Christian reflection on society, signaling a drift toward the sentimental, a forgetfulness of the sting of sin."[16] The sting of sin is actually so real that it represents a distinct caution against the presumption that we may set aside the fact that not only creation, but "we ourselves, who have the firstfruits of the Spirit, groan inwardly while we wait eagerly for adoption . . . , the

---

[15]Ibid., pp. 6-7.
[16]Oliver O'Donovan, *Common Objects of Love: Moral Reflection and the Shaping of Community: The 2001 Stob Lectures* (Grand Rapids: Eerdmans, 2002), p. 22.

redemption of our bodies" (Rom 8:23 NIV). Does Scripture, in other words, indicate that *we* are to "image" the Trinity or experience a perichoretic life of creaturely fellowship? Or does it point us in the direction of realizing that our fellowship is fraught with brokenness and sin while we look forward to our redemption in Christ? Surely, an overrealized eschatology runs the risk of offering an idealized picture of Christian fellowship, one that is ill equipped to handle the difficult work of repentance and reconciliation.

Having provided a rough sketch of Volf's project and the way in which the being of God resides in the fellowship of divine persons, we have arrived at a genuine problem. Is it correct to hold out a vision of human perichoretic personhood when the ontological difference between the triune God and the not yet fully redeemed ecclesial body has been set aside with such abandon? Put differently, has Volf broken the trinitarian rule set out at the beginning of this chapter, by offering us an account of ecclesial or social existence in which trinitarian life is now offered as a model for creaturely imitation or echo?

What is clear from all of this is that Volf offers us a doctrine of the triune God for which the immediate significance of the Trinity lies principally in being a model for us to imitate rather than being the constitutive ground of our reconciliation and promise of life. Not surprisingly, this emphasis upon perichoretic life and koinonia at the level of creatures is a mainstay of social trinitarianism. It is certainly present in the work of Moltmann and Volf. Given their appeal to the Cappadocians, it is only fitting that we turn to the work of arguably the most sophisticated and creative theologian among the Cappadocian fathers: Gregory of Nyssa.

GREGORY OF NYSSA: AN ANSWER TO ABLABIUS

The opening sentence of Michel René Barnes's essay "Rereading Augustine's Theology of the Trinity" begins thus: "It is impossible to do contemporary trinitarian theology and not have a judgment on Augustine; unfortunately, this is *not* the same thing as saying that it is impossible to do contemporary trinitarian theology and not have *read* Augustine."[17] Along

---

[17]Michel René Barnes, "Rereading Augustine's Theology and Trinity," in *The Trinity: An Interdisciplinary Symposium on the Trinity*, ed. Stephen T. Davis, Daniel Kendall and Gerald O'Collins (New York: Oxford University Press, 1999), p. 145.

similar lines, Cornelius Plantinga Jr. laments the absence of well-informed historical work on the Cappadocian fathers. To his credit, Plantinga sought to correct this deficit by examining Gregory of Nyssa's trinitarian theology. In the course of this work, Plantinga expresses the view that the social analogy of the Trinity is "respectably, even if distantly, of the house and lineage of Gregory of Nyssa."[18] Notably, this is a claim that is as dear to the heart of social trinitarians as it is false—which is to say, its verity must be judged not by contemporary utility or style, but by genuine historical analysis.

Following Barnes's example, let us see what happens when we pay close attention to Gregory's classic treatise *An Answer to Ablabius: That There Are Not Three Gods*. It is evident that the younger bishop Ablabius has a poor grasp of trinitarian grammar and accordingly finds himself unable to respond to those who have accused the Cappadocians of believing in three gods. Opponents of the Cappadocians have constructed an analogy and have challenged Ablabius to show whether or not pro-Nicene theology can answer the following question: If we speak of Peter, James and John as three individuals, then why can we not speak of the Father, Son and Spirit as three gods? In short, it is crucial to regard Gregory's treatise *Ad Ablabium* as a dogmatic response to the opponents of Cappadocian teaching.

When theologians appeal to Gregory's treatise in support of social trinitarianism, they inevitably face a number of substantial challenges. First, neither is Gregory responsible for the so-called social analogy of the Trinity, nor does he propose that we adopt its use. An example of the interpretative confusion exhibited by social trinitarians is found in Miroslav Volf's essay "Being as God Is: Trinity and Generosity." Volf asserts that one of the most significant early sponsors of the social analogy of the Trinity was this Gregory: "Gregory of Nyssa is well-known for employing social images for the Trinity."[19] Believing that an affinity or correspondence may be found between God and humanity, at the level of being and action, Volf is led to imagine that we may proceed to acquire a genuine knowledge of God from below: "This is

---

[18]Cornelius Plantinga Jr., "Gregory of Nyssa and the Social Analogy of the Trinity," *The Thomist* 50 (1986): 325. Cf. p. 341, where Plantinga maintains that Gregory's solution to the problem of how to speak coherently of the oneness of divine substance while affirming the existence of three divine persons is compatible with "three-person pluralism" or what has come to be termed "social trinitarianism."

[19]Miroslav Volf, "Being as God Is," pp. 5-6.

who human beings are as distinct from God; therefore, this is how they can correspond to God."[20] Obviously, there is much riding on the use of the social analogy of the Trinity. This was not lost on Gregory at all, and so we need to pay careful attention to how he responds to an analogy that has been given to him by those who seek to *undermine* his trinitarian theology.

Second, it is crucial to bear in mind that Gregory's opponents are focused upon a very different question than what preoccupies contemporary social trinitarians. In short, Gregory's opponents are uninterested in the contemporary query of how divine communion may be effectively mirrored in a fellowship shared by human persons. As Lewis Ayres rightly notes, Gregory's opponents are intent upon showing only "the degree of individuation the analogy reveals in Cappadocian trinitarianism."[21]

Given that Gregory finds insurmountable problems with the use of this analogy and that those responsible for the analogy were certainly *not* employing it in order to construct a social trinitarian doctrine of divine self-giving, it is difficult to forestall the conclusion that social trinitarians have misinterpreted this text in significant ways.

What then is Gregory seeking to accomplish with his treatise? This question is best answered by gaining a purchase on the argument as a whole. First, when we observe a group of persons, we readily identify distinct characteristics such as size, color, height and so forth; common language permits the recognition that a group of people is comprised of more than one individual. This leads Gregory to affirm that while we may use the plural term "persons" to reflect our sense of the plurality of individuals, we may not say that they manifest a plurality of natures, for the grammar of *nature* requires us to speak of it in the singular. Simply put, although we commonly speak of Peter, James and John as being three separate persons, we rightly maintain that their nature is indivisible. We bear in mind the fact that Gregory's principal concern is not the question of how to speak accurately of the constituent *substance* of humanity shared by all persons. Instead, he is focused upon setting forth the basic grammar of language about God. This leads him to state:

---

[20]Volf, *After Our Likeness*, pp. 198-200.
[21]Lewis Ayres, *Nicaea and Its Legacy: An Approach to Fourth-Century Trinitarian Theology* (New York: Oxford University Press, 2004), p. 345.

If therefore usage here permits this, and no one forbids us to speak of two as two or more than two as three, how is it that we in some way compromise our confession, by saying on the one hand that the Father, the Son, and the Holy Spirit have a single Godhead, and by denying on the other that we can speak of three gods? For in speaking of the mysteries [of the faith], we acknowledge three Persons and recognize there is no difference in nature between them.[22]

Having already identified the indivisibility of the divine *ousia*, Gregory proceeds to ask, "When we refer to the divine nature, why does our dogma exclude a multitude of gods, and while enumerating the Persons, not admit their plural significance?"[23] Put differently, Gregory insists that when speaking of God we must refuse to countenance the belief that language of three divine persons (consubstantial, sharing in one *ousia*) commits us to the notion that the Father, Son and Spirit are three separate distinct centers of consciousness or identity (as would be the case in existence of three human persons: Peter, James and John). Similarly, when speaking of Father, Son and Spirit, we identify three *hypostases*, but not three gods, for the divine nature is indivisible. Gregory reminds Ablabius that "we must confess one God, as Scripture bears witness, 'Hear, O Israel, thy God is one Lord,' even though the term 'Godhead' embraces the Holy Trinity."[24] This last comment signals an important transition in Gregory's argument.

Gregory's interpretation of Scripture leads us to see that an apophatic approach to God demands a particular hermeneutic:

We, however, following the suggestions of Holy Scripture, have learned that His nature cannot be named and is ineffable. We say that every name, whether invented by human custom or handed own by the Scriptures, is indicative of our conceptions of the divine nature, but does not signify what the nature is in itself.[25]

Gregory speaks of all this within the context of the Cappadocians' emphasis upon the spiritual and theological practice of *epinoia*. *Epinoia* is a

---

[22]Gregory of Nyssa, "An Answer to Ablabius: That We Should Not Think of Saying There Are Three Gods," in *Christology of the Later Fathers*, ed. Edward Roche Hardy, Library of Christian Classics (Philadelphia: Westminster Press, 1954), pp. 256-57.
[23]Ibid., p. 257.
[24]Ibid., p. 258.
[25]Ibid., p. 259.

hermeneutical practice in the service of drawing closer to God in both understanding and worship. It requires that we return again and again to reverently speak of God in a process of *ascesis* (self-discipline). It is an activity through which we offer our language back to God in a deep awareness of its frailty and inability to fully identify or name the unutterable reality of the triune God. Lewis Ayres offers us a fine example of what Gregory and Basil of Caesarea mean by *epinoia*: "From the act of mental dissection that is *epinoia* we may acquire a sense of an object that remains hidden from direct perception. We call God 'Giver of Life' and by abstraction we term God 'Life': by reflecting on God's act of creating all things we learn to speak of God as uncreated."[26] This certainly has a profound resonance with the overall argument of this chapter: that our language for God, our understanding of divine action and our worship *must* be submitted to God and offered back to him for his use. Only under these terms may we ever hope to be given God's blessing and to share in his presence. As such, the practice of *epinoia* suggests a necessary humility and awareness of the ontological distinction between God and humanity. By way of contrast, an exemplarist trinitarian theology transgresses the self-conscious commitment to reticence employed in the practice of *epinoia*. When the appeal of the doctrine of the Trinity lies principally or even secondarily in what it appears to promise us as a model for our social existence (as when claiming that "the Trinity is our social program"), we find ourselves at an obtuse angle from the early church. Listen to Ayres's cautionary remark:

> For Gregory it is vital that we build up our set of appellations for God in a way that preserves appropriate reverence and reserve: participating in the established practice of those who already undertake this discipline and sharing their assumptions about what may be reverently said of God is a prerequisite for the good use of *epinoia*.[27]

Although compressing the sophisticated historical and philosophical analysis of Gregory's work offered by Michel René Barnes undoubtedly fails to capture the nuance of his work, we can perhaps leverage Barnes's analysis in order to better grasp the way in which Gregory understands

---

[26]Ayres, *Nicaea and Its Legacy*, p. 352.
[27]Ibid.

trinitarian action. Gregory believes that by observing the economic acts of the triune God, you not only see the power of God but are also given a sense of the unity of God's nature. Along these lines, Barnes argues that Gregory draws a very close relationship between divine "nature" and "power." By focusing upon divine power, Barnes has uncovered the significance of Gregory's understanding of causality; in so doing, he leads us to see that for Gregory, divine power and nature are coextensive. On this basis, moreover, Gregory speaks of the Father's generation of the Son without entailing the subordinationism present in the work of his opponent Eunomius.

When we turn to Gregory's account of the external operations of the Trinity, we begin to see the sheer force and clarity of his line of reasoning. At the core of the argument is the claim that whatever "Godhead" *(theotēs)* or divinity means, it has to do with the fact that the Father, Son and Spirit are equally involved in the same activity. For Gregory, this means that by observing the various external operations of the Trinity we may derive a genuine understanding of the shared activity of the one God.

Gregory considers the divine activity of sight or beholding by spelling out the relationship between divine appropriation and coinherence. Well aware of the fact that participating in the same activity as others neither requires nor establishes an ontological identity, Gregory concedes that when you have a group of philosophers or orators undertaking common work, "even if many share the same operation, each one separately and by himself undertakes the matter at hand; . . . each one who follows this pursuit goes about it on his own."[28] To which he adds, "In the case of men [humanity] therefore, since we can differentiate the action of each while they are engaged in the same task, they are rightly referred to in the plural."[29] Though Gregory admits that when Scripture speaks of the divine activity of seeing, it "attributes sight equally to the Father, Son and Holy Spirit,"[30] he rightly argues that all three persons are always involved in this seeing. What are we to make of this? Once again, Gregory is laying bare the proper grammar of trinitarian theology—only this time he does so by drawing a distinction between the way in which human persons share in the same

---

[28]Nyssa, "An Answer to Ablabius," p. 261.
[29]Ibid.
[30]Gregory appeals to Ps 84:9; Mt 9:4; Acts 5:3.

activity, as individuals, and the way in which the external operations of the Trinity are undertaken by one God.

While two individuals may undertake the same kind of activity, they do not directly participate *in* the same act. Likewise, the ontological difference between God and human persons demands a further qualification. Creaturely acts are rightly characterized as being "individuated in a way characteristic of the created order"; in other words, while individuals may undertake specific acts of their own, their very existence follows from previous generations, and they themselves are mortal.[31] While this qualifies the kinds of acts undertaken by creatures, none of this, according to Gregory, is true of God. In other words, crucial distinctions obtain, all the way down—so much so that the categorical difference between God and humanity cannot be dismissed without irredeemable confusion. With this in view, let us briefly examine Gregory's trinitarian grammar of the oneness of God in the operations of the three hypostases.

The very fact that we are led to speak of Gregory's trinitarian theology in terms of his positive appraisal of divine oneness indicates the degree to which standard accounts of the putatively distinct characteristics of "Eastern" and "Western" trinitarian theology are misguided. Note that, when speaking against Eunomius, Gregory does not begin with an affirmation of the full divinity of the three persons and work his way back to their own nature—because his opponent has already insisted upon identifying divinity with one person (God) and one relation (the unbegotten Son). Instead, Gregory starts at the other end of the problem by insisting first upon divine unity before offering an account of the remarkable cooperation among the three persons in every economic action of God. Barnes is entirely correct in pointing out that this is not the "dynamic usually attributed to Gregory's (or Cappadocian or "Greek") trinitarian theology, but it is the only description that makes sense of the polemical context."[32] Listen to Gregory's classic expression of the way in which the three persons of the Trinity share in *ad extra* operations (in relation to the world):

We do not learn that the Father does something on his own, in which the Son

---

[31]Ayres, *Nicaea and Its Legacy*, p. 357.
[32]Michel René Barnes, *The Power of God: Dunamis in Gregory of Nyssa's Trinitarian Theology* (Washington, D.C.: Catholic University of America Press, 2001), p. 263.

does not co-operate. Or again, that the Son acts on his own without the Spirit. Rather does every operation which extends from God to creation and is designated according to our differing conceptions of it have its origin in the Father, proceed through the Son, and reach its completion by the Holy Spirit. It is for this reason that the word for the operation is not divided among the persons involved. For the action of each in any matter is not separate and individualized. But whatever occurs, whether in reference to God's providence for us or to the government and constitution of the universe, occurs through the three persons, and is not three separate things.[33]

There could hardly be a more positive expression of the way in which the three persons of the Trinity share in carrying out the selfsame act. While certainly not calling into question the distinct hypostatic existence of each of the divine persons, Gregory works with an understanding of divine power and causality that directly leads to the conclusion that Christians do not believe in three gods, but rather in one God in three persons. Accordingly, we should allow Gregory's account of the unity of divine power to lead us to a right understanding of the order of causality and the corresponding identity of three persons. Ayres correctly argues that Gregory's account of divine causality demands that we see the three persons "not as possessing distinct actions, but as together constituting *just one distinct action* (because they are one power)."[34] The force of this interpretation leads us to affirm that Gregory draws distinctions among the three persons without recourse to psychological language commonly associated with the metaphor of cooperation.

So where has all of this taken us? Up to this point, we have accomplished two things: first, our examination of the work of Miroslav Volf has revealed a number of crucial points at which an appeal to the social analogy of the Trinity leads us away from classical trinitarian theology toward seeing the Trinity as a model upon which we may construct patterns of social community and fellowship. Second, our reading of Gregory's treatise *Ad Ablabium* has shown that Gregory does not employ a social analogy of the Trinity. While social trinitarians accord pride of place to what they falsely adduce as a Cappadocian understanding of the perichoretic fellowship of the divine

---

[33]Nyssa, "An Answer to Ablabius," p. 262.
[34]Ayres, *Nicaea and Its Legacy*, p. 358.

persons—by insisting upon the importance of "relational properties"[35]—
they often fail to acknowledge precisely what Gregory insisted upon: the
radical ontological *distinction* that obtains between God and humanity.

For example, in their work *Beyond Foundationalism: Shaping Theology
in a Postmodern Context*, Stanley Grenz and John Franke mistakenly interpret the Cappadocian understanding of *hypostases* as being that which
denotes three "independent realities."[36] When combined with the use of the
social analogy, this leads Grenz and Franke to assert that "the community
we share is our shared participation, or participation together, in the perichoretic community of trinitarian persons."[37] Stated even more strongly,
"only in relationship—as persons-in-community—are we able to reflect the
fullness of the divine character."[38] Yet the Cappadocians did not think of
hypostases in the same way that we conceive of "individual realities." In
other words, *hypostasis* meant "person" rather than "individual."

Once we have in place Gregory's classic expression of the way in which
the three divine hypostases share in every operation *ad extra*, we are led to
see why Gregory insists that we should be more disciplined in our use of the
term *many* when we are speaking of a shared or common nature. In other
words, the fullness of what it means for three divine hypostases to share in
one *ousia* is captured in the communion of three divine persons. By comparison to the frailty of human community, the fullness of what is meant
here by divine perichoresis is beautifully displayed in Lucian Tercescu's
monograph *Gregory of Nyssa and the Concept of Divine Persons:*

> Since the Son is eternally contemplated in the Father, and the Spirit is the
> Son's Spirit, the Spirit too is eternally contemplated in the Father. All three
> persons rejoice eternally in the presence of each other and know each other
> perfectly. This is communion, and it allows for both the distinction of each
> person and the perfect unity among them.[39]

I have demonstrated why social trinitarians are mistaken in their belief

---

[35]Cf. Richard Swinburne, *The Christian God* (Oxford: Clarendon Press, 1994), 189.
[36]Stanley Grenz and John Franke, *Beyond Foundationalism: Shaping Theology in a Postmodern Context* (Louisville, Ky.: Westminster John Knox, 2001), p. 179.
[37]Ibid., p. 228.
[38]Ibid., p. 229.
[39]Lucian Turcescu, *Gregory of Nyssa and the Concept of Divine Persons* (New York: Oxford University Press, 2005), p. 117.

that the social analogy of the Trinity is of the "house and lineage of Gregory of Nyssa." Now it is time to examine the work of a theologian whose trinitarian theology is often maligned by social trinitarians: Karl Barth.

BARTH ON THE *MYSTERIUM TRINITATIS*

Our reflection upon the work of LaCugna, Volf and Moltmann shows the extent to which contemporary theology inhabits a culture in which less than adequate attention is given to the task of reading Scripture. The promise of dogmatic theology, however, lies in its commitment to carry out its work in deep conversation with the biblical witness and the classical tradition of the church as exemplified in its creedal and confessional documents. In his dogmatics, Karl Barth tirelessly sought to discover ways of giving faithful expression to the free and gracious reconciliation of humanity to God in Christ. In so doing, Barth recovered a way of speaking about God that necessitated a retrieval of the classical trinitarian categories and commitments to which I have just alluded. Given this, it should not be surprising to find that his work lies much closer to the Cappadocians than is true of various strains of social trinitarianism. With this in mind, allow me to tease out a few ways in which this correspondence takes shape.

The trinitarian grammar of pro-Nicene theology emphasizes the unity of divine nature, will and action. Here Barth and the Cappadocians alike stand in utter agreement. As we have seen, in striking contrast to contemporary social trinitarians, the Cappadocians did not ground an affirmation of the oneness or unity of the triune God at the level of hypostases or persons. Rather, they spoke of God as being indivisible. We ought to remember that before the work of the Cappadocians, theologians in the East had employed the terms *hypostasis* and *ousia* interchangeably. Reflecting upon Colossians 1:15, Hebrews 1:3 and Philippians 2:6, Basil the Great reasoned that while a differentiation can be made between the Father and the Son at the level of operations—for the Father generates the Son, and the Son is generated—the grammar of trinitarian speech demands that we speak of the three persons as one God, identical in being. Along these lines, Basil the Great, commenting upon Matthew 28:19, states:

> The words of baptism are the same, and they declare that the relation of the
> Spirit to the Son equals that of the Son with the Father. If the Spirit is ranked

with the Son, and the Son with the Father, then the Spirit is obviously ranked with the Father also.[40]

To this, Basil adds:

> There is one God and Father, one Only-Begotten Son, and one Holy Spirit. We declare each Person to be unique, and if we must use numbers, we will not let a stupid arithmetic lead us astray to the idea of many gods.[41]

Speaking in this way, the Cappadocians were able to articulate the necessary logic for drawing appropriate distinctions at the level of operations while, at the same time, affirming the unity of divine power and nature. This indicates how far removed social trinitarians are from an understanding of the Nicene Creed. Ayres captures this point: "We never find descriptions of the divine unity that take as their point of departure the psychological inter-communion of three distinct people."[42] As such, we should not expect to find detailed accounts of the way in which the ontology of divine persons corresponds to what we now conceive of as creaturely community and mutual support.

If social trinitarians betray a lack of understanding when it comes to pro-Nicene accounts of the unity and differentiation in the Godhead, there is a similarly problematic assumption that trinitarian theology can be accurately divided along the lines of Eastern and Western approaches. Here some commonly offer a supposedly matter-of-fact claim that theologians in the West articulate a doctrine of the Trinity in a way decidedly different from the style of theologians in the East. To take just one example, assuming that the East begins with an affirmation of the three persons of God and that the West begins with an account of the singleness of the divine *ousia*, Robert Jenson asserts that "notoriously, the Eastern and Western churches have joined them from opposite sides."[43] Ayres is certainly correct to argue for a much stronger continuity between East and West than has generally been recognized. It is simply not true that the West began with an

---

[40]Basil the Great, *On the Holy Spirit*, trans. David Anderson (Crestwood, N.Y.: St. Vladimir's Seminary Press, 1980), p. 70.
[41]Ibid., p. 72.
[42]Ayres, *Nicaea and Its Legacy*, p. 292.
[43]Robert W. Jenson, *Systematic Theology*, vol. 1, *The Triune God* (New York: Oxford University Press, 1997), p. 115.

emphasis upon the oneness of God and that the East began with a consideration of the three persons: the Cappadocians were just as concerned with affirming divine unity as they were with affirming distinct hypostases. Their unambiguous affirmation of the unity of divine power, nature and causality actually allows them to articulate a rich account of the operations of the three persons while maintaining that we do not worship three Gods, but one God in three persons.

Ayres recognizes that contemporary theology often betrays an overly shallow engagement with pro-Nicene theology in the service of generating narrative sketches of the period that neatly serve contemporary projects. Hence he raises a serious concern about the way in which contemporary systematic theology often fails to root a given patristic doctrine in its larger world of reference and practices. Along such lines he sensibly maintains that "reemphasizing contemplation of the Scriptures as the core of Christian life will have significant consequences for theological practice as a whole."[44]

Here Barth found genuine sources for rich dogmatic reflection in the early church. His account of divine "person" and perichoresis bears a striking resemblance to a number of characteristic features of pro-Nicene theology, and he maintains a firm grasp upon the affirmation of the unity and freedom of divine will and action, alongside a full affirmation of a divine perichoresis of three hypostases in the one *ousia*. What does this look like in less compact prose?

According to Barth, divine unity consists in the single subject whose name is Father, Son and Holy Spirit. Commenting upon Matthew 28:19, "Go therefore and make disciples of all nations, baptizing in the name of the Father and of the Son and of the Holy Spirit," Barth asserts: "The trinitarian baptismal formula could not be more wrongly understood than by understanding it as a formula of baptism into three divine names."[45] Yet Volf commits precisely this error when he claims that the social analogy works because Christians are baptized into the name of three persons.[46] With Gregory, Barth insists that the church worships one God, not three.

---

[44]Ayres, *Nicaea and Its Legacy*, p. 386.
[45]Karl Barth, *Church Dogmatics*, trans. Geoffrey W. Bromiley, vol. 1/1 (Edinburgh: T & T Clark, 1975), p. 349.
[46]Volf, *After Our Likeness*, p. 195.

Barth says, "The faith which is confessed in this formula, and similarly the faith of the great three-membered confessions of the ancient Church, is not, then, a faith which has three objects." He adds that "three objects of faith would mean three gods. But the so-called three 'persons' in God are in no sense three gods."[47] With this in hand, how does Barth go on to identify the three persons of the Trinity?

In the course of explaining what he means by the somewhat awkward locution "three-in-oneness," Barth maintains that when one fails to see that the unity of God coheres in the threeness of the persons, a strict affirmation of threeness would itself compromise divine unity. As such, for Barth, God is one divine subject who is fully himself in each person. In other words, what Barth opposes is the supposition that each "person" of the Trinity could constitute an essence or subject—and here we find a distinct parallel between the trinitarian theology of the Cappadocians and Barth. Read Barth's claim:

> The name of Father, Son, and Spirit means that God is the one God in three-fold repetition, and this in such a way that the repetition itself is grounded in His Godhead, so that it implies no alteration in His Godhead, and yet in such a way also that He is the one God only in this repetition.[48]

Barth's claim here is that the threefold repetition of God is itself grounded in the *ousia* (being) of God. Yet at the same time he maintains that it is only *as* this eternal threefold repetition of God in eternity that he is the one God. Likewise Barth maintains that "'Person' as used in the Church doctrine of the Trinity bears no direct relation to personality. The meaning of the doctrine is not, then, that there exist three personalities of God. This would be the worst and most extreme expression of tritheism." To this he adds, "The concept of equality of essence, or substance (*homoousia, consubstantialitas*), in the Father, Son and the Spirit is thus at every point to be understood also and primarily in the sense of identity of substance."[49]

Recognizing the inadequacy of all concepts with respect to the mystery of the Trinity, Barth famously employs the expression of three "modes of

---

[47]Barth, *Church Dogmatics*, 1/1:349.
[48]Ibid., p. 350.
[49]Ibid., p. 351.

being." It is absolutely crucial that we pay very close attention at precisely this point. While it is true that Barth speaks of the three-in-oneness of God as three "modes of being," he does *not* do so in order to subvert orthodox belief. Barth is not espousing a form of Sabellianism! Those who wish to accuse Barth of being a modalist have utterly failed to understand the language and argumentation of the early church in its opposition to Sabellianism. Commenting upon all of this, George Hunsinger insists that "modalism can be charged against Barth only out of ignorance, incompetence, or (willful) misunderstanding."[50] Barth employs this expression in order to faithfully reflect what he regards as being of immense worth in Hebrews 1:3, that Jesus Christ is "the reflection of God's glory and the exact imprint of God's very being" (NRSV). In more formal language, Barth draws a correspondence between the Latin term *subsistentia* (*Seinsweise* in German) and a Greek term employed by the Cappadocians *(hypostasis)* in order to convey the notion of three "modes of being." Barth's language of *Seinsweise* (modes of being) is entirely consistent with the trinitarian theology of the Cappadocians while standing in quite profound opposition to the Sabellian claim that Father, Son and Spirit are three modes of *appearance*. Excluding the right of Christians to speak of a divine fourth person, Barth comments: "The One who according to the witness of Scripture is and speaks and acts as Father, Son and Spirit, in self-veiling, self-unveiling and self-imparting, in holiness, mercy and love, this and no other is God."[51]

One final point of agreement between Barth and the Cappadocians warrants inclusion in our deliberation. Sharing the apophatic sensibility of the Cappadocian fathers—evident in Barth's account of a trinitarian "self-veiling, self-unveiling and self-imparting"—Barth reminds us that it would be impertinent and misguided to imagine that we could penetrate the mystery of the Trinity. He expresses this point in a number of ways: "When we have said what that is: Father, Son, and Spirit, we must then go on to say that we have said nothing."[52] Barth's confession of the *mysterium Trinitatis* (mystery of the Trinity) is profoundly helpful, for it points us toward the recog-

---

[50]George Hunsinger, *Disruptive Grace: Studies in the Theology of Karl Barth* (Grand Rapids: Eerdmans, 2000), p. 191.
[51]Barth, *Church Dogmatics*, 1/1:382.
[52]Ibid., p. 367.

nition of the sheer gratuity of God's freedom and love made known to us in Christ, "our paschal lamb" (1 Cor 5:7 NRSV). Returning to the triune God, Barth writes: "He in Himself is power, truth and right. Within the sphere of His own being He can live and love in absolute plenitude and power, as we see Him live and love in His revelation."[53] It is *this* God who, while retaining his utter transcendence and lordship, lives as Creator, Reconciler and Redeemer. Barth states: "He who can and does this is the God of Holy Scripture, the triune God known to us in His revelation. This ability, proved and manifested to us in His action, constitutes His freedom."[54] The implications of all that follows from this are vast, yet for our purposes we need only to indicate this: if genuine knowledge and life with God follows from divine freedom and condescension, then the ground of analogical predication rests in faith and faith alone. As Barth expresses it:

> If there is a real analogy between God and man—an analogy which is a true analogy of being on both sides, an analogy in which the knowledge of God will in fact be given—what other analogy can it be than the analogy of being which is posited and created by the work of God Himself, the analogy which has its actuality from God and from God alone, and therefore in faith and in faith alone.[55]

Barth clearly refuses to equivocate when it comes to the freedom and movement of the triune God *pro nobis* (for us). There is a genuine analogy between God and humanity, yet it is not our shared earthly community and fellowship, but rather it is *solus Christus* (Christ alone): only in Christ do "we live and move and have our being" (Acts 17:28 NIV).

CONCLUSION

The argument that I have offered in this chapter has led us through the work of a number of figures, both contemporary and ancient. Volf is certainly correct in his observation that contemporary trinitarian theology is marked by the presence of an almost self-evident proposition—that "ecclesial communion should correspond to trinitarian communion."[56] Yet the pri-

---

[53]Karl Barth, *Church Dogmatics*, vol. 2/1 (Edinburgh: T & T Clark, 1957), p. 301.
[54]Ibid., p. 303.
[55]Ibid., p. 83.
[56]Volf, *After Our Likeness*, p. 191.

mary goal of this chapter has been to show that social trinitarians in general and Volf in particular have misread the Cappadocian fathers at crucial points; because of this it would be wrong for us to follow their lead. When contemporary theology takes a long view of the history of the church, giving full weight to the church's classical creeds and confessions, it must recover a posture of humility. Lewis Ayres reminds us that "modern trinitarian theology invokes some of the formulae produced within the fourth century but simultaneously argues that the theological methods that produced those formulae are untenable in modernity." Likewise, given our reading of Gregory's counsel to his young bishop, it would be best to regard the contemporary fascination with social trinitarianism as constituting a kind of minority report that, in the end, risks being a more or less sophisticated form of what Garrett Green and, before him, Ludwig Feuerbach rightly term a projection theory, or role-model theology, for which "God is the mirror of man."[57]

Above I alluded to the existence of an apophatic sensibility in Barth. For some, this may have been a rather puzzling remark: how could someone who has written so many words be one who honors and respects the claim that, in the end, God is a mystery? For Barth, and I hope for each of you, dogmatics is a task of great privilege and blessing, for in it the church exercises faithfulness in seeking to gain a more certain grasp upon the words and acts of a loving and gracious Lord. Barth says all of this with more penetrating and elegant prose than mine, reminding us that dogmatics involves taking rational trouble over the mystery of the triune God:

> Theology means rational wrestling with the mystery. But all rational wrestling with the mystery, the more serious it is, can lead only to its fresh and authentic interpretation and manifestation as a mystery. For this reason it is worth our while to engage in this rational wrestling with it. If we are not prepared for this we shall not even know what we are saying when we say that what is at issue here is God's mystery.[58]

---

[57]Ludwig Feuerbach, *The Essence of Christianity*, trans. George Eliot (New York: Harper & Row, 1957), p. 63.
[58]Barth, *Church Dogmatics*, 1/1:368.

6

Does the Doctrine of the Trinity Hold the Key to a Christian Theology of Religions?

KEITH E. JOHNSON

Recently several Christian theologians have suggested that the doctrine of the Trinity holds the key to a Christian theology of religions.[1] According to one theologian, "God has something to do with the fact that a diversity of independent ways of salvation appears in the history of the world. This diversity reflects the diversity or plurality within the divine life itself, of which the Christian doctrine of the Trinity provides an account. The mystery of the Trinity is for Christians the ultimate foundation for pluralism."[2] Similarly, "I believe that the trinitarian doctrine of God facilitates an authentically Christian response to the world religions because it takes the *particularities* of history seriously as well as the *universality* of God's action."[3] Finally, "It is impossible to believe in the Trinity *instead* of the distinctive religious claims of all other religions. If Trinity is real, then many of these *specific* religious claims and ends must be real also. . . . The Trinity is a map

---

[1]For an overview of these developments, see Keith E. Johnson, "A 'Trinitarian' Theology of Religions? An Augustinian Assessment of Several Recent Proposals" (Ph.D. diss., Duke University, 2007); and Veli-Matti Kärkkäinen, *Trinity and Religious Pluralism: The Doctrine of the Trinity in Christian Theology of Religions* (Burlington, Vt.: Ashgate, 2004).

[2]Peter C. Hodgson, "The Spirit and Religious Pluralism," in *The Myth of Religious Superiority: Multifaith Explorations of Religious Pluralism*, ed. Paul F. Knitter (Maryknoll, N.Y.: Orbis Books, 2005), p. 136.

[3]Gavin D'Costa, "Toward a Trinitarian Theology of Religions," in *A Universal Faith? Peoples, Cultures, Religions, and the Christ: Essays in Honor of Frank de Graeve*, ed. Catherine Cornille and Valeer Neckebrouck (Grand Rapids: Eerdmans, 1992), p. 147.

that finds room for, indeed requires, concrete truth in other religions."[4]

The purpose of this chapter is to evaluate the claim that the doctrine of the Trinity offers the basis for a positive appraisal of non-Christian religions. Drawing upon the trinitarian theology of Augustine, I will critically examine the trinitarian doctrine in three recent proposals in the Christian theology of religions: Amos Yong's pneumatological theology of religions, Mark Heim's trinitarian theology of multiple religious ends and Jacques Dupuis's Christian theology of religious pluralism. Several factors have shaped my selection of these theologians. First, I wanted to limit my investigation to proposals in which trinitarian doctrine plays an *explicit* role. Second, I wanted to focus upon proposals that intend to affirm historic trinitarian orthodoxy. Finally, I wanted to select proposals that would provide a representative cross-section of the kind of appeal to trinitarian doctrine one encounters in the Christian theology of religions.[5]

Why turn to Augustine? Not only is Augustine's doctrine of the Trinity by far the most influential in the history of the West,[6] but despite popular portrayals to the contrary, his trinitarian doctrine also shares much in common with the Greek-speaking theologians of the East (e.g., the Cappadocians).[7] In turning to Augustine, one draws upon what is arguably the most representative version of trinitarian doctrine in the history of the

---

[4]Mark Heim, "The Depth of the Riches: Trinity and Religious Ends," *Modern Theology* 17 (2001): 22, emphasis in original.

[5]I also tried to select theologians who would represent diverse ecclesial affiliations: Yong is Pentecostal, Heim is Baptist, Dupuis is Roman Catholic.

[6]Not everyone views Augustine's influence as positive. According to critics, Augustine's theology "begins" with a unity of divine substance (which he allegedly "prioritizes" over the divine persons), his trinitarian reflection is overdetermined by neo-Platonic philosophy, his psychological analogy of the Trinity tends toward modalism, and he severs the life of the triune God from the economy of salvation by focusing on the immanent Trinity. Lewis Ayres and Michel Barnes, however, have convincingly demonstrated that these criticisms are based on a misreading of Augustine's trinitarian theology. See Lewis Ayres, "The Fundamental Grammar of Augustine's Trinitarian Theology," in *Augustine and His Critics: Essays in Honour of Gerald Bonner*, ed. Robert Dodaro and George Lawless (New York: Routledge, 2000), pp. 51-76; Michel R. Barnes, "Rereading Augustine's Theology of the Trinity," in *The Trinity: An Interdisciplinary Symposium on the Trinity*, ed. Stephen T. Davis, Daniel Kendall and Gerald O'Collins (New York: Oxford, 1999), pp. 145-76.

[7]See Michel R. Barnes, "De Régnon Reconsidered," *Augustinian Studies* 26 (1995): 51-79; idem, "Augustine in Contemporary Trinitarian Theology," *Theological Studies* 56 (1995): 237-50; and Lewis Ayres, *Nicaea and Its Legacy: An Approach to Fourth-Century Trinitarian Theology* (New York: Oxford University Press, 2004), pp. 273-383.

church among Protestants and Catholics.[8] In conversation with Augustine, I will argue (1) that there is good reason to question the claim that the "Trinity" represents the key to a new understanding of religious diversity and (2) that current "use" of trinitarian theology in the Christian theology of religions appears to be having a deleterious effect upon the doctrine. First, I will outline the proposals of Yong, Heim and Dupuis, paying special attention to the role of trinitarian doctrine. Then, I will evaluate the trinitarian "grammar" they each employ from an Augustinian perspective.[9] I will close by reflecting on the implications of my investigation for contemporary trinitarian theology.

TRINITARIAN DOCTRINE IN THE CHRISTIAN THEOLOGY OF RELIGIONS: THREE RECENT PROPOSALS

Amos Yong's pneumatological theology of religions. In a monograph titled *Discerning the Spirit(s): A Pentecostal-Charismatic Contribution to a Christian Theology of Religions*, Amos Yong, a Pentecostal theologian, tries to develop a "Pentecostal-charismatic" theology of religions.[10] Yong suggests that pneumatology may provide the key to moving beyond what he calls the "christological impasse," that is, "the almost irreconcilable axioms of God's universal salvific will and the historical particularity of Jesus of Nazareth as Savior of all persons."[11] The metaphysical basis for Yong's proposal is the universal presence of the Holy Spirit. Yong argues that the Holy Spirit is present and active among non-Christian religions and that Christians must learn to discern the Spirit's presence.

The "foundational pneumatology" that Yong develops in *Discerning the Spirit(s)* is predicated upon a trinitarian distinction between the "economy" of the Word and the "economy" of the Spirit.[12] It would not be an over-

---

[8]My evaluation of these proposals will draw implicitly and explicitly upon Augustine's most significant trinitarian work: *De trinitate*. All citations of *De trinitate* will be taken from Augustine of Hippo, *The Trinity*, trans. Edmund Hill, ed. John E. Rotelle (Hyde Park, N.Y.: New City Press, 1991).

[9]Space limitations will not allow me to develop the trinitarian theology of Augustine, which will be employed as the basis for my evaluation. This can be found elsewhere. See Johnson, "A 'Trinitarian' Theology of Religions?" pp. 47-110, 122-33, 175-200, 261-76.

[10]Amos Yong, *Discerning the Spirit(s): A Pentecostal-Charismatic Contribution to a Christian Theology of Religions* (Sheffield: Sheffield Academic Press, 2000).

[11]Ibid., p. 94.

[12]"The entire objective of shifting to a pneumatological framework in order to understand

statement to say that this distinction constitutes the trinitarian key to his proposal. On the basis of this distinction, Yong affirms the presence and activity of the Holy Spirit among non-Christian religions and justifies the use of nonchristological criteria for discerning the Spirit's presence. According to Yong, the economies of the Son and Spirit are "mutually related, and should not be subordinated either to the other."[13] At the same time, these economies possess a measure of autonomy inasmuch as they originate in the Father.[14]

Having established this framework, Yong turns to the problem of criteria for discerning this presence of the Spirit. Previous pneumatological approaches have foundered because they were unable to identify nonchristological criteria for discerning the Spirit's presence. Although christological criteria are clearly useful in certain contexts, they are not particularly helpful outside the church. Because the Spirit acts in an economy distinct from that of the Son, one should be able to identify aspects of the Spirit's work that are not "constrained" by the Son.[15] To this end, Yong proposes a "three-tiered process" for discerning the "religious" activity of the Spirit among adherents of other religions. The first element is "phenomenological-experiential," the second is "moral-ethical," and the third is "theological-soteriological."[16] In addition to the Holy Spirit as "divine presence," one must also acknowledge the possibility of the presence of the "demonic" as "divine absence."[17] Thus, a Pentecostal theology of religions is able to account both for the "transformative" nature of religious experience as well as negative elements.

Pentecostals must learn to "discern" the presence of the Spirit (or spirits) in other religions by cultivating a "pneumatological imagination" informed by these three elements.[18] Although there is good reason to believe that the

---

non-Christian faiths is premised upon the recognition that there is a distinction between the economy of the Son and that of the Spirit relative to the redemption of the world" (ibid., p. 61).

[13]Ibid., p. 69.

[14]Ibid.

[15]Ibid., p. 136.

[16]Ibid, pp. 250-54.

[17]Ibid., p. 131.

[18]As a test case for his proposal, Yong investigates the possibility of discerning the presence of the Holy Spirit within Umbanda, an Afro-Brazilian tradition. Traditionally, Pentecostals have dismissed Umbanda as demonically inspired; however, Yong believes that evidence of

Spirit is present and active in other religions, confirmation of the Spirit's presence can come only through concrete engagement. When the Spirit's presence is discerned, one may recognize a non-Christian religion "as salvific in the Christian sense."[19]

Mark Heim's trinitarian theology of religious ends. In a book titled *The Depth of the Riches: A Trinitarian Theology of Religious Ends*, Mark Heim, a Baptist theologian, suggests that the debate over the theology of religions proceeds on "a largely undefended assumption that there is and can only be one religious end, one actual religious fulfillment."[20] This assumption must be rejected. While Christians will experience "salvation" (i.e., communion with the triune God), adherents of other religions may experience other positive ends that must be distinguished from "salvation." These alternative "religious ends" arise from an encounter with the "complex" life of the Trinity: "I contend that distinctive religious ends sought and realized in other religious traditions are grounded in apprehension of and connection with specific dimensions of the divine life of the Triune God."[21]

According to Heim, the divine life of the triune God is "complex" in the sense that it is characterized by three dimensions: (1) "impersonal," (2) "personal" and (3) "communion." The impersonal dimension of the triune God involves the infinite divine life as it circulates among the persons. This exchange among the persons can be perceived either as an awareness of impermanence (in the case of Buddhism) or as "self without relation" (in the case of Advaita Vedanta Hindu thought).[22] A second "dimension" involves God's personal involvement in the world. Through this dimension, humans "seek God's presence, hear God's word, see God's acts, obey or disobey God's commandments, and offer praise or petition."[23] A third dimension of relation involves "communion": a "mutual indwelling, in which the distinct persons are not confused or identified but are enriched by their

---

the Spirit's presence among the Umbanda can be seen in "the movement toward personal authenticity in the lives of individuals and toward social solidarity" (ibid., p. 279).

[19]Ibid., p. 312.

[20]Mark Heim, *The Depth of the Riches: A Trinitarian Theology of Religious Ends* (Grand Rapids: Eerdmans, 2001), p. 17.

[21]Ibid., p. 9.

[22]Ibid., pp. 187-89.

[23]Ibid., pp. 192-93.

participation in each other's inner life."[24]

When a relation with God is pursued "consistently and exclusively" through one of the three dimensions, a "distinctive religious end" results.[25] Heim distinguishes four possible human destinies: (1) salvation (communion with the triune God), (2) alternative religious ends (which represent a response to an economic manifestation of an immanent dimension of the triune life), (3) nonreligious human destinies (which result from fixation on some created good) and (4) the negation of the created self. Alternative religious ends are rooted in an "authentic revelation *of* the triune God" and depend upon God's grace: "The triune God is party to the realization of alternate religious ends. They are not simply the actualization of innate human capacities; they are distinct relations with aspects of the triune life. A particular grace of God is operative within them."[26]

Jacques Dupuis's Christian theology of religious pluralism. In his book *Toward a Christian Theology of Religious Pluralism*, the late Jacques Dupuis, a Roman Catholic theologian, argues on trinitarian grounds that non-Christian religions mediate God's saving grace.[27] Because the triune God constitutes the ultimate source of all genuine religious experience, different religions are able to convey differing—yet legitimate—insights into this divine ultimate reality.[28]

Before outlining his proposal, it will be helpful to locate Dupuis's work in the context of contemporary Catholic approaches to religious pluralism. Although Vatican II clearly affirmed that non-Christian religions are—in some sense—to be viewed positively and that individuals who have never heard the gospel can experience salvation,[29] the conciliar bishops were silent regarding the means through which salvific grace is mediated apart from the church. Silence on this question has led to two conflicting positions among Catholics that can be summarized as follows: (P1) Although salvation is available outside the church, it is not mediated through non-

---

[24]Ibid., p. 196.

[25]Ibid., p. 289.

[26]Ibid., p. 275, emphasis in original.

[27]Jacques Dupuis, *Toward a Christian Theology of Religious Pluralism* (Maryknoll, N.Y.: Orbis Books, 1997).

[28]Ibid., p. 279.

[29]See Miikka Ruokanen, *The Catholic Doctrine of Non-Christian Religions According to the Second Vatican Council* (New York: E. J. Brill, 1992).

Christian religions.[30] (P2) Salvation is not only available outside the church, but it is also mediated through non-Christian religions in such a way that non-Christian religions are to be viewed as means of salvation.[31] Dupuis embraces a form of P2.

Although Jesus Christ is the "universal" Savior of humankind, he is not the "absolute" Savior. According to Dupuis, "absoluteness" can be attributed only to God the Father. Jesus Christ is Savior only in the derivative sense that "the world and humankind find salvation in and through him."[32] Thus, rather than speaking of Jesus Christ as "absolute" Savior, Dupuis maintains that it would be better to speak of Jesus Christ as "constitutive" Savior. By insisting that Jesus Christ is "constitutive" Savior, Dupuis wants to open the door to other "saviors" who somehow "participate" in the universal mediation of Christ. God's saving action, he insists, is not limited to the Christ-event. On the contrary, the "two hands" of God, the Word and the Spirit, are universally present and active in non-Christian religions.[33] A "distinct action" of the nonincarnate Logos continues following Christ's resurrection.[34] The Spirit is also universally active following the incarnation. As a result of the Spirit's inspiration, "revelation" can be encountered in the sacred writings of non-Christian religions. For example, sacred scriptures such as the Qur'an can be viewed as containing the "word of God."[35]

Building upon the foundation of Karl Rahner, Dupuis claims that non-Christian religions constitute "channels of salvation" through which efficacious grace is mediated to their adherents. Salvation does not reach human beings *in spite of* their religious traditions but *in and through* them. For example, the worship of images may constitute a means of grace for Hindus: "The worship of sacred images can be the sacramental sign in and through which the devotee responds to the offer of divine grace; it can mediate secretly the grace offered by God in Jesus Christ and express the hu-

---

[30]Catholic proponents of P1 include Gavin D'Costa and Joseph DiNoia.

[31]Catholic proponents of P2 include Karl Rahner, Paul Knitter, Hans Küng and Raimundo Panikkar.

[32]Dupuis, *Toward a Christian Theology of Religious Pluralism*, p. 293.

[33]Ibid., p. 316.

[34]"While, then, the human action of the Logos *ensarkos* is the universal sacrament of God's saving action, it does not exhaust the action of the Logos. A distinct action of the Logos *asarkos* endures" (Dupuis, *Toward a Christian Theology of Religious Pluralism*, p. 299).

[35]Ibid., p. 245.

man response to God's gratuitous gift in him."[36]

Finally, Dupuis claims that non-Christian religions share in the universal reign of God. Although they are not members of the church, adherents of other religious traditions are, nevertheless, authentic members of the kingdom who contribute to its growth and development.[37] In light of these and other factors, religious pluralism should not be viewed with suspicion but welcomed with open arms, recognizing that "God has manifested himself to humankind in manifold ways."[38]

AMOS YONG'S TRINITARIAN PNEUMATOLOGY: A CRITICAL EVALUATION

Inasmuch as Yong's pneumatological theology of religions is rooted in a distinction between the "economy" of the Son and the "economy" of the Spirit, his proposal raises important questions about the relations of the trinitarian persons both within the divine life of the triune God *(ad intra)* and in the economy of salvation *(ad extra)*. I will argue that Yong's proposal ultimately fails to offer an adequate account of the relation of the Spirit to the Father and the Son.[39]

Insufficient trinitarian framework. Although Yong acknowledges that the "mission" of the Spirit must ultimately be understood in a trinitarian context, he offers no comprehensive trinitarian framework *at the outset* within which to relate the work of the Father, Son and Holy Spirit. Although he frequently refers to the "missions" of the Son and Spirit, he offers no substantive discussion of the content of these missions from a salvation-historical perspective. Echoing several contemporary theologians, he simply asserts that the Spirit operates in an "economy" distinct from that of the Son, brackets the "mission" of the Son and then focuses almost exclusively on the "mission" of the Holy Spirit. At the level of the immanent Trinity, Yong offers no account of the relations of the trinitarian persons *ad intra* as ground for his understanding of the divine "missions." The closest he comes to a discussion of intratrinitarian relations is a brief discussion of the procession of the Spirit, in which he rejects the

---

[36]Ibid., p. 303.
[37]Ibid., p. 345.
[38]Ibid., p. 386.
[39]For a more extensive evaluation of Yong's proposal, see Johnson, "A 'Trinitarian' Theology of Religions?" pp. 158-213.

traditional Western view that the Spirit proceeds jointly from the Father *and the Son* (in order to maintain a theological basis for an independent "economy" of the Holy Spirit). Nevertheless, evidence *against* the twofold procession of the Spirit *ad intra* does not count as evidence *for* a distinct economy of the Spirit *ad extra*.

Severing the two hands of the Father. Throughout *Discerning the Spirit(s)*, Yong repeatedly appeals to Irenaeus's image of the Son and Spirit as the two hands of God as a way of conceptualizing the Son-Spirit relationship. His use of this image, however, stands in tension with his emphasis upon a distinct "economy" of the Spirit. From an economic standpoint, the two-hands imagery is not about a left hand doing one activity and the right hand doing another (which seems to be implied by associating a distinct "economy" with each "hand"). It is fundamentally about the *Father* acting through the Son and Spirit to a particular end.[40] It underscores unity of action, combining hypostatic distinction at the intratrinitarian level (i.e., Father, Son and Spirit) with unity of action at the economic level. Yong's use of this image causes one to wonder if his proposal implicitly severs the two hands of the Father.[41]

Like Irenaeus, Augustine emphasizes the unity of the divine persons *ad extra*. Father, Son and Spirit work together in a single economy of salvation. Although the sendings of the Son and Spirit are distinct in such a way that one can speak of *two* "sendings" (Gal 4:4-6), these two "sendings" have *one* ultimate goal—bringing human beings into communion with the triune God. From two "sendings" one should not infer two distinct "economies."[42]

---

[40]In the original context of Irenaeus's trinitarian theology, the two-hands metaphor served to highlight the "direct" nature of God's involvement in the world over and against Gnostics, who posited a chain of intermediaries between God and the world.

[41]In fairness to Yong, we recognize that in many places where he employs the two-hands metaphor, he explicitly acknowledges that the Son and Spirit work together. For example, in commenting on the Son and Spirit as the two hands of God, Yong explains, "As such, they are both present universally and particularly in creation, and, in the words of Congar, they 'do God's work together'" (Yong, *Discerning the Spirit(s)*, p. 116).

[42]Yong's trinitarian pneumatology is deficient not because it affirms differing economic *roles* of the Son and the Spirit (e.g., the fact that the Son alone became incarnate). Rather, it is deficient because it affirms two distinct *economies*—one associated with the Son and the other with the Spirit. From two "sendings" (Latin, *missiones*) one should not infer two distinct "economies." Yong makes the mistake of equating "mission" and "economy." Notice how he uses these terms interchangeably in the following statement: "Preliminarily then, a pneumatological theology of religions that validates the distinction between the *economy*

By positing two "economies," Yong implicitly severs the two hands and undermines the unicity of the economy of salvation.

Further evidence that Yong's trinitarian pneumatology severs the two hands can be seen in the way he relates the work of the Spirit to the Son. Although Yong emphasizes the empowering role of the Spirit in the incarnation and earthly ministry of Christ, he fails to take seriously biblical teaching regarding the Spirit's unique role in bearing witness to and glorifying the risen Christ (e.g, Jn 15:26-27; 16:7-15; Acts 1:6-9; 4:24-31).[43] In his discussion of Pentecost (Acts 2), Augustine discerns a special significance in the sign through which the bestowal of the Spirit was manifested: bearing witness to Christ in multiple languages. It offers a proleptic fulfillment of the goal of the Holy Spirit's work: leading people in every nation to believe in Jesus Christ.[44] Precisely in this sense the Spirit "universalizes" the work of Jesus Christ. This universal work of the Spirit constitutes the basis for the evangelistic mission of the church. Thus, from a salvation-historical perspective, the redemptive work of the Spirit (along with the Father and Son) among adherents of other religions must be understood in terms of *praeparatio evangelica* (preparation for the gospel).[45] No grounds exist for positing a distinct salvation-historical economy of the Spirit leading to some other end. Inasmuch as Yong's proposal tries to move beyond the latter, it severs the two hands of the Father and obscures the missionary nature of the economic Trinity.

A final way Yong's trinitarian pneumatology severs the two hands of the Father is by bracketing christological criteria for discerning God's work. If,

---

of the Word and Spirit holds the christological problem in abeyance. For now, it is sufficient to grant that there is a relationship-in-autonomy between the two divine *missions*" (Yong, *Discerning the Spirit(s)*, p. 70, emphasis added).

[43]In the Pauline epistles we see further evidence that the Holy Spirit bears witness to the Son and glorifies the Son. The Spirit glorifies Christ by witnessing to the "sonship" of the redeemed (Rom 8:1-17); empowering the preaching of the gospel (Rom 15:14-21; 1 Cor 2:2-5); enabling believers to confess Jesus as Lord (1 Cor 12:2-3); removing the "veil" so that men and women can see the glory of Christ, who is the image of God (2 Cor 3:7–4:6); enabling believers to become conformed to the image of the Son (Rom 8:26-30); producing the fruit of Christ in the lives of believers (Gal 5:15-24); enabling believers to know and experience the love of Christ (Eph 3:14-21).

[44]See Augustine *De trinitate* 4.29.

[45]Adopting this view does not require one to deny the presence of truth and goodness in the lives of adherents of other religions. These can be accounted for in terms of a Christian anthropology informed by the doctrines of creation and fall.

as Augustine rightly insists, the Father, Son and the Spirit are working to-gether in a single economy, which exists to draw men and women into the life of the triune God, then any criteria for discerning the Spirit's redemp-tive work must include a "christological" element.[46]

MARK HEIM'S TRINITY OF THREE DIMENSIONS: A CRITICAL EVALUATION

Since the patristic period, Christian theologians have drawn an important distinction between God *in se* (in himself) and God *pro nobis* (for us).[47] The latter denotes God's self-communication through the economy of sal-vation (the economic Trinity); the former refers to the intratrinitarian life of the three divine persons (the immanent Trinity). From an *epistemological* perspective, God's self-revelation in the economy of salvation constitutes the foundation for our knowledge of the immanent Trinity. From an *onto-logical* perspective, the immanent Trinity constitutes the foundation for the economic Trinity. In the discussion that follows, I will argue that the prob-lems in Heim's proposal center on the relationship between the economic Trinity and the immanent Trinity.[48]

Speculative account of the immanent Trinity. At the root of Heim's proposal is an assumption that the *immanent* life of the triune God is con-stituted by three dimensions: "impersonal," "personal" and "communion." These dimensions constitute the trinitarian foundation for multiple ends.

---

[46]In a more recent book titled *Beyond the Impasse: Toward a Pneumatological Theology of Religions* (Grand Rapids: Baker Academic, 2003), Amos Yong to a greater degree acknowl-edges the inherent relatedness of the Son and the Spirit as the two hands of the Father. Yong also seems more aware of the problems associated with a search for nonchristological criteria for discerning the Spirit's presence. Nevertheless, none of these acknowledgments leads to any explicit revision of his earlier proposal. On the contrary, he continues to affirm a distinct "economy" of the Spirit and still wants to maintain the legitimacy of nonchris-tological criteria for discerning the Spirit's presence and activity. (In a far more restrained form, similar claims can also be found in *The Spirit Poured Out on All Flesh: Pentecostal-ism and the Possibility of Global Theology* [Grand Rapids: Baker Academic, 2005], chap. 6.) Insofar as Yong emphasizes the distinct economy of the Spirit in order to gain traction for a nonchristological approach to other religions, he implicitly severs the two hands of the Father. However, insofar as he acknowledges the intrinsic relatedness of the two hands under pressure of classical Christian concerns regarding the doctrine of the Trinity, he un-dermines his quest for nonchristological criteria.

[47]Augustine, for example, carefully distinguishes "procession" (immanent Trinity) from "mission" (economic Trinity); see *De trinitate* 2-4.

[48]For a more thorough evaluation of Heim's proposal, see Johnson, "A 'Trinitarian' Theol-ogy of Religions?" pp. 111-57.

For example, through a "relation" with the impersonal dimension of the triune life, Buddhists may experience the Buddhist religious end: nirvana. What constitutes the epistemic basis for Heim's claim that the inner life of the triune God is constituted by three "dimensions"? Although Heim would likely insist that Scripture constitutes the ultimate basis for his understanding of the immanent Trinity,[49] there are good reasons to question this claim. The primary source for these dimensions is not God's self-revelation in Scripture but Smart and Konstantine's *Christian Systematic Theology in World Context* (to which Heim acknowledges his indebtedness).[50] Smart and Konstantine simply assert the existence of these three dimensions and then try to explain the "economic" activity of the triune God among other religions on this basis of this assumption. Although they insist that the Trinity is the ultimate divine reality, they are quite skeptical regarding the foundation on which this affirmation ultimately rests (i.e., Scripture).[51] Inasmuch as Heim's account of the three immanent dimensions is consciously dependent upon Smart and Konstantine, it represents a speculative account of the immanent Trinity that is inadequately rooted in Scripture.

From the immanent to the economic Trinity. A second trinitarian problem involves the way in which Heim relates the immanent Trinity to the economic Trinity. To better understand the nature of this problem, we must revisit his description of the economic Trinity. According to Heim, three "relations" characterize the economic activity of the triune God: "impersonal identity," "iconographic encounter" and "personal communion." These "real relations"[52] constitute the economic means through which al-

---

[49]Heim argues that an "impersonal" dimension can be seen in Old Testament theophanies (e.g., the "fire" through which God appears to Moses; see *Depth of the Riches*, pp. 185-86). There are at least two problems with his argument. First, these apparently "impersonal" manifestations represent one aspect of a fundamentally "personal" self-revelation: it is the God of Abraham, Isaac and Jacob who "speaks" to Moses from the "burning bush." To sever an "impersonal" aspect (e.g., "fire") from the "personal" and make it stand alone is highly problematic. Second, no epistemic warrant exists for assuming that a particular *created* form (e.g., fire) necessarily reveals something about the immanent nature of the triune God.

[50]See Ninian Smart and Stephen Konstantine, *Christian Systematic Theology in World Context* (Minneapolis: Fortress, 1991), p. 174.

[51]The following encapsulates their view of Scripture: "It therefore seems nonsense to pretend that the Bible has doctrinal or narrative authority" (ibid., p. 47). By rejecting the authority of Scripture, they reject the epistemic basis for a Christian doctrine of the Trinity.

[52]"Relations with God in *all* three dimensions we have described are real relations with God.

ternative religious ends (e.g., moksha, nirvana, etc.) obtain. Heim is clear
that God intentionally wills these economic relations.[53] In other words,
alongside God's economy of "salvation" in Christ, other divine "economies" exist: there is an economy of salvation (the Christian end), an "economy" of nirvana (the Buddhist end), an "economy" of moksha (the Hindu
end) and so forth.[54] In book four of De trinitate, Augustine explains that
the "sendings" of the Son and Spirit have as their goal restoring fallen humans into a relationship of communion with the triune God. Missio constitutes a central link between the divine persons (immanent Trinity) and the
economy of salvation (economic Trinity). By positing "economies" of divine
activity that effectively bypass the work of Christ, Heim implicitly severs
this link. No epistemic warrant exists for positing additional "economies"
of divine activity that bypass (or constitute an alternative to) this one economy of salvation effected in Christ. On the basis of a speculative understanding of the immanent Trinity, Heim outlines a deficient account of the
economic Trinity that ultimately undermines the divine oikonomia revealed
in Scripture.

A trinity of dimensions replaces the Trinity of persons. At the level of
the immanent Trinity, Heim's proposal ultimately employs two Trinities.
The first Trinity (Father, Son and Holy Spirit) is the Trinity of Christian
confession; however, this Trinity is not the one that does the real work in
his project. Heim subtly substitutes his three "dimensions" for the trinitarian "persons," effectively creating an alternate "trinity." The term "complex" plays a key role in this substitution. When Heim first introduces the
term "complex," it denotes the fact that God's being is constituted by a
multiplicity of persons; however, as his argument unfolds, "complex" shifts
to denote his three "dimensions." His substitution of "dimensions" for
"persons" can be seen most clearly in applying language usually reserved
for the trinitarian "persons" to these "dimensions." For example, Heim
claims that only "three" dimensions exist. Why three? Why not two, four
or even ten? Is it merely coincidental that there also happen to be three di-

---

They are not relations with something else (idols) or with false gods. What humans find in
such relations is truly there" (Heim, Depth of the Riches, p. 199).

[53]See ibid., p. 275.

[54]One cannot call these "economies of salvation" because Christian salvation does not represent their goal.

vine persons? Moreover, Heim suggests that "each of the dimensions is granted coequality with the others."[55] Here Heim applies the language of coequality to the dimensions; yet coequality applies only to the trinitarian persons. Finally, he claims that individuals experience "relations" with these "dimensions" in such a way that the "dimensions" effectively replace the trinitarian persons.[56] Heim's immanent "trinity of dimensions" has subtly replaced the Trinity of persons.

JACQUES DUPUIS'S TRINITARIAN CHRISTOLOGY: A CRITICAL EVALUATION

Although, at first glance, Dupuis appears to be faithful to the Catholic trinitarian tradition, I will try to demonstrate that a close reading reveals that his proposal gains traction only by introducing subordinationism into the Father-Son relationship and undermining the unicity of the economy of salvation.[57]

Subordinationism in the Father-Son relationship. In order to make space for other "saviors" and "mediators," Dupuis appeals to a "trinitarian Christology" in which Christ is recognized not as "absolute" Savior but merely as "constitutive" Savior. That Jesus Christ is "constitutive" Savior means, among other things, that he is not the *goal* of salvation but merely the constitutive *means* of salvation.[58] What is troubling about the latter claim is the obvious attempt to distinguish the salvific role of the incarnate Son (constitutive Savior) from that of the Father (absolute Savior) by limiting the Son to an *instrumental* role in salvation. To suggest

---

[55]Ibid., p. 213.

[56]Heim's equivocation on this point is quite revealing. On one hand, he insists that individuals relate to the triune God (ibid., p. 199). On the other hand, he also claims that individuals experience a relation with an "aspect" of God's nature. Multiple religious ends result from an "intensification of a particular kind of relation with an *aspect of divine life*" (ibid., p. 289, emphasis added). Thus it is unclear whether the "relation" exists with the triune God or merely with an "aspect" of God.

[57]In addition to Jacques Dupuis's *Toward a Christian Theology of Religious Pluralism,* I will also draw upon a more recent work of his: *Christianity and the Religions: From Confrontation to Dialogue,* trans. Phillip Berryman (Maryknoll, N.Y.: Orbis Books, 2002). For a more thorough evaluation of Dupuis's proposal, see Johnson, "A 'Trinitarian' Theology of Religions?" pp. 158-236.

[58]"[Christocentrism] never places Jesus Christ in the place of God; it merely affirms that God has placed him at the center of his saving plan for humankind, not as the end but as the way, not as the goal of every human quest for God but as the universal 'mediator' (cf. 1 Tim 2:5) of God's saving action toward people" (Dupuis, *From Confrontation to Dialogue,* p. 88).

that the salvific role of Jesus Christ is *merely* instrumental sounds suspiciously subordinationist. Inasmuch as Jesus Christ is Savior as God incarnate (*homoousios* [of the same substance] with the Father), one must affirm (on the basis of the unity of action *ad extra*) that the Son also willed salvation along with the Father.[59] If one instead maintains that Jesus Christ is merely a *constitutive means* of salvation and did not also will it (along with the Father and the Spirit), then it would seem that some form of subordinationism is unavoidable.

Dupuis is aware of this problem. To avoid positing subordinationism in the immanent life of the triune God, he appeals to the distinction between the human and divine natures of Jesus Christ as the basis for his claim that Jesus Christ is "constitutive" Savior.[60] Although this move may solve the problem of subordinationism, it does so only by undermining the unity of the two natures in *one* person. It was not a *nature* that the Father sent to save the world but a *person*. It was not a *nature* that died on the cross but a *person*. That person was the Son of God.

At the end of the day, Dupuis faces a serious dilemma. He cannot continue to affirm that Jesus Christ is merely "constitutive" Savior and uphold an orthodox trinitarian Christology. On the one hand, if he suggests that Jesus Christ is merely the constitutive *means* of salvation and did not will it along with the Father, he necessarily introduces subordinationism into the immanent life of the triune God. On the other hand, if he tries to overcome this problem by emphasizing the "unbridgeable distance" between God the Father and Jesus Christ in his human nature, he undermines the unicity of the two natures.

Undermining the unicity of the economy of salvation. Central to Dupuis's proposal is a distinction between the work of the Logos *ensarkos* (the incarnate Logos) and the work of the Logos *asarkos* (the nonincarnate

---

[59]One of the fundamental axioms of Augustine's theology—an assumption he shares with the Cappadocians—is that the Father, Son and Holy Spirit act with *one will* in the economy of salvation (see *De trinitate* 4.30).

[60]"The unique closeness that exists between God and Jesus by virtue of the mystery of the incarnation may never be forgotten, but neither can the *unbridgeable distance* that remains between the Father and Jesus in his human existence. . . . While it is true that Jesus the man is uniquely the Son of God, it is equally true that God (the Father) stands beyond Jesus" (Dupuis, *From Confrontation to Dialogue*, p. 92, emphasis added).

Logos).[61] On the basis of this distinction, he claims that an enduring work of the Logos *asarkos* (distinct from the Logos *ensarkos*) continues following the incarnation.[62] The distinction Dupuis draws between the economic activity of Logos *ensarkos* and economic activity of the Logos *asarkos* prompts a crucial question from an Augustinian standpoint: Does the work of the Logos *asarkos* constitute a *second* economy of salvation existing in parallel with the first?

Although Dupuis would insist it does not, the way he employs the Logos *ensarkos* / Logos *asarkos* distinction seems to require two parallel economies of salvation.[63] This can be seen by comparing the economic activity of the Logos *asarkos* with that of the Logos *ensarkos*. Through the work of the Logos *ensarkos* (and the Spirit),[64] the Christian Scriptures contain the Word of God. Through the work of the Logos *asarkos* (and the Spirit),[65] the Qur'an and other non-Christian scriptures contain the Word of God.[66] Through the work of the Logos *ensarkos*, there is one mediator between humans and God. Through the work of the Logos *asarkos*, other mediators exist between humans and God. Through the work of the Logos *ensarkos*, the church mediates salvific grace. Through the work of the Logos *asarkos*,

---

[61]His distinction between the work of the Logos *ensarkos* and Logos *asarkos* following the incarnation is grounded, to a significant degree, in the distinction between the two natures of Christ: "Admittedly, in the mystery of Jesus-the-Christ, the Word cannot be separated from the flesh it has assumed. But, inseparable as the divine Word and Jesus' human existence may be, they nevertheless remain distinct. While, then, the human action of the Logos *ensarkos* is the universal sacrament of God's saving action, it does not exhaust the action of the Logos" (Dupuis, *Christian Theology of Religious Pluralism*, p. 299).

[62]"There is a salvific working of the Word as such, distinct from that of the Word operating through his human being in Jesus Christ, risen and glorified, though in 'union' with it [the human nature of Jesus Christ]" (Dupuis, *From Confrontation to Dialogue*, p. 139).

[63]I am not suggesting that any kind of distinction between the Logos *ensarkos* and Logos *asarkos* necessarily implies two economies of salvation; rather, I am arguing that the specific way Dupuis employs this distinction requires two economies.

[64]Although I am focusing on the work of the Logos, Dupuis is careful not to sever the action of the Logos from the action of the Spirit. It will become clear that Dupuis does not sever the unicity of the economy of salvation by severing the Word from the Spirit (as in the case of Yong) but rather by severing the work of the Logos *ensarkos* from the work of the Logos *asarkos*.

[65]See the previous footnote. In the rest of this paragraph, it should be understood that the Spirit is included when I speak of the work of the Logos *ensarkos* or the Logos *asarkos*.

[66]See Dupuis, *From Confrontation to Dialogue*, pp. 115-37. Dupuis suggests that while Jesus Christ represents the "qualitative fullness" of revelation, he does not represent the "quantitative fullness" of revelation.

the worship of Hindu images mediates salvific grace.[67] Through the work
of the Logos *ensarkos*, men and women are reconciled to God and incorporated into Christ's church. Through the work of the Logos *asarkos*, men
and women are not incorporated into the church but become members of
"the kingdom of God."[68] Following Christ's resurrection, how can one be
savingly related to the Father without concomitantly being included in
Christ's church? The latter contrast seems to suggest a second parallel economy.[69] From an Augustinian perspective, no epistemic warrant exists for
positing a second economy of salvation in parallel with that of the incarnate Word.[70] Inasmuch as Dupuis implicitly posits two economies, he undermines the unicity of the economy of salvation.[71]

CONCLUSION

The purpose of this chapter was to evaluate the claim that a proper understanding of "the Trinity" provides the basis for a new understanding of
religious diversity. To this end I have critically examined the trinitarian
doctrine in three recent proposals in the Christian theology of religions.
Under pressure to accommodate religious pluralism, Amos Yong, Mark
Heim and Jacques Dupuis reinterpret trinitarian doctrine in order to support their constructive accounts of religious diversity. To argue for a distinct economy of the Spirit, Yong severs the two hands of the Father. To
argue for the validity of "other" religious ends, Heim substitutes a trinity

---

[67]Dupuis, *Christian Theology of Religious Pluralism*, p. 303.

[68]Moving beyond Karl Rahner, Dupuis no longer wants to talk about "anonymous Christians."

[69]The net result is two parallel economies that converge only eschatologically; in the present
stage of salvation history, they exist more or less in parallel.

[70]Augustine is quite clear that the sending of the Son and the sending of the Spirit have one
goal: bringing men and women into fellowship with the triune God by leading people in
every nation to confess Jesus as Savior and Lord (see *De trinitate* 4.29 [pp. 174-75]).

[71]Moreover, if it is true that Dupuis distinguishes the work of the Logos *asarkos* and Logos *ensarkos* in a way that undermines the unicity of the economy of salvation, this also
suggests a further deficiency in his Christology (inasmuch as the distinction between the
work of the Logos *asarkos* and Logos *ensarkos* is grounded in the distinction of the divine
and human natures). When one combines Dupuis's emphasis on the "unbridgeable gap"
between "God" and Jesus Christ in his human nature as the basis for his "constitutive"
Christology with his insistence upon the distinction between the divine and human natures
as the basis for a distinct and continuing action of the Logos *asarkos*, it appears that his
"trinitarian Christology" may implicitly undermine the unity of the divine and human
natures of Jesus Christ in a "Nestorian" fashion.

of dimensions for the Trinity of persons. To argue that non-Christian religions are channels of salvation, Dupuis posits subordination in the Father-Son relationship and undermines the unicity of the economy of salvation. An inverse relationship exists between the orthodoxy of the trinitarian doctrine employed in these proposals and the extent to which trinitarian doctrine can be used to support the independent validity of other religions. Thus, contemporary use of trinitarian theology in the Christian theology of religions appears to be having a deleterious effect upon the doctrine. Inasmuch as the proposals of Yong, Heim and Dupuis are representative of current appeals to trinitarian doctrine in the Christian theology of religions, there seems to be good reason to question seriously the claim that "the Trinity" offers the key to a new understanding of religious diversity.

Nevertheless, the methodological problems documented in this chapter are not limited to the theology of religions. Similar problems can be seen in attempts to relate trinitarian doctrine to other areas including personhood, ecclesiology, gender, politics and society.[72] I will briefly register two concerns. First, problems arise anytime one attempts to draw a straight line from a speculative construal of the immanent Trinity to some created reality in a way that bypasses (or in some cases even undermines) the economy of salvation revealed in Scripture. Heim's proposal exemplifies the latter problem: he draws a straight line from a speculative account of the immanent Trinity (i.e., three "dimensions") to multiple religious ends. Similarly, a number of contemporary proposals draw a straight line from a speculative understanding of the immanent life of the triune God (e.g., "perichoresis") to some beneficial practice (e.g., egalitarian human relations, countering individualism, etc.). Yet Scripture does not exhort Christians to imitate the *immanent* life of the triune God apart from the economy of salvation. Rather, imitation takes place on the *economic* level: it is a redemptive relation with the triune God precisely *in* the economy of salvation that constitutes the "blueprint" for Christian imitation (i.e., an *imitatio Christi*). Thus, Paul exhorts Christians to imitate him not as he imitates the *intratrinitarian life* of the triune God (immanent Trinity) but rather to imitate

---

[72]For further discussion of these methodological problems, see Johnson, "A 'Trinitarian' Theology of Religions?" pp. 311-43.

him as he imitates the *incarnate* Christ (economic Trinity).[73] Furthermore, the Creator/creature distinction disallows direct movement from the immanent Trinity to created realities.[74] Moreover, as Karen Kilby rightly notes, some proposals that directly appeal to the immanent Trinity end up "projecting" aspects of human relatedness into the immanent life of the triune God in a way that opens the door to Feuerbach's "projection" critique.[75] Finally, by treating the *immanent* Trinity as a ready-made blueprint for societal, ecclesial, political and even interreligious structures, some theologians sever the immanent Trinity from the economic Trinity.

My other concern centers on the *end* to which trinitarian doctrine is currently being used. One cannot help but wonder if the recent "usefulness" of trinitarian doctrine is sometimes driven more by Jamesian pragmatism[76] than a compelling vision of the triune God as the ultimate good. Here contemporary theologians can learn an important lesson from Augustine. His trinitarian reflection in *De trinitate* is driven by a quest to know and enjoy the triune God.[77] He wants to draw his readers more deeply into the life of the triune God.[78] Augustine challenges contemporary theologians to consider whether their "functionalizing" of trinitarian doctrine leads their readers "to know and enjoy, and not merely use, the strong Name of the Holy Trinity."[79]

---

[73]See 1 Cor 4:15-16; 11:1; Phil 3:17; 1 Thess 1:6.

[74]See Augustine *De trinitate* 15.

[75]Karen Kilby, "Perichoresis and Projection: Problems with Social Doctrines of the Trinity," *New Blackfriars* 81 (2000): 432-45.

[76]See Matthew W. Levering, "Beyond the Jamesian Impasse in Trinitarian Theology," *The Thomist* 66 (2002): 395-420.

[77]One of the biblical texts that frames Augustine's quest is Ps 105:4, "Seek his face." Augustine cites this text at several key points in *De trinitate*. John Cooper has argued that one of the most basic notions in Augustine's thought is that of a spiritual quest; see "The Basic Philosophical and Theological Notions of Saint Augustine," *Augustinian Studies* 15 (1984): 93-113.

[78]See A. N. Williams, "Contemplation: Knowledge of God in Augustine's *De trinitate*," in *Knowing the Triune God: The Work of the Spirit in the Practices of the Church*, ed. James J. Buckley and David S. Yeago (Grand Rapids: Eerdmans, 2001), pp. 121-46.

[79]C. C. Pecknold, "How Augustine Used the Trinity: Functionalism and the Development of Doctrine," *Anglican Theological Review* 85 (2003): 141.

7

Trinity and Missions

Theological Priority in Missionary Nomenclature

ROBERT K. LANG'AT

THE DISLOCATED EVANGELICAL THEOLOGY OF MISSIONS

The doctrine of the Trinity has become even more relevant as missions has taken center stage in the global church. This necessitates grounding the economic Trinity in relation to missionary praxis within the immanent Trinity in relation to missionary theory.[1] Missions, however, has historically become captive either to evangelical individualistic imperialism or else liberal pluralistic relativism. Many consider the doctrine of the Trinity too speculative to provide practical guidelines for any missionary project. Sometimes, in attempts to contrast ontological over and against practical matters, preference is given to "practical divinity" over the philosophical roots of Christian praxis. In this attempt to make Christianity more user-friendly, the trinitarian moorings, as Stephen Lewis has noted, do not seem "palatable to seeker-sensitive congregations."[2] The rise of the church-growth and the megachurch movements within evangelical ecclesiology may not truly represent a trinitarian theology of the Christian church and its missional implications. The driving force for these churches has been "success" rather than theological underpinnings. Any gospel that is made a

---

[1]Karl Rahner, *The Trinity*, trans. Joseph Donceel (New York: Crossroad, 2002), pp. 101-3.
[2]Stephen Lewis, "Being, Becoming, and Doing: A Trinitarian Approach to Spiritual Formation in Christian Higher Education," a paper presented at the 35th Annual Meeting of the Wesleyan Theological Society, Azusa Pacific University, March 3-4, 2000.

slave to market demands, however, cannot a sustain a trinitarian missiology. The above, together with the prosperity gospel, are driven by individualistic modern ideologies that are foreign to a trinitarian understanding of missionary engagements. There is always something blunted when the gospel focuses on Christian comfort rather than suffering and sacrifice.

Though it is not true that missions was simply a product of the Western colonial enterprise, the fact that it coincided with the era of modern inquiry and with the absence of adequate trinitarian reflection on matters of coessentiality—a fact that was true of the eighteenth and the nineteenth centuries—meant that it easily lost the trinitarian relational essence of the *imago Dei*. The missionary movement gradually led to a "don't care" imperialistic attitude on the part of the sending agencies, or else fostered a "missionary, go home" moratorium among the natives, who were dissatisfied with the whole enterprise. It is no surprise to find the good old evangelical missions being reminded that their time is up in some parts of the world because their presence has lost redemptive theological meanings. Missionary theories that had been held dear by evangelicals for many years could not be sustained past the scrutiny of the civil rights and independence movements of the 1960s. They could not be sustained either when viewed from a biblical, trinitarian perspective: they are not interdependent enough. For instance, the late nineteenth-century concept of the "four-selves"—self-supporting, self-propagating, self-governing and (added much later) self-theologizing—as our objective, a theory engaged by almost all evangelical missions, is ultimately irreconcilable with a trinitarian theology of coessentiality. It is not even clear if the later addition of "the fourth self," to appease the third world by opening opportunities to contextualize theology, was useful in redressing the paternalistic Western standards of the first three. These concepts may have led instead to the postmodern affirmation of various disconnected realities that adore pluralism as a way of life.

Over the years such theories have been fed by a skewed missiology—studied largely as a branch of the social sciences rather than a branch of theology. Missions as an academic subject has thus been suffocated by reductionistic categories of inquiry and dislocated from its theological origins. Missions is, therefore, offered in many seminaries and universities through the departments or schools of intercultural studies. Departmental allocation is not so much of a problem, in and of itself, as the secularist assumptions that undergird the academic perspectives used to study missions-related subjects. In an attempt to develop a missions curriculum, it is easy to have courses such as anthropology taught from social science perspectives rather than theologically. One has to keep a keen eye and ear on the postmodern world political stage to understand that there is a dualistic interplay between totalitarianism, which subverts the interest of the many in the name of societal interests, and individualistic demands, which offer unfettered freedoms and personal expressions that restrict any communal responsibility. Both of these, when allowed to form the basic framework of Christian mission, frustrate the latter's relational character.

THE ONE AND THE MANY IN THEOLOGY OF MISSIONS

Missionaries from all Christian persuasions had to articulate the meaning of the doctrine of the Trinity for specific missionary contexts. This has not always been an easy task and in a number of instances has elicited theological and methodological differences.[3] The most subtle destructive force against the doctrine, however, has not come from genuine evangelical attempts to communicate an elusive doctrine in a foreign context. It has rather come from deliberate attempts to create an imbalance against its missional implications. While African theologians have embraced Christology, albeit with tendencies toward constructing it on the base of African ancestral veneration, the doctrine of the Trinity is seen by many liberal theologians in this context as "a relic of medieval Christianity," and a "western trinitarian formula of the Divinity" which needs to be dismantled.[4] This is often done with less attention to the biblical text and the classical formulation of the doctrine outside the modern West.

Many theologians believe that one of the greatest religious tensions in

---

[3]Chinua Achebe, *Things Fall Apart* (London: Heinemann, 1985), p. 130. Achebe analyzes a situation of a missionary arguing about the inability of an African flock to understand the doctrine of the Trinity and the sacraments due to the failure of his predecessor to articulate those doctrines well within a missionary context.

[4]See *African Theology en Route: Papers Presented by the Pan-African Conference of Third World Theologians*, December 17-23, 1977, Accra, Ghana, ed. Kofi Appiah-Kubi and Sergio Torres (Maryknoll, N.Y.: Orbis Books, 1979), pp. 64-65; and Kevin Daugherty, "Missio Dei: The Trinity and Christian Missions," *Evangelical Review of Theology* 31, no. 2 (2007): 151.

our world is the tension between "the one" and "the many" as two ways of looking at reality. Christianity itself is "one" religion that is in constant confrontation with the "many" others in the mission fields. In praxis it has encountered enormous challenges among living religions "undergirded by intellectual systems" and in relation to conversions except among polytheistic and animistic religions.[5] In theory, this theological problem has produced two diametrically opposed religious interpretive paradigms: polytheism versus monotheism, or their close variations. Neither of these two polarities presents a helpful theological paradigm in Christian missions. One has to wrestle with these two realities not only in the mission fields of Africa and Asia but also, in our contemporary world, "many Europeans and Americans, disillusioned by the manifest failures of the Christian west, are turning toward the East and the South for fresh ways" of looking at God.[6] They are in essence moving "out of the frying pan into the fire." Terrified by years of Western dominance, they have the tendency to give in too much and in the process end up "being missionized instead of missionizing." This is an aspect of unnecessary guilt on the part of evangelicals, especially those who have historically presented the gospel as having a liberating agenda in and of itself, without any propping up from any of the modern "isms."

The debate about God in Africa and Asia has been dominated by these two opposite poles: God as singular, absolute and personalistic (monotheistic terms); or as multiple, relative and separatistic (polytheistic terms). On the one hand, polytheism perverts and imbalances the triunity by focusing on "the many" and thus cannot affirm the one God of the gospel who alone can save. Proponents of the pluralistic theory have had the audacity to conclude that it is no longer necessary for Christians to claim the "finality" and "normativity" of Christ and that "relational truth" is to become "a revolution in mission and global theology."[7] On the other hand, radical monotheism perverts and imbalances the triunity by focusing on "the one" and thus cannot easily affirm the relational and communitarian God,

---

[5]Paul F. Knitter, *No Other Name? A Critical Survey of Christian Attitudes Toward the World Religions* (Maryknoll, N.Y.: Orbis Books, 1985), p. 4.
[6]Cited in Norman Anderson, *Christianity and World Religions: The Challenge of Pluralism* (Downers Grove, Ill.: InterVarsity Press, 1984), pp. 144-46.
[7]Knitter, *No Other Name?* p. 230.

whose dynamic love magnetically draws people to himself in missions. The modern religion of deism, for instance, is unitarian in nature and is known to be at "the root of totalitarian or repressive forms of social order."[8] This order has been more pervasive, as noted here by Colin Gunton, in modern evangelical missionary enterprise than has been accounted for.

Likewise Vinoth Ramachandra has done extensive work on critiquing both Western individualism and Asian pluralism in the light of biblical missions and the trinitarian theological mandate. He says that "absolutising of the individual" is at the core of this problem perpetuated from the Western world as a "dogma that I can be myself without my neighbor."[9] In many parts of the world this has led to what Gunton calls "revolt of the many against the one, and at the same time that of humanity against divinity." For this reason we see the emergence of many "black Messiahs" identified with the African Initiated Churches (AICs) because those known historically as recipients of the missionary enterprise are dissatisfied with "the God" of Christendom in its oppressive "monotheistic form," and they are in a quest for "a place to feel at home," as it were.[10]

It is said in Africa, "It takes a village to raise up a child." In many cultures of the world, to be alone is to be cursed (meaning to be without truth). Extended family is important in Africa to the extent that reality is summed up in the statement "I am because we are," or as the Xhosa of South Africa have in their proverb *Umuntu ngumuntu ngabantu*, which means "a person is a person through [relationship with] other people." This affirmation in itself needs to be celebrated as providing a fertile ground for enactment of trinitarian missionary theology.

A few scholars have captured this fertility and developed various paradigms that depict an African understanding of the Trinity in ways ranging

---

[8]Colin E. Gunton, *The One, the Three, and the Many: God, Creation, and the Culture of Modernity; The 1992 Bampton Lectures* (Cambridge: Cambridge University Press, 1993), p. 25.

[9]Vinoth Ramachandra, *Gods That Fail: Modern Idolatry and Christian Mission* (Carlisle, U.K.: Paternoster, 1996), p. 22. As a matter of fact, mission work has been in the forefront, reaching out to the uttermost parts when churches come to realize that they are their neighbor's keeper.

[10]Gunton, *The One, the Three, and the Many*, p. 27. See also F. B. Welbourn and B. A. Ogot, *A Place to Feel at Home: A Study of Two Independent Churches in Western Kenya* (London: Oxford University Press, 1966).

from "I dance, therefore I am," to "I belong, therefore I am," and "I am related, therefore I am."[11] The evangelical gospel has been contextualized by Africans to the extent that God is seen as indeed a brother, a sister, an aunt, a grandfather, a nephew and even a mother. When African Christians celebrate all rites of life (birth, circumcision, death, etc.) in a social sense it is not only because they subscribe to a communal view of the biblical God but also because they truly have let that triune God "baptize" their African sociability so that it becomes a genuine Christian fellowship. Perhaps this, in a sense, is what Stephen Williams calls "benefit from extra-Christian conceptuality in [triune] elucidation."[12]

Here it needs to be granted that there are a number of cases where this is purely syncretistic and at the intellectual level may be used as a disguised affirmation of pluralism. Those who have been more radical about the possibilities of finding *"vestigia trinitatis* [vestiges of the Trinity] in African traditional cultures" have turned to the African Traditional Religions (ATRs) for help.[13] Relativism, which supports loosely or unconnected pluralistic divine collectivism, is sometimes being read into the African understanding of community in relationships in ways that undermine the missionary witness and curtail a serious African trinitarian theology.

Indeed, a new way of conceptualizing the Deity as a "community of gods" is emerging to enrich African trinitarian discussions. Foremost here is A. Okechukwu Ogbonnaya's opposition to polytheism and monotheism by positing a third African way: talking about the divinity as *Communotheism.* This third thesis, while an improvement, does not provide the balance between "the one" and "the many" as understood within the trinitarian reality.[14] If Ogbonnaya is willing to say that "gods are fundamen-

---

[11]Roderick T. Leupp, "God in the Midst: Trinitarian Theology in a Global Context," a paper presented at the 35th Annual Meeting of Wesleyan Theological Society, Azusa Pacific University, March 3-4, 2000, pp. 42-45.

[12]Stephen Williams, "The Trinity and 'Other Religions,'" in *The Trinity in a Pluralistic Age: Theological Essays in Culture and Religion,* ed. Kevin J. Vanhoozer (Grand Rapids: Eerdmans, 1997), p. 29.

[13]See Mika Vahakangas, "African Approaches to the Trinity," in *African Theology Today,* ed. Emmanuel Katongole (Scranton, Penn.: University of Scranton Press, 2002), p. 69. In addition to this, evangelical Africans often think that the problem of the feminine/masculine pronouns, so enigmatic in contemporary theological circles, is a Western problem.

[14]A. Okechukwu Ogbonnaya, *On Communitarian Divinity: An African Interpretation of the Trinity* (St. Paul: Paragon House, 1998), p. 71.

tally related to one another and ontologically equal while at the same time distinct from one another by their personhood and functions," then it becomes mere speculation simply to reduce this multiplicity to a triad and come up with a trinitarian framework.

African creation myths and stories, nevertheless, trace human origins to some divine source. It is only fair to say that the divine having a Son resonates with the African anthropomorphic center of reality, which traces the origins of humanity to the divine.[15] It should then be easier to see African evangelization as restoration of the divine image or presence, which most of the African tribes believe has been distanced from humanity because of sin. But even Ogbonnaya himself realizes that the "the African communal orientation tends to be based squarely on tribal loyalty," and perhaps tribal ancestry, rather than global human origins. This "communitarian divinity" eventually becomes parochial and lacks universalistic value. Kipkoeech Araap Sambu has added his voice by trying to argue that the deity of the Kalenjiin of Kenya, called Asiis, "according to some myths, existed as a divine triad"[16] with collegiate functions, but in the end has to contend with the contradiction of malevolent as well as benevolent members making up that trinitarian formulation. Thus I recognize that something about the triune God as believed in Christianity is unlike that in any pagan religion.

Affirming possibilities for collective theistic beliefs that do not necessarily provide ground for trinitarian thought, scholars such as M. William Ury claim that "plurality can exist where there is no Trinity. Indeed duality itself is plurality."[17] Although it cannot be denied that anthropological data may illustrate relational and communal elements in African and human experience analogous to those found within the divinity, to postulate that "African ancestral relationship is a replica of a similar relationship in the Trinity"[18] does not do justice to the doctrine of the Trinity. Yet, unfortu-

---

[15]Mika Vahakangas, "Ghambageu Encounters Jesus in Sonjo Mythology," *Journal of the American Academy of Religion* 76, no. 1 (March 2008): 122.

[16]Kipkoeech Araap Sambu, *The Kalenjiin Peoples' Egypt Origin Legend Revisited: Was Isis Asiis?* (Nairobi: Longhorn, 2007), p. 28.

[17]M. William Ury, *Trinitarian Personhood: Investigating the Implications of a Relational Definition* (Eugene, Ore.: Wipf & Stock, 2002), p. 198.

[18]Charles Nyamiti, *Jesus, the Ancestor of Humankind: Methodological and Trinitarian Foundations*, Studies in African Christian Theology (Nairobi: Catholic University of Eastern Africa, 2005), p. 93.

nately, there has been little trinitarian reflection engaged in the African Christian witness.

A thorough analysis of most African theological treatises reveals that they are heavily guided by a sociopolitical agenda that is paradigmatically controlled by Western liberalism and Marxist tendencies. James H. Cone could still advocate "taking seriously the trinitarian view of the Godhead" yet try to justify "a trinity from below" position. God is viewed to be black and is narrowly seen as the Creator, who identified with oppressed Israel; the Redeemer, who became the oppressed one; and the Holy Spirit, who continues the work of liberation in black society by creating a community of "encounter with the whites."[19] This is inadequate in expressing coessentiality, yet African theologians have basically and uncritically sung to the tune of such paradigms. Meanwhile a number of theologians are beginning to call for a paradigm shift from liberation to reconstruction.[20]

Similar examples of what Gunton calls "the tyranny of homogenizing God," which is a pervasive tendency of most postmodern world systems whether totalitarian or democratic, can be found in Indian theology.[21] As Lesslie Newbigin would state, the triune reality cannot be "verified by reference to the axioms of our culture."[22] The trinitarian formulation evoked by "specific historical claims about Jesus of Nazareth" is lost in a relativized theological environment. The gospel is unique in its teaching of the Trinity to the extent that there is no equivalent analogy in pagan cultures. In a missionary context, therefore, "the doctrine of the Trinity 'guards' the Christian experience of God."[23] The greatest success of Greek patristic thought, for instance, has been a shift from individualistic and monistic paradigms to identification of truth with communion or community.[24] While the church affirmed even Judaism's monotheism, it was radically different in that within

---

[19]James H. Cone, *A Black Theology of Liberation* (Maryknoll, N.Y.: Orbis Books, 1997), p. 64.
[20]See J. N. K. Mugambi, *From Liberation to Reconstruction: African Christian Theology after the Cold War* (Nairobi: East African Publishing House, 1995).
[21]Colin Gunton, *The Promise of Trinitarian Theology* (Edinburgh: T & T Clark, 1991), p. 163.
[22]Lesslie Newbigin, *The Open Secret* (Grand Rapids: Eerdmans, 1978), pp. 20-31.
[23]William H. K. Narum, "The Trinity, the Gospel, and Human Experience," *Word and World* 2, no. 1 (1982): 372.
[24]John D. Zizioulas, *Being as Communion* (Crestwood, N.Y.: St. Vladimir's Seminary Press, 1997), p. 101.

its missionary context, where nonracial fellowships brought both Jews and Gentiles together, the Christians used language of divinity in worship of Christ as an affirmation of their trinitarian theology.[25]

We concur with Augustine that God as taught by Christianity is thought of "in such a way that our thoughts strive to attain something, than which there is nothing better or more sublime."[26] When one remembers the struggle of pioneer missionaries in Africa and other parts of the world to teach this doctrine to the extent that a Kalenjiin woman praying, having been to no theological institution, can affirm in her own language *kipsomok che kosegei iit* (literally, the "threeness that is in agreement"), this indicates that there is a mystery that transcends human understanding in crosscultural conceptualization of the triune God.

In order to reengage the trinitarian foundation, therefore, missions has to replace "the psychology of separateness" with an "epistemology of participation" by way of "retrieval of togetherness, interdependence and symbiosis."[27] Since it is impossible to formulate a trinitarian theology of missions from the axioms of our culture, we must turn to the biblical narratives to see if these can be of help. Scrutiny of these materials reveals that the missionary nomenclature as historically expressed cannot be understood without unfolding the doctrine of the Trinity. Words such as *love, holiness, community, fellowship, outreach, sending, service, sacrifice* and *self-giving* are essentially missional terms, but they are essentially trinitarian words as well. We will now examine three missionary "engines"— sending, relationships and love—since they relate the triune God and missions in this way.

THE IDEA OF SENDING IN TRINITY AND MISSIONS

In our modern world, as noted by David Bosch, the word *mission* has been used in relation to Christian missions in a variety of ways—sending of missionaries, activities of missionaries in the field, a particular geographical

---

[25]Vinoth Ramachandra, *The Recovery of Missions: Beyond the Pluralist Paradigm* (Grand Rapids: Eerdmans, 1997), p. 226.

[26]Augustine of Hippo, *Teaching Christianity*, trans. Edmund Hill, ed. John E. Rotelle (Hyde Park, N.Y.: New City Press, 1996), pp. 108-9.

[27]David Bosch, *Transforming Mission: Paradigm Shifts in Theology of Mission* (Maryknoll, N.Y.: Orbis Books, 1991), p. 362.

area where evangelistic activities take place or the non-Christian world in general, the sending agencies themselves. The dislocation of the idea of "mission" from its biblical origins and its concreteness in the above categories has rendered its theological significance almost meaningless. It is now clear that the term itself is a point of contention. Christopher J. H. Wright, while arguing for "the theological priority of God's mission," has expressed his dissatisfaction with the use of the term "solely in relation to human endeavors of various kinds."[28] Until the Jesuits employed this kind of usage in the 1600s, *mission* was used in reference to the doctrine of the Trinity, to imply the Father's sending of the Son, and the Father and the Son's sending of the Holy Spirit. In John 20:21 we find those words of great encouragement yet with a sense of commission: "Peace be unto you: as my Father hath sent me, even so send I you" (KJV). Mission or evangelization, therefore, is essentially the believers' task of continuing the *missio Dei*. As the Father sent Christ to the world, so Christ sends the church to the world. We cannot separate the church's triune origins from our mission to the world.[29] This concept is clearly developed in the Holy Scriptures.

Some Scriptures are quite explicit about the triune foundations of mission and lend themselves as readily available as proof texts. A number of Old Testament scholars have understood Isaiah's threefold proclamation of God as Holy, and the fact that God asked "Whom shall we send?" before commissioning the prophet, to have something to do with trinitarian connection to missions.[30] Yet Isaiah "saw the Lord" and not "the Lords," as if there were many. He saw that "the train of his robe," not "their robes," filled the temple (Is 6:1 NIV). Isaiah moved from there to record the seraph's threefold declaration of the holiness of God, which a number of interpreters see as proclaiming Father, Son and Holy Spirit as sharing in the character of holiness (Is 6:3). But perhaps more congenial for our consideration is Isaiah 6:8, where the Lord asks a missiological question, "Whom shall I send? And who will go for us?" (NIV). The use of the words "I send" and

---

[28]Christopher J. H. Wright, *The Mission of God: Unlocking the Bible's Grand Narrative* (Downers Grove, Ill.: IVP Academic, 2006), p. 22.

[29]Bosch, *Transforming Mission*, pp. 389-93.

[30]The recently published *Africa Bible Commentary*, ed. Tokunboh Adeyemo (Nairobi: WordAlive Publishers; Grand Rapids: Zondervan, 2006), p. 814, points out that "this is interpreted by some as a veiled allusion to the Trinity."

"go for us" depicts a singularity and plurality of the senders in the same setting. When this is mentioned in the context of Jewish monotheism, it can only be reconciled in the light of a divine community commissioning the prophet. Missions and the idea of sending, furthermore, constitute the central message of the Old Testament such that it is possible to see these ideas within every context where God communicates his nature and provides his mandate to human agents.

The implication is that Christian mission is triune mission; from that center comes the incarnate Christ, and subsequently from him it comes to us through the power of the Holy Spirit. This is as much the message of the New Testament as of the Old Testament. The "sending," missionary understanding of the divine enables us to conceptualize why "God did . . . send his Son into the world" (Jn 3:17 NIV) and why "the Counselor comes, whom I will send to you from the Father" (Jn 15:26 NIV), as Jesus puts it. Within this context we understand well the trinitarian economy within the Christian community, which Bill Ury refers to as "the activity of the Father, Son and Holy Spirit" or "a community where the implications of our personhood is [sic] worked out."[31] There is a mutual obedience and submission also expressed in Johannine literature (Jn 14:26). Andreas J. Köstenberger is accurate in pointing out that "John's entire Gospel is pervaded by divine mission," with the Son being sent by the Father and with the Holy Spirit playing a crucial role in the mission of Christ and the witness of the church.[32] The Lukan account in 4:17-18 records that Jesus made reference to the Father sending him in the power of the Holy Spirit. Unrolling the scroll of the prophet Isaiah, he found the place where it is written: "The Spirit of the Lord is on me, because he has anointed me to preach good news to the poor" (Lk 4:17-18 NIV). What this means is that the term *missions* was basically a processional word: of the Son earlier and of the Holy Spirit later. This is the *missio Dei* in which the saved humanity is invited to participate through various avenues.

Missions as Relationship with the Triune God

From its very foundation the biblical canon clearly disclosed that the es-

---

[31]Ury, *Trinitarian Personhood*, p. 280.

[32]Andreas J. Köstenberger, "John's Trinitarian Mission Theology," *Southern Baptist Journal of Theology* 9, no. 4 (Winter 2005): 16.

sence of our relationship with our Holy God is for him to come and dwell among us, to fellowship with us "in the cool of the day" (Gen 3:8 NIV). The ultimate meaning of being lost is "being without relationship with the Father" rather than burning in hell. If that is true, it also implies that the ultimate goal of redemption is "being in relation with the Father," not just enjoying the bliss of heaven. This understanding thus sets forth the terms and conditions of missionary service. This relationship is founded on the creation of humanity in the triune image of God: "Let us make man in our image" (Gen 1:26 NIV). The first two chapters of Genesis demonstrate this amazing harmony between God and his creatures, especially between Adam and his Creator. Adam understood his mission very well, to "be fruitful and . . . fill the earth and subdue it" (Gen 1:28 NIV). Even when God gave him his other "special mission" of loving and caring for Eve, he accepted it perfectly well. Adam affirmed, "This at last is bone of my bones, and flesh of my flesh; she shall be called Woman, because she was taken out of Man" (Gen 2:23 RSV). He thus was affirming not just respect for himself and his wife but also the perfection of the triune God, who gave him such a gift. Missions, therefore, is the process of re-creating this harmonious relation between humanity and the divine.

It is the revelation of God as triune that empowers this process of participation in the life of God. The concept of "God the Father" as the first person of the Trinity is connected to the promise that Abram was to be "a father of many nations" (Gen 17:5 NIV). Here we find that the "glorious gospel of the Abrahamic covenant is that God's mission is ultimately to bless all the nations."[33] When Abraham obeyed the test to "take your son, your only son, Isaac, whom you love, . . . and sacrifice him . . . as a burnt offering," God intervened and pointed out again that "through your offspring all nations on earth will be blessed, because you have obeyed me" (Gen 22:2, 18 NIV). This was not only a missional encounter but also a trinitarian encounter. God revealed that he is God like none other. Other gods had taken life; the triune Yahweh gives life. God revealed his plan of redemption within a moment of ultimate human consecration. Since this anticipates the sacrifice of the second person of the Trinity, Abraham was

---

[33]Wright, *Mission of God*, p. 207.

basically reminded that it was not for him to purchase his own redemption since it was by faith, by a divine plan. God revealed a plan not just to bless Abram and his nation Israel but also the entire world.

There is a Father-Son relationship, which further supports this Genesis concept, explicated in Psalm 2 in ways showing that mission to the ends of the earth is a product of this trinitarian connection. The Father presents the Son as the anointed one, the one to be kissed and the one from whom to take refuge. This psalm opens up for the Son possibilities of reaching out to all nations, with the words in Psalm 2:8: "Ask of me, and I will make the nations your heritage, and the ends of the earth your possession" (RSV). This is what connects the Trinity with missions not only in a definitive ontological way but also in an extended practical and geographical sense. Dennis F. Kinlaw states that this "Father-Son relationship existed within the Trinity long before there were subjects for the King."[34]

It was also in the context of the return of the seventy-two that Jesus underscored the interconnectedness of the trinitarian reality in the redemption of the world:

At that time Jesus, full of joy through the Holy Spirit, said, "I praise you, Father, Lord of heaven and earth, because you have hidden these things from the wise and learned, and revealed them to little children. Yes, Father, for this was your good pleasure. All things have been committed to me by my Father. No one knows who the Son is except the Father, and no one knows who the Father is except the Son and those to whom the Son chooses to reveal him." (Lk 10:21-22 NIV)

This implies that the redemptive nature of missionary engagement must be in relation to the Father through the Son and in the power of the Holy Spirit. It also implies the creation of human relations that are imbued with the power of the Holy Divine. In expounding the above passage, Samuel Escobar has argued, "This is one of those passages in the Gospels that has a missionary as well as a trinitarian thrust, because the biblical foundation of mission is trinitarian, which explains why great movements of missionary advance are born in the cradle of spiritual revival."[35]

---

[34]Dennis F. Kinlaw, *The Mind of Christ* (Wilmore, Ky.: The Francis Asbury Society, 1998), pp. 26-27.
[35]Samuel Escobar, *The New Global Mission: The Gospel from Everywhere to Everyone*

MISSIONS COMPELLED BY TRIUNE LOVE

It is no surprise that the passage we have come to know as the Great Commission combines the dynamic process of disciple making with a trinitarian baptismal formula (Mt 28:19). This is not an accidental addendum but an intricate ground for our Christian witness. The Christian church took this dual mandate seriously: through history it has not only been involved in evangelization and discipleship but also in baptizing and incorporating people into the church in the triune name of God. This implies that the Trinity must continue to reshape the ecclesiastical creedal statements as well as missionary theology for our contemporary witness. Most of us depend on this First Gospel account of the Great Commission for a missional mandate, but when we also look at John 3:16, a well-known verse in Christian circles, the trinitarian missionary dictates are very clear. John affirms four great ontologically trinitarian statements: "For God so loved the world that he gave his one and only Son, that whoever believes in him shall not perish but have eternal life" (NIV). The concept of love is so pertinent to missionary drive, and its usage in this Johannine Scripture is indicative of the perichoretic interpenetration within the triune reality as a source of missions. That God "gave his . . . only son" affirms a missionary idea of "sending," as a byproduct of love within that triune reality. "That whoever believes" not only points to the universality of the missionary message but also affirms that establishment of "relationship" based on the veracity of the gospel is an entrance into the triune life of God. This relationship is not perishable and is eternal because it is established by undying reciprocal love with the triune God.

In the community of the saints, "love is forever given and forever enjoyed; . . . the love of God is actually tested and known."[36] This also carries the inevitable idea that Christian testimony arises out of a trinitarian understanding, recognizing that "Jesus manifested a relationship of unbroken love and obedience to the one he called the Father, a love and obedience sustained by the unfailing love and faithfulness of that Father; and those who believe and follow have been enabled through the presence of the Spirit actually to participate in this shared life of mutual love, which is the being

---

(Downers Grove, Ill.: InterVarsity Press, 2003), p. 95.

[36]Newbigin, *Open Secret*, p. 149.

of the Trinity."[37] The relational aspects of a loving Father and the idea of sending are seen in the Father's giving of the Son.

THE MISSIONAL IDENTITY OF CLASSICAL THEOLOGY

Indeed, a study of Pauline missiology also reveals that missionary calling is related to the Trinity: look at the beginning of every one of Paul's epistles. Though not always clearly indicated, the triune origin of missions and the communal nature of our witness are intricate and implicit parts of his understanding of missions. In Galatians 1:1, Paul lays down the foundation of apostolic calling as he terms himself "Paul, an apostle— sent not from men nor by man, but by Jesus Christ and God the Father, who raised him from the dead" (NIV). In Romans 1:1, he speaks of himself as "Paul, a servant of Christ Jesus, called to be an apostle [missionary] and set apart for the gospel of God [the Father]" (NIV). He shows that this ministry has an origin, a conveyor, with himself as an agent and others as recipients. This is how we ought to understand Pauline words such as "For to me, to live is Christ" (Phil 1:21 NIV), and "Those who live should no longer live for themselves" (2 Cor 5:14-20 NIV). The Scripture points to both triune cooperation in the redemption of humankind and the divine-human cooperation in the redemption of the world. It thus strongly proclaims "that God [the Father] was reconciling the world to himself in Christ" and that "he has committed to us [the church/Christians] the message of reconciliation" (2 Cor 5:19 NIV). This missional process has pneumatological implications, especially when viewed as closely tied to trinitarian interests.[38] The formation of a Christian community and the Trinity in Acts 1:8 and numerous other incidences in the rest of the book of Acts are indicative of the triune God creating the church as an alternative missional community. The Bible says in Acts 1:7-8, "It is not for you to know the times or dates the Father has set by his own authority. But you will receive power when the Holy Spirit comes on you; and you will be my witnesses in Jerusalem, and in all Judea and Samaria, and to the ends of the earth" (NIV). At this juncture Christ, the second person of the

---

[37]Ibid., p. 89.
[38]Dennis F. Kinlaw, *Preaching in the Spirit* (Wilmore, Ky.: The Francis Asbury Society, 1985), pp. 19-21.

Trinity, is speaking of the Father's design to establish his authority on earth through the power of the Holy Spirit; Christ will use human agency to carry his missional witness around the world.

There has been a notion that the speculative nature of trinitarian theology may not have been central to the church's missional self-understanding. In sifting through modern missionary literature, it may not be easy to find any serious engagement with the Trinity for missions. Yet this is, perhaps, the tragedy of a world that is becoming more and more distanced from its theological origins. In early Christianity, theological discussions were within the realm of the marketplace of ideas. That is why the church saved civilization by protecting its culture and art and by humanizing the world through giving it the concept of "a person." The ultimate worth of human persons, which becomes part of the motivating factor in reaching to the uttermost parts of the earth, cannot be understood without its divine origins. When a United Nations Secretary General talks of the sanctity of human life, he is basically affirming a gift that the church gave the world.

Theology was specifically trinitarian in content and was formulated within the context of missions as the early church wrestled to share the life of God within a pagan environment.[39] Almost all conciliar agreements, classical creedal formulations and theological articulations in relation to Christology and pneumatology were developed within the context of the church's struggle for identity in the missional matrix among Judaizers, secularists and the pluralistic religious world of the Greco-Roman society. This is often forgotten when the heretical and polemical battles of the era take center stage in interpreting Christian history. The church needed clarification of its role in the world in the light of heresies and other religious and ideological dictates. As the gospel came in contact with Stoic and Platonic thought, for instance, the place of Christ within the Godhead had to be clarified. How was the church to describe the relational uniqueness of Yahweh God while avoiding the plurality of the gods of the missionary context and safeguarding Judaic monotheism? Most of the church councils' universal consensuses took place as the church was expanding itself beyond

---

[39]Lesslie Newbigin, *Trinitarian Faith and Today's Mission* (Richmond, Va.: John Knox Press, 1964), p. 33.

the borders of Palestine. This missionary expansion raised questions that had never been faced before as the gospel sought truly universal claims. As noted by Thomas C. Oden, it was actually "as the church moved further [missionally] into the Greco-Roman world that it was required to answer highly specialized queries" on the doctrine of the Trinity.[40] Thus theology as such began as reflection on mission. George G. Hunter III says of Celtic Christianity and its missionary witness that the "doctrine of the Trinity became the foundational paradigm for Celtic Christianity." This awareness was accentuated by their openness, as in the African situation, to the triune God owing to fascination with "rhetorical triads" that informed earlier Irish superstitious beliefs.[41]

One could ask, Did not the Christian doctrine of God become syncretized with pagan thoughts during this period? The answer is that when the gospel arrived in the Hellenistic world, the Nicene fathers redefined or "baptized" the Greek categories, rather than simply affirming them, in order to carry the full import of the new trinitarian "wine." By so doing, they were actually setting a precedent that was to be critical in the missionary expansion of later years. They had "realized that if they allowed the dualist ways of thought in the prevailing culture to cut the bond between Christ and God the Father, then the whole gospel would be lost."[42] This is a sensitivity that the acid of modernity gradually dislodged, as shown by the way missions has been practiced in the twentieth century.

The early church understood very well the role of the *pneuma* (Spirit) in the missional church. The Holy Spirit is the key that enlightens our minds and makes the triune God approachable. As John 17:21 puts it missionally, the eternal union between the Father and the Son provides for a relationship that introduces us to the Godhead so "that all of them may be one, Father, just as you are in me and I am in you. May they also be in us so that the world may believe that you have sent me" (NIV). There is a mutual self-giving love between the Father and the Son, whose perichoretic missional movement is intimated by the Holy Spirit. Irenaeus named the Trinity as

---

[40]Thomas C. Oden, *Systematic Theology*, vol. 1, *The Living God* (San Francisco: Harper-SanFrancisco, 1992), pp. 202-9.
[41]George G. Hunter III, *The Celtic Way of Evangelism* (Nashville: Abingdon, 2000), pp. 20, 82.
[42]Thomas F. Torrance, *The Trinitarian Faith* (Edinburgh: T & T Clark, 1995), p. 7.

the foundation of faith and said that the Holy Spirit had been poured out in the end times "in a new manner upon humanity over all the earth, renewing man to God"; through this God has "opened the testament of adoption of sons."[43] It is through this dynamic outworking of adoption of sons that God calls a community to himself. The community thus constituted is called the church.

"For Tertullian, the notion of the Trinity is ideologically connected to the fact of salvation as embodied in the church community. The Trinity is the witness of faith."[44] In *De baptismo*, Tertullian pointed out that "by the benediction we have the same mediators of faith as we have sureties of salvation. That number of the divine names of itself suffices for the confidence of our hope. Yet because it is under the charge of three that profession of faith and promise of salvation are in pledge."[45] The church's calling as a missionary, salvific entity is located within a trinitarian understanding of ecclesiology, of the church as the image of God.[46] The practice of missions in any given church therefore needs to recapture "the relational," "the loving dynamism," "the other-orientation," "the self-giving" and the self-emptying "kenotic" nature of the triune reality. That is why the patristic concept of perichoresis with its emphasis on involvement, interpenetration, reciprocity and interanimation makes sense in understanding the triune involvement in world missions.[47]

In classical theology, Christian missions has not been tangential to the church but definitive of its very essence. The church is God's mission to the world. This is God's initiative, to restore and heal creation through the sent agency of the church.[48] John D. Zizioulas, who has spent significant effort in trying to understand the church's way of "being as communion," discusses the relationship between "Ministry and Communion" by asserting that ministry is "initiated by the Father, who actually sends the Son in or-

---

[43]Irenaeus, *Proof of the Apostolic Preaching*, trans. Joseph P. Smith (New York: Paulist Press, 1952), pp. 49-54.

[44]Ogbonnaya, *On Communitarian Divinity*, p. 59.

[45]Tertullian, *Homily on Baptism*, trans. Ernest Evans (London: SPCK, 1964), p. 17.

[46]See Kärkkäinen's interpretation of Jürgen Moltmann in Veli-Matti Kärkkäinen, *An Introduction to Ecclesiology* (Downers Grove, Ill.: InterVarsity Press, 2002), p. 127.

[47]Gunton, *The Promise of Trinitarian Theology*, p. 163.

[48]Darrell L. Guder, ed., *Missional Church: A Vision for the Sending Church in North America* (Grand Rapids: Eerdmans, 1998), p. 4.

der to fulfill and realize the eternal design of the Holy Trinity to draw man and creation to participation to God's very life."[49] As the third person of the Holy Trinity, the Holy Spirit has a role in this economy in that there is "the interdependence between ministry and the concrete community of the church as the latter is brought about by *the koinonia* of the Spirit."[50] It is the "indwelling Trinity that makes the believer 'a god by adoption and grace.' . . . The inner presence of the Trinity, like a magnet, draws man's 'conscious attention.'" In his *Treatise on the Least of the Commandments,* Symeon the New Theologian (949-1022) examined the fact that the Holy Trinity is not just a treasure we possess; we are adopted and possessed by God through the triune reality, which "unites us to Himself and makes us cleave to Himself."[51] In faith "we rest ourselves upon the reality of the Trinity" and thus become "enmeshed in the true world of God."[52]

Within the holiness movement, there has been an interest in the doctrine of the Trinity. This is not a mere modernist theological development. Where the Scriptures clearly reveal God's missional character, they also reveal his holy character. This line historically passes through the missional self-conception of such groups as the desert fathers, monastic movements, religious orders, the pietists, the evangelical revivalists, the charismatics of the twentieth century. The annual meeting of the Wesleyan Theological Society at Azusa Pacific University in 2000 focused on "the Holy Trinity." In one of the presentations, T. A. Noble stated that "the heart surely of a Christocentric and therefore trinitarian basis for the Wesleyan doctrine of Christian holiness as perfect love" is rooted in the Cappadocian understanding of trinitarian holiness. This doctrine was basically the revivalist doctrine of the evangelical circles of the eighteenth and the nineteenth centuries. It is thus possible to see that, while those two centuries may not have been the best in trinitarian reflection, nevertheless the holy character of God informed the self-giving, sacrifi-

---

[49]Zizioulas, *Being as Communion*, p. 211.
[50]Ibid., p. 212.
[51]Symeon the New Theologian, *The Discourses*, trans. C. J. de Cantanzaro (New York: The Missionary Society of St. Paul, 1980), pp. 35, 288.
[52]Dallas Willard, *The Divine Conspiracy: Discovering Our Hidden Life in God* (San Francisco: HarperCollins, 1998), p. 318.

cial nature of the emergent missionary movement.[53]

When talking of the Trinity, Kinlaw likewise sees that "perichoresis and agape love can only be understood in terms of interrelatedness of persons." From this argument, Kinlaw establishes that in missions Christians "must lose their lives in something and for someone(s) beyond themselves." He states that in reality the "pagan world is filled with data" to support that agape love, which is a product of trinitarian relationship, supports the principle of giving oneself for someone else.[54] The concepts of love, sharing and communication inform Kinlaw's thinking: "Love is his inner life, the divine life, which the three persons of the blessed Trinity co-inherently share." God's love communicates because by nature the dynamism of love cannot allow it to keep quiet. Communication is an essential element in missions. Missionaries have historically struggled to have their message understood. As we have seen, some of their failures are related to attempts to safeguard the integrity of the gospel as communicated in a foreign context.

When God communicates, it is creative.[55] This is what produces mission. No wonder then that missionary and holiness movements have always been characterized by trinitarian piety: the monastics, the pietists, the puritans, the holiness and the Pentecostal movements in their times have been the most keen in the missionary enterprise. These movements have been structured along "loose fellowship" formats that render the communicative nature of the Trinity easily shared at home and in other parts of the world. This is because the ultimate expression of the full life of God in a person subsequently leads to the ultimate sacrifice in missions (*My Utmost for His Highest*, as Oswald Chambers, that onetime missionary to Egypt, would put it). It is within a selfless and unegotistic environment where commitment to God becomes commitment to his mission in the world: the more one is at "the disposal of God, the Church, and his neighbor, the more his heart is open to the needs of others" in missions.[56] Christian faith is intrin-

---

[53]T. A. Noble, "The Cappadocians, Augustine, and Trinitarian Holiness," a paper presented at the 35th Annual Meeting of Wesleyan Theological Society, Azusa Pacific University, March 3-4, 2000, p. 19.

[54]Dennis F. Kinlaw, *Let's Start with Jesus* (Wilmore, Ky.: The Francis Asbury Society, 2005), p. 134.

[55]Ibid., pp. 28-32.

[56]See Stephen Ackermann, "The Church as Person in the Theology of Hans Urs von Balthasar," *Communio: International Catholic Review* 29 (Summer 2002): 245.

sically missionary because the dynamism within the Trinity carries with it the unveiling of that truth and love to the world. Missions is about God's self-communication as he establishes relationship with the world. So, since theology is the queen of the sciences, "mission is the mother of theology." Articulation of missions as being at the heart of God, therefore, speaking of the triune God as a "self-giving" missionary God—this is a crucial Christian undertaking. The doctrines, then, that convey the utmost Christian consecration to the transforming holiness of God must logically connect to the dynamic outworking of this utmost trinitarian love.

CONCLUSION

Christian faith is intrinsically missionary because the dynamism within the Trinity carries with it the unveiling of that truth and love to the world. Yet this chapter began by demonstrating that evangelical understandings of mission have frequently been dislocated from their properly trinitarian home. This neglects the important issues of the one and the many that surface in missionary contexts. We have explored these issues with particular reference to the African theological context. After raising these questions, the chapter next unfolds three trinitarian missionary "engines": sending, relationship and love. In each of these cases a variety of Scripture passages—in the Old Testament, the Gospels and the Pauline epistles—make connections, at least implicitly, between trinitarian doctrine and mission. Moreover, the church's classical trinitarian understanding has come about in the context of missionary encounter with Greco-Roman paganism. Likewise, today trinitarian understanding also has the potential of protecting missions from the impotence of giving in to a pluralistic and relativistic world. The holiness-oriented movements are able to promote active mission as they embody the relational dynamic of God's own life. Thus the trinitarian mandate has much to inform the church's ontological missionary character, the contents of the missionary message and the methods of missionary engagement.

PART THREE

WORSHIP

Church Practices and the Triune Mission

8

The Sacraments and the Embodiment
of Our Trinitarian Faith

GORDON T. SMITH

INTRODUCTION

There is a deep longing in the contemporary Christian community to recover and embrace a thoroughly trinitarian understanding of the nature of God and of our experience of God. Part of what makes this whole conversation so animating is that it is such an ecumenical exchange: Christians from remarkably diverse traditions seek to learn from one another. Nowhere is this more apparent than when it comes to how our faith in a triune God finds expression through our participation in the sacraments of the Lord's Supper and baptism. The last fifty years of conversation between faith communities has led to a wealth of insight on this topic, and this chapter is meant to do nothing more than capture the primary threads of this conversation.

This interplay between conversation about the Trinity and the nature of the sacraments is appropriate and indeed essential. Sacramental theology reminds us that at some point we move beyond rational discourse and debate into practice and that perhaps we do not understand the doctrine of the Trinity unless and until it is embodied. So the sacramental actions of the church—notably baptism and the Lord's Supper—are given to us specifically so that the trinitarian character of the living God might be formed in us.

The sacraments enable us to move beyond our propensity to think things through in an effort to understand the Trinity; instead, they enable us to enter into the mystery from within, to actually live it even as we come to understand the mystery more fully. What does it mean to say "These three are one"?[1] Its meaning comes to us not so much by critical reflection on the confession of the church—though that is needed; its meaning, rather, is *embodied* in us through the sacramental actions of the church. Through the sacraments, the mystery of the triunity of God becomes the mystery in which we live. Through baptism and the Lord's Supper, women and men are both invited and graced to enter into intimate communion with the triune God, their Creator and the giver of all good gifts; who is revealed to them through the incarnate, crucified, risen and ascended Christ; and through the Spirit, the Lord and giver of life is present and known.

The force of these recent ecumenical discussions on the sacramental actions of the church—evident most notably in the benchmark publication of *Baptism, Eucharist and Ministry (BEM)* in 1982—is that we need to see the Lord's Supper and baptism as both an activity of the triune God and as a means by which the church responds to this saving activity. And I fear that the church traditions that have ignored this discussion because of their antipathy to the World Council of Churches or to any kind of ecumenical dialogue have missed out on this extraordinarily rich conversation.

For some, this has meant that they have continued to adhere to a form of christomonism rather than a christocentric trinitarianism in their practices of baptism and the Lord's Supper. For others, it has meant that they have not been enriched by the strong call to appreciate the dynamic role of the Spirit in the celebration of the Lord's Supper or the vital place of chrismation in the practice of baptism.

Further, by bringing together both trinitarian theological discussions and sacramental theology, we have moved forward the continued, nagging question about the efficacy of the sacraments. Part of the abiding dilemma of the church has been to delineate who is the actor in the event of baptism or the Lord's Supper. For sacramentalists, as they are often called, the assumption is that God is the actor and that the sacrament is a means of grace.

---

[1] I am borrowing this phrase from William C. Placher's chapter heading in *The Triune God: An Essay in Postliberal Theology* (Louisville, Ky.: Westminster John Knox Press, 2007), p. 119, which he acknowledges as borrowed from a book with the same title by David S. Cunningham: *These Three Are One: The Practice of Trinitarian Theology* (Malden, Mass.: Blackwell, 1998).

Those who have rejected such a perspective have done so largely out of a concern that it violates the principle of faith—the conviction that without faith we cannot know the salvation of God. And they have, on the whole, endorsed a vision of these actions as fundamentally human: at baptism a person testifies to the salvation of God; the Lord's Supper is an occasion to celebrate the salvation of God and to remember and renew one's covenant commitments (the renewal of baptismal vows). This is typically articulated with an insistence that there is nothing inherently redemptive in the elements of or in the acts of baptism and the Lord's Supper.

But must we choose between these? Are we inevitably torn between the one and the other, or is there a resolution, perhaps precisely in a full recovery of the trinitarian character of our faith and of the events themselves, the sacramental actions of baptism and the Lord's Supper? The way forward is likely twofold:

First, we need to affirm that we must, regardless of where we stand on this polarity (i.e., is it the action of God or a human response to the [prior] action of God?), insist that this is not purely an individual, interior and expressive effect. Surely, this is an act of the church; it is a church event, and as individuals, our participation in the sacraments is one and the same a participation in both God's gracious work (however this is defined) and the communion we have with fellow Christians.

Second, we need to affirm that God remains sovereign (as Karl Barth insisted) and so is not constrained by the sacraments, which are located within the church but not owned by the church. Hence, the church together responds in thanksgiving to God as the summit of our common life in Christ. But more, this act of response is not merely with an *idea* that we have; it is not purely cerebral—something we are remembering or recalling, or even a principle with which we are identifying (such as the cross)—but rather, it is a real-time encounter with the living Christ, crucified, risen and ascended, and therefore it is necessarily salvific. We can only speak this way, however, if we enter our celebration of these sacred acts with a consciousness of their trinitarian character.

The grace of God is inherently trinitarian; the grace of God is communicated to humanity by the Father, through the Son and in the Spirit. This is, in truth, the only way we can conceive of the sacraments. It suggests something further, that we cannot fully know the grace of God except by the sacramental actions of baptism and the Lord's Supper.

Typically, the heirs of the Protestant Reformation recoil at such a suggestion. How can something tangible and tactile—the water, the bread and the wine—be necessary for our salvation? We are so adamant that the salvation of God can be known on no other basis than the interior response of repentance and faith. But the language of the New Testament, while insisting on faith and repentance, is not so inclined to affirm that we must choose. For example, the simple language of Acts 2:38—"Repent and be baptized"—suggests that the sacramental dimension of our response is not optional or secondary. This is not just a case of good advice, some recommendations from the Scriptures: these things are ordained, mandated. We can and should also appeal to the trinitarian character of our faith to appreciate why these actions are so essential to the very faith we long to express and sustain.

The Lord's Supper as Participation in the Life of the Triune God

If the Lord's Supper is to be a means by which we witness to the salvation of a triune God and respond to that salvation, then we are wise to be explicitly trinitarian in our celebration of the Lord's Supper—especially in the rubrics that shape our practice and give understanding to our experience of this event. And thus the wisdom that coalesces in the *BEM* publication suggests that our language in worship—our rubrics—need to affirm God as Creator and giver of all good gifts; God as the Son, in whom and through whom we know the salvation of God; and God the Spirit as the Lord and giver of life. Increasingly we are witnessing the emergence of liturgies that reflect the kind of ecumenical dialogue that led to *BEM*, that the very structure of our participation in the Lord's Supper is threefold: we give thanks to the Father-Creator (this is a Eucharist), we do this in remembrance of Christ *(anamnēsis)* as we invoke the presence of the Spirit *(epiklēsis)*. And the unity of this structure demonstrates that these three are one.

Giving thanks to the Creator. In the Lord's Supper we give thanks, certainly, for the gift of the Son and the work of Christ on the cross; but *BEM* reminds us that this meal is a Eucharist in which this specific act of thanks is located within the great thanksgiving for all of God's providential work as Creator and benefactor.[2] Everything is from God, who is good and whose mercies endure forever. So we give thanks, we offer a eucharistic sacrifice of praise and thanksgiving to the Creator. And the church does this on behalf of the whole of creation, bringing the fruits of the earth—bread and wine—as offerings, along with a hymn of praise to the one who gave us these gifts and the capacity to cultivate them into bread and wine.

In remembrance of Christ Jesus. Though we begin and end with eucharistic praise, the pivot on which everything rests, the focus of our attention, is the second person of the Trinity—in whom and through whom we give our thanks, and by whom we know the salvation of God. And when we speak of Christ Jesus, it is imperative that we acknowledge the full scope of his redemptive work—from incarnation through Pentecost, through the full realization of his reign.[3] The crucified one is the incarnate Christ, who is the risen and ascended one and whose wounds are "yet visible above," as suggested by Charles Wesley and Matthew Bridges.

But the work of Christ is always perceived through a trinitarian lens—for what we see and enter into is, precisely, the dynamic that exists between Father and Son; this is the heart of the matter—and in this dynamic our salvation is found. For the work of Christ is an offering to the Father, and the Lord's Supper is but a proclamation of this work and, further, a participation in the relationship that exists between the Son and the Father.

The ascended Christ is the operative agent of Christian worship: Christ our high priest calls us into worship and then leads us into the presence of the Creator God. Our worship is a participation in the communion that has existed for all of eternity within the triune God. The sacramental actions of the church make this reality visible and enable this reality to be embodied—and thus to be lived. James B. Torrance asks the rightful and probing question: Is our worship truly trinitarian, or is it in effect unitarian?[4] He contends that everything depends on who we think is the operative agent in

---

[2] *Baptism, Eucharist and Ministry [BEM]*, Faith and Order Paper No. 111 (Geneva: World Council of Churches, 1982), "Eucharist," 2.3-4 (pp. 10-11).

[3] For this perspective I am indebted to the work of Louis-Marie Chauvet, *The Sacraments: The Word of God at the Mercy of the Body* (Collegeville, Minn.: Liturgical Press, 2001), p. 156.

[4] James B. Torrance, *Worship, Community and the Triune God of Grace* (Downers Grove, Ill.: InterVarsity Press, 1996), pp. 20-21.

baptism and the Lord's Supper. He insists that we are fundamentally unitarian if this event is no more than a human act, a human accomplishment. If it is truly trinitarian, it is a participation in what is already happening. This worship is Spirit generated and sustained—which I will come to—and this worship is participation in the communion that already exists between Father, Son and Spirit.

Yet so many of us within free-church or what might typically be called evangelical theological traditions (and this would mean low-church Anglican as much as Baptist and Christian and Missionary Alliance) have deeply ingrained in our consciousness the idea that the work of the Lord's Supper and that of baptism is fundamentally *our* work. And the irony (perhaps even the tragedy) is that we have done this to preserve the doctrine of justification by faith, and perhaps inadvertently we have established in both baptism and the Lord's Supper a justification by works.

Not so for Calvin and Luther, who were well aware of the grace that is found in Christ and is appropriated through the ministry of the Spirit in the sacraments. John Calvin is as good as Calvin gets in the fourth book of the *Institutes*, where he develops his theology of the sacraments, addressing specifically the Lord's Supper. Calvin speaks of the extraordinary exchange—Christ takes what is ours (our broken humanity) and cleanses us with his life, which he offers back to the Father. And then Christ comes to us in the power of the Spirit and urges us to eat in remembrance of him—so that his death becomes our death, so that his life indeed becomes our life. At both baptism and the Lord's Supper, the grace we seek is one of radical identification with Christ: immersed in the life of Christ in the waters of baptism, then Christ is taken deeply into our bodies as we eat and drink his body and blood. We consume so that we are consumed by Christ.

Thus, the gospel is not only known, thought or understood but also *embodied*—first, the gospel was embodied in Christ; now, through the sacramental actions of baptism and the Lord's Supper, the gospel is embodied in us.[5] And what is begun in baptism is then sustained through the Lord's Supper. Calvin puts it this way:

---

[5]John Calvin, *Institutes of the Christian Religion*, trans. Henry Beveridge, vol. 2 (reprint, Grand Rapids: Eerdmans, 1972), 4.17.2.

For as God, regenerating us in baptism, ingrafts us into the fellowship of his Church, and makes us his by adoption, so we have said that he performs the office of a provident parent, in continually supplying the food by which he may sustain and preserve us in the life to which he has begotten us by his word.[6]

And thus Christ, "having received our mortality, . . . has bestowed on us his immortality; . . . having undertaken our weakness, he has made us strong in his strength."[7]

The grace we seek, as in Philippians 3:10-11, is "to know Christ and the power of his resurrection" (RSV): that death might be at work in us so that life might be at work in us. Notice then that trinitarian thought becomes practice; it establishes for us and within us that "religion" is not ultimately our task, but only our participation in the work of God. On this the church rests, on the work of the triune God. So Lesslie Newbigin has aptly observed: "The Church . . . is not constituted by a series of disconnected human responses to supernatural acts of divine grace in the word and sacraments. It is the continuing life of Christ among" us, in the life and witness of the church.[8] And as Newbigin stresses, it is precisely through these tangible things—water, bread, wine—that we are incorporated into the life of God.

Indeed, how we celebrate the Lord's Supper and baptism (along with our approach to preaching, by the way) reflects how we think the church is sustained, and at heart, whether we see the church as the product of our efforts or the fruit of God's work. It is crucial that we intentionally signal what we believe: this is not fundamentally our work, but the work of the triune God. Hence, there is a deepening consciousness of the presence of the ascended Christ, remembered as in the Revelation of John as the slain Lamb who is now seated on the throne, remembered so that we are conscious that the one in our midst is the crucified Lord and Savior (there is no other). Indeed, the whole of Christ's work—from incarnation through to the consummation of the kingdom—is present to us in the meal, but the

---

[6]Ibid., 4.17.1.
[7]Ibid., 4.17.2.
[8]Lesslie Newbigin, *The Household of God: Lectures on the Nature of the Church* (London: SCM Press, 1953), p. 77.

presence is cruciform and by this form brings us into fellowship with the Father. If the work of salvation is God's and if this is effected in us through Christ by the Spirit, then this needs to be patently evident in our rubrics and practices surrounding the sacramental actions of the church.

And the Spirit is the giver of life. The Lord's Supper reminds us of this extraordinary exchange between the Father, who is God; and the Son, who is God. How then do we participate in this life-giving exchange? Only by God who is the Spirit—only by the enabling of God's very self. So that we might know the grace that Christ effects in the cross, the Father and the Son send another, the Comforter, the Spirit of truth.

Christ Jesus is the revelation of God, and as the action (or Word) of God, Christ stands and mediates between God's very self and humanity, between God and the church. Yet it is by the Spirit that we see, understand and live—the same Spirit who inscripturates the Word of God, the same Spirit by whom Christ is conceived in the womb of Mary, by whose anointing Jesus moves into the desert and then into the world, and by whose filling the church becomes the "body" of Christ and a living witness to the world of the inbreaking of the kingdom.

We do not understand or participate in the work of God in the world without a dynamic theology of the Spirit; it is by the Spirit that Christ is present in the world, and it is by the Spirit that Christ is present in the Lord's Supper.

The life of the church, therefore, pivots on the dual reality of the Ascension-Pentecost—the risen Christ *and* the outpouring of the Spirit. And the sacraments are but the gifts of God for the people of God, by which the church participates in this twofold triumph over the forces of darkness. Only by grasping this—the mutuality of relations between the ascended Christ and the Spirit given—can we appreciate what it means to call God triune, as this finds expression in the Lord's Supper.

God longs to give the very Godself to us; and this is offered to us through the ministry of the Spirit. Thus the work of God in the Lord's Supper is the work of the Spirit; this is all about the Spirit's ministry in our midst and in our lives. It is by the Spirit that Christ is present. It is by the Spirit, further, that we are able to see Christ, believe in Christ and then turn from the meal and witness to Christ in the world. Ultimately, it is not we who witness to or for Christ; rather, it is the Spirit who glorifies the Son, and our witness is but participation in the ongoing ministry of the Spirit to make Christ known—in the world.

The Spirit does not replace Christ in the Lord's Supper. Rather, as John Calvin helps us to see, the Spirit is the means to the end, the one who unites us with Christ, who enables us to participate in mysteries that our minds cannot possibly comprehend, who strengthens our faith so that in this meal Christ can be received.[9] And it is the Spirit who unites us as one people, one body, such that our communion with Christ is reflected in our unity with one another. This is all of the Spirit.

James Torrance observes that we fall into a less-than-subtle form of utilitarianism when we emphasis our work over against the work of Christ at the Lord's Supper. T. F. Torrance echoes this: "If our worship and witness are conspicuous for their lack of [the] Holy Spirit, it is surely because we . . . have become engrossed in our own subjectivities and the development of our own inherent potentialities."[10]

Yet on the whole churches of the West tend to make no explicit reference to the ministry of the Spirit at the Lord's Supper. I am struck by the cry of Hans Urs von Balthasar, when he bemoans the neglect of the *epiclesis*—the prayer for the coming of the Spirit—and the lack of emphasis on the ministry of the Spirit in the celebration of the Lord's Supper within the Roman Catholic church. He observes that "there is in the Roman Mass a painful lack of this recalling of Pentecost and the Spirit's perfecting activity in the Church." We echo this sentiment in our own settings where there is a similar neglect, a similar "painful lack."

We then rightly affirm those streams of our common history that have more intentionally sustained this awareness; here I am obviously thinking of the Eastern Orthodox Church and of Calvin's persistent references to the Spirit as the means of Christ's presence at the Holy Meal. And certainly, as the Pentecostal and charismatic movement comes into greater theological maturity, it will surely help all of us appreciate this dimension of participation in this meal. Each of these streams highlights for us that in our celebra-

---

[9]Calvin, *Institutes* 4.17.10.

[10]Thomas F. Torrance, *Theology in Reconstruction* (Grand Rapids: Eerdmans, 1965), p. 245.

tion we rightly, if not naturally, cry out for God to be among us and to strengthen us; and this cry is the cry for the Spirit: "Come, O Lord and giver of life!"

This then raises the ancient and recurring question: Does the *epiclesis* belong in the rite—the words or rubrics spoken and the prayers offered— when we celebrate the Lord's Supper? Is there a place for the prayer asking that the Holy Spirit would be among us, make Christ present, unite us in our response to Christ and enable us to know God's grace that would empower us to be God's people in the world? Do we need to be explicit on this, or can it be assumed? From the second century it has been integral to the liturgical rubrics of the Eastern church. But should it be integral to all Christian celebration of the Lord's Supper?

The *BEM* calls for an *epiclesis*.[11] Rightly so—if for no other reason than for purposes of catechism and instruction, which would be justification enough for it to be included in our liturgies. One of the great needs of the Western church is clear catechetical instruction about the character and meaning of the Holy Trinity; and one of the most effective ways to accomplish is through the liturgy, particularly in the celebration of the sacraments—not that these are occasions for lectures or talks (God forbid!) but rather as opportunities in our rubrics to signal the movement and work of God in our midst. Christians of the Pentecostal and charismatic heritage often need a good reminder that the work of the Spirit is but one of making the crucified, risen and ascended Christ present; they need a christological pneumatology. Yet Christians of so many other traditions can go through the Lord's Supper with scant, if any, reference to the third person of the Trinity; they need to be awakened to the pneumatological character of their Christology! We also teach and learn by demonstration, by living and worshiping with a growing consciousness of the character of God. Indeed, T. F. Torrance insists that without this kind of "transparence" (his word), baptism (and the same would apply to the Lord's Supper) become "blind and meaningless."[12]

---

[11]*BEM*, "Eucharist," 1.14 (p. 13), specifying that we pray this prayer, confident of the promise of Jesus, praying to the Father so that the faith community would be strengthened for its mission in the world.

[12]T. F. Torrance, *Theology in Reconstruction*, p. 258.

And surely one of the most crucial ways by which we teach the Trinity and the trinitarian character of the Lord's Supper is by incorporating the epiclesis in our liturgies and forms or rites. Participation in both baptism and the Lord's Supper is thoroughly pneumatological; thus the epiclesis is of utmost importance: by it the church declares that we enter into these symbolic actions or gestures by the grace known only through the Spirit. Any other participation is an affront—fraudulent; thus a growing number of believers sense that there cannot be a eucharistic celebration without an epiclesis; there cannot be a baptism without it—since we are born again of water and the Spirit (Jn 3:3, 5).

But it is not merely for catechetical purposes that we would include the epiclesis; it just makes good theological sense. All of our natural instincts lean us toward assuming that we are the actors—that *we* somehow make this happen. We therefore need to be reminded, week in and week out, that Christ is present by the Spirit, that the transformative power of this event resides not in a priest or a pastor or in the right words of institution, that the quality of our response rests not on our sincerity or even our faith, but rather in the Spirit.

This work of the Spirit is necessarily in the church itself—for Pentecost is, at one and the same time, the inauguration of the church. As Louis-Marie Chauvet notes, "The Spirit, which makes the church, connects each member through the sacraments to the 'body of Christ' and thus counteracts the temptation to an individualist participation."[13] And Chauvet makes an intriguing point: the work of the Spirit is always simultaneously universal and particular—universal in that the Spirit cannot be contained or constrained by the church or a building or an institution (it has no boundaries); and always particular, in Christ, then in the church, then in this particular celebration of baptism or the Lord's Supper.[14] And so we are learning together, coming together to know our God through God's self-revelation in the simple acts of baptism and the Holy Meal.

The Holy Spirit makes this sacramental event one of true encounter with Christ. Indeed, baptism and the Lord's Supper are precisely the means, crucial and vital means, as necessary complements to the Word, by which the

---

[13]Chauvet, *The Sacraments*, p. 169.
[14]Ibid.

Spirit does what we so long for the Spirit to do: to make us one with Christ so that Christ abides in us even as we abide in Christ, so that the church knows the transforming grace of Christ. As a widening number of theologians—Orthodox and Catholic, to be sure, but also Protestant, Evangelical and Pentecostal—are asking: Could it be said that all we long for from the Spirit is offered to us in these events and that we indeed cannot fully know the grace of God except through this remarkably simple yet extraordinary act?

And so we act: we baptize and we celebrate the Lord's Supper. But we do so in response to the Spirit and in the enabling of the Spirit. Neither baptism nor the Lord's Supper is, finally, a pious creation for our own self-perfecting so that we might be "worthy"; rather, however much we truly testify to our acts of response to God's gracious initiative, these are first and foremost acts by which we testify to Christ's work, even as we accept—yea more, submit to—the Spirit's work in our lives and in our midst. As such, it simply makes no sense to neglect an explicit and deliberate prayer: "Come, Holy Spirit, come Lord and giver of life, come!"

The three are one. Using language that reflects the economy of God, *BEM* thus summarizes what occurs in the Lord's Supper with these words:

> The Father . . . is the primary origin and final fulfillment of the eucharistic event. The incarnate Son of God by and in whom it is accomplished is its living centre. The Holy Spirit is the immeasurable strength of love which makes it possible and continues to make it effective.[15]

The reference to the "living centre" is noteworthy. Our participation in baptism and the Lord's Supper is an act of encounter not with three gods, but with one God. And thus we ask: How through our participation are we coached and formed into a deepening awareness of the unity of the triune God?

Surely this is through an intentional and focused "christological concentration" (to use a phrase from Michael Welker).[16] Christ Jesus is the dynamic center and thus the unifying center of both baptism and the Lord's

---

[15]*BEM*, "Eucharist," 1.14 (p. 13).
[16]Michael Welker, *What Happens in Holy Communion?* trans. John F. Hoffmeyer (Grand Rapids: Eerdmans, 2000), p. 174.

Supper. This is our passion and focus; we are baptized into Christ, and in the Holy Meal we are in fellowship with Christ. At least the christomonists have the right bent in their focus on the second person of the Trinity! Their neglect of the fullness of the triune God is a great and devastating loss; the sacrament is, in a sense, no longer a Christian event. Yet the focus is right. Through these events, to the glory of and in thanks to the Father, and through the power of the Spirit, we are brought into fellowship—into real-time communion—with the crucified, risen and ascended Christ. All things begin and end with the Father, the Creator and source of all good gifts; and all things come to us by the Spirit, through whom, by the grace of God's love, we offer back to God these very gifts and enter into the life of God that is extended to us in these events. But all of this is in and through and by the one who is before us, behind us, first in our hearts; thus the great liturgical line: "through him, with him, in him."

Hence, to be truly trinitarian, we are radically christocentric. And this becomes dramatically apparent through our participation in baptism and the Lord's Supper. God comes to us, and through Christ we come into communion with God. The pivot point is the person and work of Christ. Christ is the sacrament of God—the one who offers himself to the world in obedience to the Father, then also the one through whom the church responds in love, thanksgiving and obedience to the Father. The sacramental rite is without doubt a human act: we take and eat; we enter the water of baptism. But what is critical is that this is an act of response to the gracious initiative God in Christ, and our act of response is enabled by the Spirit.

Further, in our participation we are also reminded that we are looking forward to the day of Christ's appearing. In baptism, we are initiated into a new life, and yet we are aware of how far we still have to go; in the Lord's Supper we are so keenly aware of the disconnect between the beauty and simplicity of the Meal and the fragmentation around us and in our world: the whole creation groans as in childbirth, awaiting the day of our redemption (Rom 8:19-23). We know that we are on the way, and we eagerly celebrate this event in anticipation, in hope as God enables us, in confidence that one day all will be made well and that justice and peace will embrace.

What we look forward to is the day of Christ's appearing, when the entire created order will again be brought under the authority of its rightful ruler. And now, through Word and sacrament, we live in dynamic union with our living head.

And baptism initiates the church into the life of the triune God. The life that is celebrated and nurtured through the celebration of the Lord's Supper finds its initiation in water baptism. Baptism initiates the Christian and indeed the church into the life of the triune God.

Baptism is an act of the church; an act of self-offering by the one who is coming to faith in Christ. Yet it is in Christ that we do this. As Alexander Schmemann puts it: "We offer . . . ourselves to God. But we do it *in Christ* and *in remembrance of Him.*"[17] For Christ is the offering to God; we are but participants in his high-priestly sacrifice, performed once and for all, now opened for us through the sacramental actions of the church. Through baptism we enter into and participate in the death and resurrection of Christ. Thus we are included in the offering of Christ to the Father, and thus we enter into the life that exists between the Father and the Son. That life becomes ours! And in the extraordinary language of Paul, now our "life is hidden with Christ in God" (Col 3:3 NIV). Baptism is, then, integral to conversion and Christian initiation.

Yet what has so frequently happened in the history of the church is that here, too, as with the Lord's Supper, there is minimal reference to the ministry of the Spirit: sometimes the Father and Spirit are only mentioned as part of the threefold baptismal formula! Without the formula, it could easily sound as though it is an event of "me and Jesus." No more. And here, too, what a loss! We need to make explicit that through baptism we are entering into the work of Christ, offered to the Father, and that we enter into this fellowship through the ministry of the Spirit.

Thus we surely acknowledge that by the Spirit we have come to this day: drawn and wooed to this moment, seeing truth that we would not see apart from the Spirit, coming into a faith that is nurtured and sustained within us by the Spirit. But do we not need to go further and affirm that on this day we enter into union with Christ in his death and resurrection and that in this union we find God's very life given to us in the Spirit? This union with Christ that draws us into fellowship with the Father is ultimately evident in

---

[17]Alexander Schmemann, *For the Life of the World: Sacraments and Orthodoxy* (Crestwood, N.Y.: St. Vladimir's Seminary Press, 1998), p. 35.

the very life of God given to us by the Spirit—as the Spirit is indeed given to us.

On the day of Pentecost, in reply to the question "what shall we do?" (Acts 2:37 NIV), Peter called for repentance and baptism: the interior and exterior dimensions of Christian initiation. But his words on that day also included "and you will receive the gift of the Holy Spirit" (Acts 2:38 NIV). A question naturally arises: What is the connection between the reception of the gift of the Spirit and water baptism? The Roman Church has historically separated baptism from confirmation. Many contemporary traditions also, especially those that are heirs to the holiness movement of the nineteenth century and the Pentecostal and charismatic movements of the past century, have almost insisted on separating them: there is the act of repentance and baptism into Christ, counted as the first "act"; then later, after baptism and as a distinct experience, there is "act" two, the reception of the gift of the Spirit. These two acts are regarded as separate and distinct.

Then the host of other Western Protestant and evangelical traditions tend to be silent on these matters, just as they are silent about the Spirit at the Lord's Supper. When pressed, they insist that one can count on receiving the gift of the Spirit at baptism; it is taken for granted as integral to the experience of baptism, even if no explicit reference is made to receiving this gift.

Is this acceptable: either the split, with the Spirit presumed to be a gift to come later; or the silence, the assumption that this gift is integral to baptism? Or do we need to find ways to be explicit in bringing the two together and, indeed, in demonstrating in tangible ways that in conversion-initiation we are entering into fellowship with the triune God? And the extraordinary wonder is that the very life of God is given to us, the trinitarian life of God; the life of God is evident in that as we come to faith in Christ, we receive the gift of the Spirit, of God's very self. Why would we not make this explicit?

The apostle Peter made it explicit in the words spoken on the day of Pentecost. And surely this is the very least we could do: speak of the gift of the Spirit, even if the nonsacramentalists among us insist that it is not causal or instrumental—even if, in other words, we are not prepared to link the water directly with the gift of the Spirit. But whether or not we are sacramental, we need to declare at baptism that the life of God is known through the gift of the Spirit—and that, at the very least, it is anticipated by our baptism and that the baptized one can expect to receive the gift of God's very self, the gift of the Spirit. Surely we can at least go this far.

But should we go further and re-present this more vividly, in our sacramental *actions* and not merely in the words spoken? The early church made the link verbally, but it was also re-presented in the acts of those who preside and participate. Up until the fourth century or so the primary reference for baptism/initiation was the baptism of Jesus in the Jordan: it was assumed that the "the baptism of Jesus orders, structures, Christian baptism" and that his baptism was the event of his anointing by the Spirit, and thus baptism for the early church was the "locus of the imparting of the Spirit."[18] Thus, typically, it was explicit for the early church, both in the words spoken and in their gestures and rituals. The early liturgies, the rites of initiation of Tertullian and Hilary and others, include both the imposition of hands and the anointing, along with an explicit call for the gift of the Spirit. Indeed, all initiation rites, East and West, included this in some form or another.[19] Does the contemporary church need to recover this practice, the act of chrismation? Do we need to include the imposition of hands and the anointing with oil and the prayer of the Spirit in our rites or practices of baptism?

Interestingly enough, this is included in the Roman Catholic Rite for the Christian Initiation of Adults (the RCIA). It was a wonder-filled experience for me to see the demonstration of this at St. Paul the Apostle Church in Manhattan at the Easter vigil (2007). Those baptized as adults along with those already baptized as infants were confirmed through a remarkable act of chrismation: their heads were bathed in oil, with the minister breathing on them and announcing the gift of the Spirit, the very life of God, given to them! They are doing something right: making this explicit in word and deed, in the words spoken and prayers offered and in the gestures by which the trinitarian character of our faith is embodied.

The signs of our sacramental encounter with the triune God. We bap-

---

[18]Kilian McDonnell and George T. Montague, *Christian Initiation and Baptism in the Holy Spirit: Evidence from the First Eight Centuries,* 2nd rev. ed. (Collegeville, Minn.: Liturgical Press, 1994), p. 340.
[19]Ibid., pp. 341-42.

tize in the name of the Father, the Son and the Spirit; and then, in the Lord's Supper, we give thanks to the Father as we come into real-time fellowship with the ascended Christ, through the gracious ministry of the Spirit. We surely need to ask, What difference does all this make? Or better, What indications or signs would assure us that, through baptism and the Lord's Supper, we are being drawn into fellowship with the triune God? At the very least, they would be two: trinitarian joy and trinitarian fellowship.

First, most notably from the Eastern church, we are reminded that when we enter into the triune life of the living God, we enter into the joy of God—a joy found in the exquisite communion of Father, Son and Spirit; this joy is now ours, a joy made complete in us, yes, but made complete precisely because we are in fellowship with God. Yet it is not only Eastern theologians who profile this; Raniero Cantalamessa, the "preacher" to the Pope, in a recent publication on the Trinity as object of contemplation, quotes Pius XII, who observed that because God is triune, we are able "to rejoice with happiness like to that with which the holy and undivided Trinity is happy."[20] Christ came that our joy might be made complete; it is made complete as by the Spirit we are drawn into the trinitarian joy of God. This is a resting place, our true home—re-presented to us in water and in a festive meal. We have come home to the Father and received the grace that is so poignantly longed for in the words of Philip when he says to Jesus (Jn 14:8 NASB): "Show us the Father, and it is enough for us." Baptism and the Lord's Supper are ultimately all about bringing us back into fellowship with the Creator, the source of life and of all good gifts, the Lord who is good and whose mercies endure forever. We enter into God's gates with thanksgiving and then return to the world with joy and thanksgiving.

This certainly is so because God is love, which then highlights a second critical indicator of our encounter and communion with the triune God: trinitarian fellowship. Our Christian heritage affirms that in baptism and the Lord's Supper we are drawn into the unity of God, a oneness that both exemplifies the character of true unity and positions us in turn live in community, most notably the communion we have in the fel-

---

[20]Raniero Cantalamessa, *Contemplating the Trinity*, trans. Marsha Daigle-Williamson (Ijamsville, Md.: Word Among Us Press, 2007), p. 35.

lowship of the Spirit as sisters and brothers in Christ.[21]

There is one body, one Spirit, one hope; one Lord, one faith, one baptism; one God and Father of all (Eph 4:4-6). But what is clear is that this unity is one that incorporates dynamic diversity—a mutuality of giving and receiving, reflecting indeed the very dynamic that is found in God. This is reinforced for us each time we break bread together, with the single loaf reminding us of our common identity in Christ. And thus these sacramental actions are formative, embodying the life of the triune God, the life of love and community, within and among us. For the Trinity is not three who become one, as best they can; rather, the Trinity is three who *are* one. In similar fashion, we who are many are one; as amazing as it might seem, that is as much a fact of the cosmos as the Trinity. There is one body, one church, one people of God; and by the grace we know through baptism and the Lord's Supper, we are increasingly enabled to maintain this unity through the bond of peace (Eph 4:3). In other words, what enables us to keep the unity of the Spirit is not so much that we mimic a mental picture of the Trinity. Rather, through baptism and the Lord's Supper we actually enter into the living dynamic of the fellowship of the Trinity. In the Lord's Supper, we all partake of one loaf; as such, we who are many are one body (1 Cor 10:16-17).[22]

In this joy and in this fellowship we are bought into the mission of God, the purposes of God in the world. We return to the world in joy and peace. Baptism marks our identity and the Lord's Supper confirms this identity: we are in the world as participants in the kingdom purposes of God. As Schmemann puts it: the Eucharist is both the end and the beginning of Christian mission—representing both the goal of mission and the point of departure for the church, for we go into the world as those who have met and encountered the living ascended Christ.[23] And the gift of

---

[21]*BEM* puts it this way: "Through baptism, Christians are brought into union with Christ, with each other and with the Church of every time and place. . . . The union with Christ which we share through baptism has important implications for Christian unity" ("Baptism," 2.6 [p. 3]).

[22]See further on this in John D. Zizioulas, *Being as Communion: Studies in Personhood and the Church* (Crestwood, N.Y.: St. Vladimir's Seminary Press), pp. 145-49: for Zizioulas, precisely this vision of the Eucharist establishes that the church has a eucharistic identity wherein the whole church is united in Christ as the body of Christ.

[23]Schmemann, *For the Life of the World*, p. 45.

the Spirit then rests upon us as we depart.

This identity in the world—marked by joy and Christian fellowship—is truly a trinitarian identity; it is formed in us slowly and incrementally, as through these actions we experience the mystery of God that is embodied within us. Wayne L. Roosa speaks of the arts in a way that would be equally pertinent to baptism and the Lord's Supper:

> It is the office of the arts to thus bear witness to the terms and dynamics of being, more through the analog of form and sign than through the proving of logic and analysis. This is part of the *distancing* needed by self-conscious beings to finally perceive themselves; it is the predicate required to establish the properties of existing, so that the subject—our selves—might be enabled to determine their *relation* to it.[24]

Slowly, incrementally but surely, we grasp it. We find our true joy; we catch the meaning of true community—of what it means that our identity is one of participation in the lives of others. We come to know and feel that we live our lives in radical dependence on God, not as autonomous beings. We come to know that our deep joy is found in God and in God alone; thus we walk into and live in the reality of unity with diversity and how, indeed, this is the life. We come increasingly to appreciate, deep within our being, that our salvation comes from God and is not self-constructed. And it all surely comes not so much by thinking about these things—this mystery—but by enactment, by gesture, by sharing together in these ordained means of grace.

How does one respond to the extraordinary wonder and mystery of trinity? Abraham the patriarch, was confronted with the threefold angelic visitation (Gen 18:1-15), which the church has consistently viewed as a vision of what would yet be revealed more fully in the incarnation and Pentecost. His response is interesting: he did not mount a theological conference to understand this amazing phenomenon—three, who are one. Rather, he set out a meal.

---

[24]Wayne L. Roosa, "A Meditation on the Joint and Its Holy Ornaments: Distance and Relation," *Books and Culture* 14, no. 1 (January/February 2008): 16-23, emphasis added.

9

Preaching as a Trinitarian Event

PHILIP W. BUTIN

On the Saturday evening before Palm Sunday, I got into a dinner conversation with my new pastor about preaching. "One of the most important things I learned in seminary," she said, "was that preaching is not about me telling other people what *I* do and don't believe." Her sentence contained an implied contrast between preaching personal opinions or interpretations on one hand, and preaching God's Word on the other hand. I did not bat an eye. As far as the comment went, it resonated well with the Reformed theology of preaching that I had always heard, taught and practiced.

That does not mean that all Christians would agree. What has long been assumed as a truism within one stream of Christian tradition may well be a source of confusion in another. I remember a Roman Catholic member of my doctoral dissertation committee who—in a sincere effort to presume common ecumenical ground between her tradition and the Reformed tradition—argued strenuously that I must have misunderstood Calvin. She welcomed my articulation of the trinitarian basis of Calvin's view of revelation.[1] But until we took the time to work through some primary texts together, she could not imagine that a seminal Protestant theologian like Cal-

---

[1]See Philip W. Butin, *Revelation, Redemption, Response: Calvin's Trinitarian Understanding of the Divine-Human Relationship* (New York: Oxford University Press, 1995), p. 60 and footnotes. Among the strongest historical and theological claims regarding Calvin's views on preaching are those of the older treatment of T. H. L. Parker in *The Oracles of God* (London: Lutterworth, 1947), pp. 45-64, who there uses explicitly trinitarian vocabulary to describe how, for Calvin, God speaks in preaching. Parker's early reading of Calvin is influenced by Karl Barth; his later reflections in his work *Calvin's Preaching* (Louisville, Ky.: Westminster John Knox, 1992), pp. 1-53, represent a more inductive and measured historical approach.

vin might say anything like the following:

> When a person goes up into the pulpit, . . . it is in order that God may speak to us through the mouth of a human being, and may be so gracious as to present himself here among us, having willed an ordinary human to be his messenger.[2]

PREACHING AS GOD'S OWN SPEECH

The idea that human preaching could characteristically convey God's own speech obviously seemed grandiose and presumptuous to my Roman Catholic mentor.[3] But it has never been particularly controversial in Presbyterian circles. To the contrary, it constitutes a bright thread that has been consistently woven throughout both the Lutheran and Reformed confessional tapestry. Luther, Bucer, Melanchthon, the Augsburg Confession, Calvin, Knox and many other sixteenth-century Protestant voices all regarded right preaching as a—and in many cases even *the*—primary identifying mark (*nota*) of a true church.[4] Perhaps Heinrich Bullinger of Zurich articulated this particular Reformed trajectory most forcefully and memorably. In his influential Second Helvetic Confession, he placed in parallel an

---

[2]John Calvin, *Calvini Opera*, in *Corpus Reformatorum* 53.266: Sermon 22 on 1 Tim 3:2, "apt to teach." See also John Calvin, *Opera Selecta*, ed. P. Barth and W. Niesel (Munich: Chr. Kaiser, 1926), 5:7-12; ET, *Institutes of the Christian Religion* (1559), ed. John T. McNeill (Philadelphia: Westminster Press, 1960), 4.1.5-6. Here, in discussing the possibility that human weakness might detract from the preacher's ability to clarify God's truth, Calvin says, "To make us aware, then, that an inestimable treasure is given us in earthen vessels, God himself appears in our midst, and, as Author of this order, would have us recognize him as present in his institution [the preaching of the gospel]." "Among the many excellent gifts with which God has adorned the human race, it is a singular privilege that he deigns to consecrate to himself the mouths and tongues of human beings in order that his voice might resound in them." "The church is built up solely by outward preaching."

[3]These conversations were in the late 1980s, yet authoritative Roman Catholic views of the relationship of preaching to the Word of God have gradually come much closer to Reformation Protestant views since Vatican II; compare the second encyclical of Pope Paul VI, *Mysterium Fidei*, §36: "In still another very genuine way, He is present in the Church as she preaches, since the Gospel which she proclaims is the word of God, and it is only in the name of Christ, the Incarnate Word of God, and by His authority and with His help that it is preached, so that there might be 'one flock resting secure in one shepherd.'" See <www.vatican.va/holy_father/paul_vi/encyclicals/documents/hf_p-vi_enc_03091965_mysterium_en.html>.

[4]See Calvin, 1559 *Institutes* 4.1.4; and my extended discussion and the notes in Philip W. Butin, *Reformed Ecclesiology: Trinitarian Grace According to Calvin* (Princeton, N.J.: Princeton Theological Seminary, 1994), pp. 19-22.

initial section title declaring that "Scripture is the Word of God" with a second and unexpectedly bold section title: "The Preaching of the Word of God Is the Word of God."[5] What has been less noticed, perhaps, is the delicate, trinitarian balance that Bullinger sought to maintain between the Word—including the necessity and authority of its articulation in outward preaching—and Christ's own bestowal of the Holy Spirit, with the Spirit's inward illumination of the human heart.[6] This view has since become deeply imbedded in the Reformed tradition. To cite just one twentieth-century example from 1955, Jean-Jacques von Allmen summarized what he regarded as a Reformed consensus regarding the trinitarian character of preaching by saying, "God is not so much the object as the true source of Christian preaching. Preaching is thus speech *by* God rather than speech *about* God." He continued:

> There is no true preaching unless God is at work in it through His Holy Spirit. . . . The Holy Spirit, indeed, has as His chief ministry to make effective today—with all that that implies—what Jesus Christ said and did, and also what He will say and do. Christian preaching cannot therefore be under-

---

[5]*The Constitution of the Presbyterian Church (U.S.A.),* part 1, *Book of Confessions* (Louisville, Ky.: Office of the General Assembly, 1999), 5.004. Parker apparently overlooks this widely influential Reformed confession and the fact that it began as Bullinger's own personal summary of his beliefs while he (Parker) engages in an extensive discussion of the question of whether and how right preaching has the capacity to be God's own speech in the early Reformed tradition (*Calvin's Preaching,* pp. 17-22). As a result, he links Bullinger and Thomas Hooker, asserting that the Zurich traditions are a source of Hooker's influential but inadequate view of the relationship of Scripture and preaching. According to Parker, Hooker makes a sharp principled distinction between Scripture and preaching in the theology of the Word; preaching is other than and less than God's Word itself (pp. 20-21). Parker's main point is well taken: he is right to emphasize the influence of Bullinger's particular polemical context in Zurich, where various enthusiasts pitted inner illumination over/against the authority and importance of outward preaching. However, my own research has not substantiated his attempts to attribute Hooker's view to Bullinger's influence.

[6]In addition to chapter 1 of the Second Helvetic Confession, see also Heinrich Bullinger, *The Decades of Henry Bullinger, Minister of the Church of Zurich,* vol. 1, *The First and Second Decade* (Cambridge: Cambridge University Press, 1849), pp. 38-39: Bullinger emphasizes the character of the word of God as God's own personal speech ("The Word of God is truth: but God is the only wellspring of truth: therefore God is the beginning and cause of the Word of God"). He stresses that God in Jesus Christ incarnates that Word ("the Son of God the Father, being incarnate, walked about in the earth; and being very God and man, taught the people"); and that the Holy Spirit—"which is of the Father and the Son"—inspired the Old Testament writers and prophets, as well as the apostles. He concludes by emphasizing that the Scriptures have their oral basis in preaching. In *Revelation, Redemption, Response,* pp. 55-61, I have sketched the trinitarian dynamics as Calvin apprehends the interplay of revelation, Scripture and preaching.

stood apart from the doctrine of the Trinity: on the basis of the past work of His Son, and in the perspective of the work he is yet to do, God the Father gives us today, through the Holy Spirit, faith in the salvation which has been accomplished and hope in the salvation yet to be revealed.[7]

Historically speaking, this consistent affirmation of the inseparable relationship of Word and Spirit in the dynamics of divine revelation has been the most significant way that the doctrine of the Trinity has influenced Reformed theological understandings of how God speaks through human preaching in the context of corporate worship.

From the other direction, Reformed rhetorical and homiletical traditions dating all the way back to Calvin have pursued the same interrelationships, showing equal fascination with preaching's more obviously human dynamics in seeking to articulate God's Word. As the center of the global Reformed tradition has shifted to Korea in the past fifty years, a strong focus on the theological basis of preaching—including consideration of the question of how human words can convey God's Word—has emerged in the teaching and writing of Chung Changbok. Chung comments: "The same Word of God which became flesh in Jesus Christ and which is attested in the Scriptures is proclaimed through the ministry of preaching."[8] He sees one of the primary challenges of the preacher as that of discerning through the Holy Spirit on a weekly basis, "Is this God's Word for this moment?"[9]

Closer to home, a recent U.S. volume edited by Jana Childers and including contributions from many influential American homileticians focused on the *Purposes of Preaching*. Childers writes there, "What could be more obvious than to say that whatever it means to 'preach Christ,' it at least means that the preacher will allow the Word or the Spirit or *Something* to

---

[7]Jean-Jacques von Allmen, *Preaching and Congregation*, trans. B. L. Nichols (Richmond, Va.: John Knox Press, 1962), pp. 7-8; the original French book was published in 1955.
[8]Chung Changbok, *Preaching for Preachers: A Study of Preaching with Particular Reference to the Korean Cultural Context* (Seoul: Worship and Preaching Academy, 1999), p. 137. Chung's concern that the preacher must discern God's word for *this context and this moment* reflects and extends Barth's understanding of proclamation as event, which will be developed below. See also the trenchant articulation of "Preaching as the Word of God" by James F. Kay in *Preaching and Theology* (St. Louis: Chalice, 2007), pp. 7-23.
[9]Ibid., p. 143.

work *through* him or her?"[10] There is an important emphasis here that is
properly the business of the discipline of homiletics, but to which a trinitarian theology of preaching must also pay attention. Its theological root
is the incarnation.

Childers goes on to sketch its shape, using the words of Phillips Brooks
from his 1877 Yale *Lectures on Preaching*: "The truth must really come
through a person, not merely over his lips, not merely into his understanding and out of his pen. It must come through his character—his affections—
his whole intellectual and moral being." Brooks is pushing toward the view
that it is only when the Word of God is incarnated in the human preacher
that the preacher can be a "real messenger of God."[11]

When a contemporary Presbyterian theologian starts talking about the
relationship of the divine and the human in preaching, Karl Barth is probably lurking somewhere in the background. Knowing this, you will not be
surprised that I want to turn to him for a few moments as I finish setting
the historical stage for my more constructive development in the second
part of this chapter.[12] In his *Church Dogmatics* I/1, published in 1932 from
lectures begun in Bonn a year earlier,[13] Barth weighed in on the same historic Reformed discussion begun by Calvin, Bullinger and the Reformed
confessions, probing the interrelationships of revelation, the Word of God,
Scripture and proclamation in familiar yet fresh ways.[14] In a manner that

---

[10]Jana Childers, ed., *Purposes of Preaching* (St. Louis: Chalice, 2004), p. 44.

[11]Phillips Brooks, *Lectures on Preaching* (Grand Rapids: Baker, 1969), p. 8. There is much of
value on this subject in classic older British and American treatments of preaching. In deliv-
ering a later series of Yale Beecher Lectures on Preaching in 1907, P. T. Forsyth emphasized
that the Holy Spirit is "preacher to the preacher" as the Spirit of Christ (*Positive Preaching
and the Modern Mind* [Grand Rapids: Baker, 1980], pp. 23-24). H. H. Farmer expands
these ideas in his discussion of preaching as personal encounter: God's love and God's claim
encounter the hearers of preaching through the direct address of the human preacher (*The
Servant of the Word* [New York: Scribners, 1942], pp. 65ff.).

[12]A much more comprehensive and always provocative treatment of Barth's perspectives on
preaching, by a United Methodist, is that of William H. Willimon, *Conversations with
Barth on Preaching* (Nashville: Abingdon, 2006).

[13]For the chronology and context, see Eberhard Busch, *Karl Barth: His Life from Letters and
Autobiographical Texts*, trans. John Bowden (Philadelphia: Fortress, 1976), pp. 209-16.

[14]Note Karl Barth's explicit discussion of the Reformed confessional tradition on this point
in his much earlier 1923 Göttingen lectures, published recently in English as *The Theology
of the Reformed Confessions*, trans. Darrell L. Guder and Judith J. Guder (Louisville, Ky.:
Westminster John Knox, 2002), esp. pp. 53-55. Here, Barth affirms ("Preaching regulated
by the Bible is the central function of the church, according to the Reformed view; . . . it
is the actual Reformed sacrament.") but wrestles mightily with ("It is obvious that this 'is'

some have characterized as Chalcedonian, Barth sought to properly appreciate and understand the subtlety and complexity of the relationship of the divine and the human in both Scripture and preaching. You no doubt are familiar with his influential articulation "The Word of God in Its Threefold Form." The discussion began with "The Word of God Preached." It continued with consideration of "The Word of God Written." Finally it culminated in "The Word of God Revealed."[15] The order was significant. Barth was suggesting (rightly, I think), that preaching in the context of the worshiping community is believers' primary and most consistent point of access to the Word of God. In order for preaching to communicate the Word of God, it must be a faithful witness to Scripture. And Scripture is the Word of God to the precise extent that it bears faithful witness to God's once-for-all revelation in Jesus Christ.

More specifically, what then is the relationship of preaching to revelation? Barth's answer was more complex and subtle than many of his Reformed predecessors. Neither Scripture nor preaching can be directly equated with revelation itself.[16] Rather, Scripture has the potential to "become" revelation in the "event" of proclamation. Barth's category of "proclamation" has a twofold form: it encompasses both preaching and sacrament. He is particularly concerned to hold together his theological articulation of the two. "Proclamation must ever and again become proclamation." "And because the event of real proclamation is the function of the church's life which governs all others, we have to say that in this event the Church itself must ever and again become the Church." "The presupposition of this event is the Word of God."[17] The connection between revelation and the Bible cannot be presupposed or anticipated. Rather, "it takes place as an event when and where the biblical word becomes God's Word, i.e., when and where the biblical word comes into play as a word of witness."

At this point in his discussion, Barth alludes to the well-known image of

---

must be understood as 'signifies' in analogy to the words of institution of the Lord's Supper.") the Zurich reformer Bullinger's claim that "the preaching of the Word of God is the Word of God," in anticipation of his later concern to do justice to the humanity of preaching within its capacity to convey divine speech.

[15] Karl Barth, *Church Dogmatics*, ed. Geoffrey W. Bromiley and T. F. Torrance, vol. 1/1 (Edinburgh: T & T Clark, 1975), pp. 88-120.

[16] Ibid., p. 112.

[17] Ibid., p. 88.

the painting of Grünewald's *Crucifixion*, from the Isenheim altar (now in Colmar), a reproduction of which hung in his study. In this image, John the Baptist's long index finger points away from himself "impressively and completely" and points "impressively and realistically to what is indicated."[18] The freedom of God is what Barth is most concerned to honor here, and the appropriate relative priority between proclamation, Scripture and revelation must be preserved. "Revelation . . . is itself the Word of God, which the Bible and proclamation are as they become it."[19] In the witness of Scripture and proclamation, the church "really recollects past revelation, and in faith receives, grasps, and really proclaims the biblical witness of it as the real promise of future revelation." "It is Jesus Christ Himself who here speaks for Himself and needs no witness apart from His Holy Spirit and the faith that rejoices in His promise received and grasped."[20]

Barth wanted to avoid what he regarded as a uniquely Protestant temptation to teach a sort of transubstantiation with respect to the divine and human dynamics of preaching. Instead, on the premise that church proclamation has the twofold form of preaching and the sacraments, he wanted to exercise the same care in relating the divine and the human in preaching that the sixteenth-century Swiss reformers had taken in discussing the presence of God in the sacraments. The eucharistic analogy was crucial:

> It is the miracle of revelation and faith when . . . proclamation is for us not just human willing and doing characterized in some way but also and primarily and decisively God's own act, when human talk about God is for us not just that, but also and primarily and decisively God's own speech.

Barth went on to encapsulate this subtle relationship between the divine and the human: "Human talk, with its motives and themes and the judgment among which it stands as human talk, is there even while God's Word is there." In contrast to "the Roman Catholic principle of change," we must acknowledge that "the willing and doing of proclaiming man . . . is not in any sense set aside in real proclamation." "Bread remains bread and wine [remains] wine, to put it in Eucharistic terms."[21]

---

[18]Ibid., p. 113.
[19]Ibid., p. 118.
[20]Ibid., p. 120.
[21]Ibid., pp. 93-95.

On the other hand, through the new robe of righteousness thrown over it, even in its earthly character it becomes a new event, the event of God's own speaking in the sphere of earthly event, the event of the authoritative vicariate of Jesus Christ. Real proclamation as this new event, in which the event of human talk is not set aside by God but exalted, is the Word of God.[22]

Barth's expansion of these same thoughts for the practice of preaching can be traced further in his nearly simultaneous Bonn lectures titled "Exercises in Sermon Preparation," given in 1932-1933.[23] There, in bringing his own pastoral experience to bear on the preparation of pastors for the task and responsibility of preaching, he emphasized that preaching must "conform to revelation" as it is given to us in and between "Christmas and the day of Christ." God speaks in preaching to the extent that it is faithful to the decisive historical revelation of the incarnation and to the anticipated and hoped-for revelation of the Second Advent. "It is in the double movement, namely, that God *has* revealed himself and *will* reveal himself, that preaching conforms to revelation in the New Testament sense."[24]

It remains to bring forward one more aspect of Barth's exposition of the "threefold form of the Word": the economic-trinitarian understanding of God and God's revelation and speech that underlies it. Barth is bold enough to say,

There is only one analogy to this doctrine of the Word of God. Or, more accurately, the doctrine of the Word of God is itself the only analogy to the doctrine which will be our fundamental concern as we develop the concept of revelation. This is the doctrine of the triunity of God.[25]

Thus Barth indicates his conviction that the theological dynamics of the doctrine of the threefold form of the Word of God derive from the more basic theological dynamics of the doctrine of God's triunity. In a comment summing up the point that God's Word is God's act—an event—Barth moves again to trinitarian language. Because God's Word is God's act in

---

[22]Ibid., p. 95.

[23]Karl Barth, *Homiletics*, trans. Geoffrey W. Bromiley and Donald Daniels (Louisville, Ky.: Westminster John Knox, 1991) esp. pp. 47-55.

[24]Ibid., p. 50. See the context provided by Busch in *Karl Barth*, pp. 219-20, as well as that in the introduction to the English translation of the lectures: Barth, *Theology of the Reformed Confessions*, 7.

[25]Barth, *Church Dogmatics*, 1/1:121.

the event of revelation, we come under a lordship "when and where Jesus Christ becomes contemporaneous through Scripture and proclamation." "The 'God with us' is said to us by God Himself." Barth goes on to point out that the Western understanding of the divine triunity pushes toward this event-centered understanding of God's speech, because the Holy Spirit cannot be separated from the Word: "His power is not a power different from that of the Word but the power that lives in and by the Word."[26]

With this historical background, the remainder of this chapter will build on the themes we have identified in Calvin, Bullinger and Barth in order to propose an understanding of preaching as a trinitarian event that can be of help in theologically articulating the claim that God speaks through the human speech of preaching. Our constructive reflection will begin with consideration of the way biblical metaphors of divine speech and divine illumination interact in several key biblical texts. I will focus on this interacting verbal and visual imagery as a conceptual resource for later more thoroughly developed Reformed trinitarian theology, as it came to articulate the mutuality of Word and Spirit in divine revelation, speech and self-communication. My constructive proposal is that it is precisely the acknowledgment of preaching as a trinitarian event that can best allow both the human and the divine aspects of preaching to be theologically articulated and coordinated in the context of corporate worship.[27] The chapter will culminate in a reflection upon the trinitarian Prayer for Illumination within Reformed liturgical tradition and its potential contribution to theological efforts to deepen our understanding of how God's Word can be proclaimed and heard in and through human preaching.

DIVINE SPEECH AND DIVINE ILLUMINATION IN SCRIPTURE

From the majestic, undulating, poetic repetition of the phrase "Then God

---

[26]Ibid., pp. 149-50.

[27]To fully appreciate this point, it is important to recognize the mutual complementarity and interdependence of trinitarian theology and Christology, of Nicaea and Chalcedon. For a Reformation example, see my extended discussion of how this interconnection emerges in Calvin's theology in *Revelation, Redemption, and Response*, pp. 39-49, 62-75, 127-28. Perhaps the most focused recent study of preaching written from a trinitarian perspective is that of Michael Pasquarello III, *Christian Preaching: A Trinitarian Theology of Proclamation* (Grand Rapids: Baker, 2006), in which Wesleyan perspectives and concerns take primary place.

said" in Genesis 1, to the thunderous prophetic "thus says the Lord" that appears throughout the Old Testament, the Word of the Lord is a determinative aspect of the divine-human relationship throughout the biblical witness.[28] With only a few dramatic exceptions, it is by speaking through human beings that God speaks to human beings.

Beginning in Genesis 1, the intricate interrelationship between God's creative speech and accompanying divine illumination seems to be intentionally reflected. "Let there be light" is the first word uttered as God speaks the creation into being. "And God saw that the light was good; and God separated the light from the darkness" (Gen 1:3-4 NRSV). The absence and then presence of the light becomes a pattern of articulation that orders the poetic structure of the entire priestly creation account: "God called the light Day, and the darkness he called Night. And there was evening and there was morning, the first day" (Gen 1:5 NRSV). Each consecutive stage of creation is patterned around the sequential rhythm of evening and morning, determined by the absence followed by the presence of the light.

A similar intentional interweaving of metaphors of divine speech and divine illumination is reflected in the prologue of the Fourth Gospel. There the writer gathers up and seeks to recapitulate the interplay of verbal and visual metaphors within the creation account, through a dramatically fresh refocusing of the existing Greek concept of *ho logos* (Jn 1:1-3).[29] Later Christian theological articulations of the Word of God, divine self-revelation and God's speech find a primary source here. The dominant metaphor of *ho logos* as God—and at the same time as God's primary and decisive self-revelation—is elaborated and intensified through interweaving of divine

---

[28]See Terence Fretheim, "Word of God," in *The Anchor Bible Dictionary* (New York: Doubleday, 1992), pp. 961-68.

[29]For a recent mainstream summary of the critical and dating issues, see Raymond E. Brown, *An Introduction to the Gospel of John* (New York: Doubleday, 2003). Broader questions of the background of *ho logos* provide perhaps one of the most debated subjects in studies of the Fourth Gospel. In the Prologue, obvious allusions to Gen 1 suggest a straightforward background in Old Testament Septuagint language for God's speech (root verb *legō*) and the Word *(ho logos)* of God. My theological reflections here have been encouraged and informed by the thorough, careful and creative recent rethinking of many traditional positions related to the Fourth Gospel, its sources and its Prologue by Herman Waetjen, particularly in *The Gospel of the Beloved Disciple: A Work in Two Editions* (London: T & T Clark, 2005), esp. pp. 61-87. See also idem, "Logos pros ton theon and the Objectification of Truth in the Prologue of the Fourth Gospel," *Catholic Biblical Quarterly* 63 no. 2 (April 2001), esp. pp. 271-74.

speech with divine illumination in John 1:4-9. The life that was in *ho logos* was the light of all people and was not overcome by the darkness (Jn 1:4-5). This true light is said to "enlighten everyone" through its coming into the world (Jn 1:9).

While a carefully articulated doctrine of the Trinity as we know it today would not emerge in Christian history until the fourth century, a significant root of the emerging trinitarian apprehension of God that grasped the early Christians is obvious in this seminal text. Longstanding Old Testament ideas of the prophetic Word of God as divine speech and divine-human communication, as well as archetypal Hebrew and Greek associations of light with divine revelation, undergird and inform these emerging reflections in the developing trinitarian awareness of the early church. If *ho logos* is in some sense the givenness—the decisive articulation or clarification—of God's eternal purpose for the world, present and immediate divine illumination is required alongside it in order for that eternal divine purpose to take shape in time and space, to find temporal, contextualized instantiation within the creation. We find embryonically present here a conceptual matrix that provides a fertile environment for the later theological refinement of perichoretic interaction and interrelationship between Word and Spirit, which is so prominent in Reformed understandings of how God speaks through human preaching.

As the prologue continues, God's self-communication as *ho logos* is epitomized—not in additional words—but rather in the claim that *ho logos* "became flesh and lived among us, and we have *seen* his glory, the glory as of a father's only son, full of grace and truth" (Jn 1:14 NRSV, my emphasis).[30] The Word become flesh is ipso facto available to the ordinary human knowledge we gain through sensory experience, especially sight. So we see the intentional intertwining of verbal and visual imagery involved in the claim that a tangible, visible divine incarnation within the

---

[30]Waetjen, "Logos pros ton theon," emphasizes the translation of *egeneto* as "happened," correcting the usual translation "became." The question at stake is whether the Word stopped being Word at its occurrence as flesh; and both Waetjen and Barth agree that the answer is "no." Waetjen's terminology facilitates interpretation emphasizing Barth's category of "event." Cf. Karl Barth, *Witness to the Word*, trans. Geoffrey W. Bromiley (Grand Rapids: Eerdmans, 1986), pp. 84-102.

creation is the ultimate form of divine speech.[31]

Although the Holy Spirit is not mentioned within the specific focus of the Johannine Prologue itself,[32] it is thematically central in the Fourth Gospel. The Spirit's dramatic introduction into the narrative at the baptism of Jesus sets Word and Spirit in striking literary parallel to each other; they are the two divine realities of the narrative to which John the Baptist bears authoritative witness. A milieu is thus further clarified here for deepening articulation of theological themes that were to become a rich source of later trinitarian theology. For our purposes, it is sufficient to note that the context of these prototrinitarian source reflections is a constructive and integrative poetic elucidation of the apparent contradiction of the union of the divine and the human in the incarnation. Given the clear presentation of the incarnation as a speech-act,[33] the implications of these connections for a theology of Christian preaching as a trinitarian event are significant. Verse 18 offers a fitting climax, particularly given the emphasis of the Prologue on divine illumination and the visual. "No one has seen God at any time. The only-begotten God who is in the bosom of the Father, He has explained [exegeted/revealed] Him" (Jn 1:18). Here the necessary Old Testament caution against fixing human perceptions of the living God in static visual imagery is juxtaposed and contrasted with the clarity of verbal revelation—divine speech—available to those who receive God's self-manifestation as the Word, which entered created time and space as flesh and pitched its tent among us.

In 2 Corinthians 2:14–4:15, the apostle Paul wrestles profoundly with the question of how his human words, expressed both orally and in his let-

---

[31]This point is underscored in later Byzantine tradition, as the issue of icons comes to focus in the East in the claim that to deny the theological appropriateness of visible icons of Christ constitutes a denial of the incarnation; cf. John of Damascus, *On the Divine Images* (Crestwood, N.Y.: St. Vladimir's Seminary Press, 1980); and Theodore the Studite, *On the Holy Icons* (Crestwood, N.Y.: St. Vladimir's Seminary Press, 1981).

[32]Likely for reasons of rhetorical strategy; compare the strategic reservation of the term "[Holy] Spirit" for introduction at the baptism of Jesus in John 1:32 (ESV): "And John bore witness: I saw the Spirit descend from heaven like a dove, and it remained on him." Thus John the Baptist becomes the authoritative witness to both the Word and the Spirit.

[33]Waetjen, "Logos pros ton theon," considers the entire Prologue to be concerned to articulate a divine speech-act; he speaks intriguingly of the Logos as "God's activity of speech" and of the light that it engenders as "its hermeneutical performance" (pp. 271-72).

ters, could communicate the truth and authority of God.[34] This passage contains a fascinating if intricate Pauline argument—rich in verbal and visual imagery—that explicitly interconnects Word and Spirit, reflecting concern for both divine speech and divine illumination, and focused on Christian preaching.[35] In his efforts to articulate how God's Word and authority can be present in and active through human words and speech, Paul here introduces theological patterns that provide a rich conceptual reservoir for later trinitarian reflection. Critics and skeptics in the recipient church had persistently questioned his authority to claim to speak on God's behalf. The self-examination to which he subjected himself in these exchanges greatly heightened his awareness of his own human weaknesses. In response, Paul articulated a subtle and multivalent understanding of the relationship of the human and the divine in Christian preaching, using patterns that later Christians could not help but identify as trinitarian. I draw attention to these anticipatory Pauline apostolic glimpses of what would later be called trinitarian thinking because I believe they had a significant influence on the early church's eventual ability to break through polarized conceptual dichotomies between the divine and the human—which tended toward unfruitful contests between conflicting human claims to authority in the church—and instead to develop a theologically coherent understanding of how and under what conditions human preaching might be(come) God's own speech.

In this section of 2 Corinthians, Paul's unique insight is that because of

---

[34]The following discussion has been informed by John Calvin, *The Second Epistle of Paul to the Corinthians, and the Epistles to Timothy, Titus, and Philemon*, trans. T. A. Smail (Grand Rapids: Eerdmans, 1964); cf. John Calvin, *Opera Exegetica*, vol. V.XV; idem, *Comentarii in Secundam Pauli Epistolam ad Corinthios*, ed. Helmut Feld (Geneva: Librairie Droz, 1994); Ralph Martin, *2 Corinthians*, Word Biblical Commentary (Waco, Tex.: Word, 1986); Victor Paul Furnish, *II Corinthians*, Anchor Bible (New York: Doubleday, 1984); Frances Young and David Ford, *Meaning and Truth in 2 Corinthians* (Grand Rapids: Eerdmans, 1987). Redaction-critical issues related to the unity of the letter are not controlling here, since all seem to agree that these chapters are part of a [relatively] coherent literary unit.

[35]Note especially the following observation of Calvin about this text, from the 1559 *Institutes* 4.14.11: "Paul excellently explains [the interrelationship of Word and Spirit] in various passages. For when he wishes to remind the Corinthians how effectively God uses his work, he glories that he has the ministry of the Spirit [2 Cor 3:6], as if the power of the Holy Spirit were joined by an indissoluble bond to his preaching for the inward illumination and moving of the mind."

the normative gospel pattern of the incarnation of God in Jesus Christ, divine revelation is *most profoundly, authentically and characteristically* communicated in and through ordinary, created, mortal human words and leaders. His remarkable metaphor elegantly expresses the paradox. In his words, the "treasure" of God's revelation in Jesus Christ normally and dependably comes to us in and through ordinary "earthen vessels"—common, rough-hewn, breakable, everyday clay pots (2 Cor 4:7). This happens for a specific theological reason: "so that it may be made clear that the extraordinary power belongs to God and does not come from us" (2 Cor 4:6-7 NRSV). The language used to articulate this crucial point is explicitly visual and appropriately focuses on divine illumination. Notice how the point is articulated as verse 6 describes the revelation of God, which is the basis of our proclamation of "Jesus Christ as Lord": "For it is the God who said, 'Let light shine out of darkness,' who has shone in our hearts to give the light of the knowledge of the glory of God in the face of Jesus Christ" (2 Cor 4:6 NRSV).[36]

Have you ever hidden money or jewelry in a sock? In the ancient Near East, houses were very small and there was almost no place to hide something valuable. There were no reliable locks. So when a family needed to leave the house, they were not likely to put their most valuable treasure in a beautiful container that would attract a thief's gaze. Instead, they would often put a valuable piece of jewelry or a bottle of perfume in the most ordinary looking pot, hoping that no one would notice. In a similar and striking way, Paul suggests, God has chosen to conceal the extraordinary power of God's revelation in Jesus Christ—to conceal it in the ordinary, common clay pots of fallen, fallible, vulnerable, imperfect human words and lives.

This principle of revelation as a treasure in common clay pots is evident first and foremost in Jesus Christ. In the incarnation, Jesus Christ was fully and authentically human. He was subject to all the uncertainties and ambiguities of the same human life we live. In the present context, it is crucial to emphasize that the humanity that Jesus assumed was not only created,

---

[36]Christopher Morse offers a detailed exposition of this verse and its implications for how God speaks in and through preaching: see *Not Every Spirit: A Dogmatics of Christian Disbelief* (Valley Forge, Penn.: Trinity Press International, 1994), pp. 87. Compare the discussion of Morse's development in Kay, *Preaching and Theology*, pp. 10-14.

mortal humanity; it was also fallen, fallible, vulnerable, imperfect, broken, even sinful humanity.[37]

At the same time, Jesus Christ was fully and authentically divine. He was the ultimate treasure in an ordinary, everyday clay jar. He was the one in whose face "the light of the knowledge of the glory of God shone." In his incarnation, it was through his constant empowerment by and embodiment of the Holy Spirit that God's glory shone through his ordinary human life and words and ministry, revealing God uniquely and decisively to all who awaited the messianic coming with eager expectation.

And the same principle applies, Paul says, to our human efforts to communicate God's Word (2 Cor 2:17; 4:2), glory (2 Cor 3:7-18; 4:4, 6), truth (2 Cor 4:2) and light (2 Cor 4:4, 6) to others in and for the church. Paul's encapsulation of the relationship of the preacher's humanity to the divine focus of the proclamation holds in tension the same paradoxes that later concern Calvin, Bullinger or Barth: "For we do not proclaim ourselves; we proclaim Jesus Christ as Lord and ourselves as your slave for Jesus' sake" (2 Cor 4:5). It turns out that God has a radical, unexpected, unlikely way of communicating with human beings. It is through the sincere (2 Cor 2:17), unadorned (2 Cor 3:1-2), humble (2 Cor 3:4-6), transparent (2 Cor 3:18), authentic (2 Cor 4:2), vulnerable (2 Cor 4:8-11) human communication of God's glory shining "in the face of Jesus Christ." It is through the recognition that the Lord is the Spirit; through the freedom of being where

---

[37]Careful wording is important here. The human createdness and mortality that God assumed in Christ established a crucial solidarity between the Word and every human preacher. In terms of Christology, the fact that human nature is also fallen poses an important but pregnant and potentially fruitful theological tension: Christian theology confesses that in Jesus Christ, God assumed fallen, fallible, broken human nature—but without any commission or deserved guilt of sin on Jesus' part; and this was precisely in order to redeem sinful human nature. Hence comes Gregory of Nazianzus's axiom of Christology contra Apollinarianism: "What has not been assumed cannot be healed; it is what is united to God that is saved" (*Epistles* 101.7). See *Nicene and Post-Nicene Fathers* [*NPNF*], series 2, vol. 7 (Peabody, Mass.: Hendrickson, 1994), p. 440. Cf. also Gregory of Nyssa: "By becoming exactly what we are, he united the human race through himself to God. For since that new Human being who was created after God—and in whom dwelt all the fullness of the Godhead bodily—had through purity brought our nature into intimacy with the Father, he also drew all of that same nature who partake of the same body and are his kin into the same grace" (*Contra Eunomius* 12, in *NPNF*[2] 5:241; cf. Migne, *Patrologia graeca* 45:889). Or in Paul's more direct words in the same section of 2 Corinthians we are discussing: "For our sake he became sin who knew no sin, so that in him we might become the righteousness of God" (2 Cor 5:21 NRSV).

the Spirit of the Lord is (2 Cor 3:17). And finally, it is through the transparency of refusing to conceal or minimize our humanity, our shortcomings and our inadequacies. Instead, with unveiled faces, we behold the glory of the Lord as though reflected in a mirror, and in this beholding we are transformed into the same image from one degree of glory to another (3:17-18). God's Word assumes and transfigures our human words. Or to put it more explicitly in the language of trinitarian event: *by the Spirit, God's Word in Jesus Christ can characteristically assume and transfigure our human words, as the Scriptures are faithfully proclaimed in the context of a gathered community of worship.* Thus Christian preachers have a reliable and well-grounded expectation that God's Word will be spoken in and through our human words, to the exact extent to which we embrace and acknowledge our humanity, confident that it has already been assumed, encompassed and transfigured by the humanity of God in Jesus Christ.

TRINITARIAN PRAYERS FOR ILLUMINATION

One of the often overlooked points at which the Reformed tradition has best reflected the biblical integration of divine speech and divine illumination, as well as the trinitarian dynamic of the preaching event, is in the customary Reformed Prayer for Illumination. This is a specific and unique prayer, typically included in the historic structure of Reformed worship just before the reading of scripture and the sermon. Given the case we have made so far, the theological significance of this traditional prayer deserves special notice.

Historically speaking, the Prayer for Illumination appears to have been deliberately introduced for theological reasons early in the sixteenth-century sources of the Reformed tradition. It normally centered in the invocation of the Holy Spirit through metaphors of divine illumination used to articulate the congregation's dependence upon the Holy Spirit as the basis of the assurance that God's Word would be spoken in and through the human preacher in the trinitarian event of proclamation.

A basic presermon prayer for God to "open his holy and eternal Word to us" was indicated in the rubrics for Huldrych Zwingli's preaching service of 1525.[38] But the considered liturgical custom of saying a trinitarian prayer just before the reading and preaching of Scripture, focused on asking the living God to speak through human preaching, emerges over the next decade along the Rhone and the Rhine to the West and can be traced to Martin Bucer, William Farel and John Calvin. This custom seemed novel enough in Strasbourg in 1545 that a visiting Roman Catholic student provided the following firsthand description of Calvin's regular practice of prayer before entering the pulpit to preach after corporate singing of the Ten Commandments:

> When this has been finished, the minister kneels before a wooden table, made like an altar. . . . This altar is placed in the midst of the church where the minister is, as I have told you, facing the people, praying for them in their own language in a loud and clear voice which everyone understands. When he has finished praying, he goes to the pulpit and preaches a sermon which lasts from half past seven till nine o'clock. These sermons are wonderfully fine to hear.[39]

The rubrics from Calvin's *Forme des prières et chantz ecclésiastiques*[40] explicitly direct the minister "to pray, beseeching God for the grace of the Holy Spirit, that his Word may faithfully be expounded to the honor and glory of his Name and for the edification of the church, and be received with the humility and obedience which it deserves. The form is left to the minister's discretion." A written example of an actual prayer of Calvin's, borrowed for Genevan use from his mentor Martin Bucer's Strasbourg worship resources, is preserved as follows:

> Almighty and gracious Father, since our whole salvation stands in our knowledge of your Holy Word, strengthen us now by your Holy Spirit that our hearts may be set free from all worldly thoughts and attachments of the flesh, so that we may hear and receive that same Word, and, recognizing your gracious will for us, may love and serve you with earnest delight, praising and

---

[38]The most detailed treatment of Reformation practice and its precedents is found in Hughes Oliphant Old, *The Patristic Roots of Reformed Worship* (Zurich: Theologischer Verlag, 1975), pp. 208-18.

[39]Émile Doumergue, *Essai sur l'histoire du culte reformé* (Paris: Librairie Fischbacher, 1890), pp. 16-17; translation from Howard Hageman, *Pulpit and Table* (Richmond, Va.: John Knox Press, 1962), pp. 27-28.

[40]Jean Calvin, *La forme des prières et chantz ecclésiastiques* (Geneva: [Jean Girard], 1542).

glorifying you in Jesus Christ our Lord. Amen.[41]

The practice of praying for the special illumination of the Holy Spirit before the reading and preaching of Scripture does not come from Western, Latin traditions.[42] Interesting and instructive examples do exist, however, of trinitarian prayers preceding the reading and proclamation of Scripture from ancient Egyptian and Syriac liturgies and prayer manuals.[43] At least in the Latin West, any earlier practice that may have existed was lost before the Reformation, since the medieval pattern of placing an assigned collect for the day before the reading of Scripture was based on the liturgical calendar and became normative. In contrast, a formal and intentional prayer seems to have been a regular facet of Reformed worship at least in sixteenth-century Strasbourg and Geneva. The available examples emphasize seeking the presence and illumination of the Holy Spirit for the proclamation of the Word, according to a pattern that regards the triune God

---

[41]Bard Thompson, *Liturgies of the Western Church* (Philadelphia: Fortress, 1961), p. 209. I have updated archaic language. There is a striking resonance between the liturgical rhythm of the Prayer of Illumination and Calvin's carefully articulated theology of Word and Spirit regarding both Scripture and preaching. See the 1559 *Institutes* 1.8.4-5; and especially regarding preaching, see 4.14.8-11: "Faith is the proper and entire work of the Holy Spirit, illumined by whom we recognize God and the treasures of his kindness, and without whose light our mind is so blinded that it can see nothing" (4.14.8). "So that the Word may not beat your ears in vain, and that the sacraments may not strike your eyes in vain, the Spirit shows us that in them it is God speaking to us, softening the stubbornness of our heart, and composing it to that obedience which it owes the Word of the Lord. Finally, the Spirit transmits those outward words and sacraments from our ears to our soul. Therefore, Word and sacraments confirm our faith when they set before our eyes the good will of our Heavenly Father toward us, by the knowledge of whom the whole firmness of our faith stands fast and increases in strength. The Spirit confirms it when, by engraving this confirmation in our minds, he makes it effective. Meanwhile, the Father of lights cannot be hindered from illumining our minds with a sort of intermediate brilliance through the sacraments, just as he illumines our bodily eyes by the radiance of the sun" (4.14.10).

[42]Old, *Patristic Roots*, p. 213.

[43]Gregory Dix, *The Shape of the Liturgy* (San Francisco: Harper and Row, 1945), pp. 446-48, translates a prayer by bishop Serapion of Thmuis ("Send 'holy Spirit' into our mind and give us grace to learn the divine scriptures from holy Spirit, to interpret cleanly and worthily") and one from the Greek liturgy of St. Mark, a medieval text descended from a fourth-century Alexandrian rite ("Send forth Thy light and Thy truth, and illuminate the eyes of our understanding for the comprehending of Thy holy oracles, and enable us to hear them so that we be not hearers only but doers also of the word"). Old, *Patristic Roots*, pp. 208-18, also provides translations from F. E. Brightman, *Liturgies Eastern and Western* (Oxford: Clarendon, 1896) of Syrian Jacobite (p. 79) and Nestorian liturgies (pp. 255-56) that include overtly trinitarian Prayers of Illumination characterized by a notable integration of emphasis on divine speech and divine illumination.

more as the speaking subject of the sermon than as its object, as reflected in the von Allmen quotation early in this chapter.

The formal inclusion of a written or prepared Prayer for Illumination became less frequent in Puritanism and various other streams of the Reformed traditions that were strongly influenced by the Westminster Directory for Worship. There "the illumination of the Holy Spirit" is mentioned theologically, but nowhere is its invocation in worship before the preaching suggested or required liturgically.[44] But many Puritan ministers did retain the individual practice of articulating a brief spontaneous or memorized spoken or silent prayer at the beginning of the preaching event.[45]

Today, as earlier Reformed examples from the sixteenth century have been recovered, the Prayer for Illumination has been formally restored to normative status in some historically Reformed denominations.[46] John Witvliet regards the Reformed Prayer for Illumination as an ongoing example of efforts in the history of worship to adequately acknowledge worship's dependence upon the reality and presence of the Holy Spirit in the gathered liturgical assembly. In particular, he sees parallels between the Reformed Prayer for Illumination and the ancient Eastern eucharistic epi-

---

[44]*Directory for the Publick Worship of God* (Edinburgh, February 1645) <http://www.covenanter.org/Westminster/directoryforpublicworship.htm>.

[45]Cf. Horton Davies, *Worship and Theology in England* (Grand Rapids: Eerdmans, 1996), 1:189, 410, 531.

[46]A survey of contemporary mainline denominational worship books indicates that a Prayer of Illumination is recommended as normative for worship most strongly in the Presbyterian Church (U.S.A.) (*Book of Common Worship* [Louisville, Ky.: Westminster John Knox, 1993], pp. 36, 60, 90-91); in the Reformed Church of America: <http://images.rca.org/docs/worship/lordsday.pdf> and <http://images.rca.org/docs/worship/worshipdirectory.pdf>, pp. 6-7; and with somewhat less consistency in *The United Methodist Book of Worship* (Nashville: United Methodist Publishing House, 1992), pp. 22, 34. It is offered as an option for the worship of the United Church of Christ (*Book of Worship: United Church of Christ* [Cleveland: UCC, 1986], p. 114), perhaps in deference to its historical German Evangelical and Reformed constituency. The Evangelical Lutheran and American Episcopal traditions retain the medieval practice of recommending a Prayer of the Day according to the lectionary, sometimes trinitarian but not specifically focused on invoking the Spirit's illumination for the proclamation of the Word (*Evangelical Lutheran Worship* [Minneapolis: Augsburg Fortress, 2006]; *The* [Episcopal] *Book of Common Prayer* [New York: Church Hymnal Corporation, 1979]). In the late nineteenth and early twentieth centuries, Presbyterian use of prayer books heavily borrowed Anglophile patterns derived from Episcopalian traditions. Presbyterian prayer books from this period are missing an explicit Prayer of Illumination. The omission is rectified in *The Worshipbook: Services and Hymns* (Philadelphia: Westminster Press, 1972), pp. 27-28. The sixteenth-century pattern is fully restored with multiple choices in PC(USA)'s *Book of Common Worship*.

clesis, in which the Father is asked to send the Holy Spirit to realize the presence of Christ in the Communion.[47] Because the Reformed theology of the Eucharist places special emphasis on the role of the Holy Spirit in realizing the presence of the risen Christ in the gathered community, special liturgical interest has been recently focused on possible commonalities between Reformed and various Eastern liturgical traditions in this respect.[48]

At this point, let us recapitulate the constructive proposal of this chapter. It is in the acknowledgment of preaching as an intrinsically trinitarian event that both the human and the divine aspects of preaching can best be theologically articulated and coordinated in the context of corporate worship. With this in mind, the disciplined ecclesial practice that is embodied in the liturgical tradition of the Prayer for Illumination takes on pivotal importance. As the congregation anticipates and prepares for the event of preaching, the human preacher and the human congregation intentionally pray together that human speech, by the Holy Spirit's work, would become God's Word spoken through the preacher to the congregation. They pray that in this unique event in this gathered Christian community in this time and place, the triune God would be Speaker, Word and Breath. They pray that the extraordinary power of God's revelation would be manifest in Jesus Christ in the ordinary, common clay pots of fallen, fallible, vulnerable, imperfect human words and lives.

In this trinitarian prayer, the preacher offers faith-filled words, and the congregation offers attention and responsiveness—faithful hearing—in anticipation of the possibility that the living, triune God will actually communicate the divine Word through human speech by the Holy Spirit. The intentional human act of acknowledgment manifested in a conscious, deliberate Prayer for Illumination is crucial, because human preaching is certainly not inevitably or intrinsically or automatically the Word of God. It becomes the Word of God only as a result of the triune God's gracious and sovereign action in the event of preaching, in the context of corporate worship.

---

[47]See John Witvliet, *Worship Seeking Understanding* (Grand Rapids: Baker Academic, 2003), pp. 273-76. In *Patristic Roots*, p. 213, Old also notes this parallel.

[48]Barth seems to have had at least an intuitive sense of this connection in the comments quoted above (see n. 21 above) regarding preaching and the sacraments taken together as constituting the category of "proclamation," and specifically regarding the risks of presuming some kind of "transubstantiation" of human words into the divine word in preaching.

Perhaps this proposal may best be illustrated and confirmed by actually presenting for meditation and reflection some particularly helpful contemporary trinitarian Prayers of Illumination, which can focus our attention in conclusion on (a) preaching as a trinitarian event in which, by the Holy Spirit, the living God speaks the divine Word through the human act of preaching; (b) the importance of the intrinsic interrelationship of Word and Spirit as the Scriptures are read and proclaimed in the worship of the gathered community; and (c) the way in which, because of the normative gospel pattern of the incarnation of God in Jesus Christ, divine revelation is most profoundly, authentically and characteristically communicated by the Spirit in and through ordinary, created, mortal human words and leaders.

> Guide us, O God,
> by your Word and Spirit,
> that in your light we may see light,
> in your truth find freedom,
> and in your will discover your peace,
> through Jesus Christ our Lord.[49]

> God our helper,
> by your Holy Spirit, open our minds,
> that as the Scriptures are read
> and your Word is proclaimed,
> we may be led into your truth
> and taught your will,
> for the sake of Jesus Christ our Lord.

> God, source of all light,
> by your Word you give light to the soul.
> Pour out upon us
> the spirit of wisdom and understanding
> that, being taught by you in Holy Scripture,
> our hearts and minds may be opened to know the things
> that pertain to life and holiness,
> through Jesus Christ our Lord.[50]

---

[49]PC(USA), *Book of Common Worship*, p. 90; Reformed Church of America, "Order of Worship for the Lord's Day" <http://images.rca.org/docs/worship/lordsday.pdf>, p. 6.
[50]The last two prayers are from PC(USA), *Book of Common Worship*, pp. 90-91.

10

The Church's Proclamation as a Participation in God's Mission

LEANNE VAN DYK

It is a common feature of the Protestant landscape—perhaps especially among evangelicals—for a preacher to assume that the sermon is the word of the Lord. These preachers might assume further that their preaching is the actual self-communication of God. I do not dispute that Protestant assumption; rather, I affirm it because it highlights the faithfulness of God in communicating through the "clay jars" of human agents. Modesty and honesty compel us to admit, however, that such an assumption carries significant ambiguity and multiple opportunities for error. God has the attribute of perfection, but preachers do not.

Christian proclamation, therefore, finds its source not in human capacities but in God's own self-communication. This means that proclamation is grounded in the triune life of God. In trinitarian terms, Christian proclamation is explicitly focused on Jesus Christ, is animated by the power of the Holy Spirit and ultimately seeks the glory of God. Christian proclamation in such a trinitarian framework embodies and enacts the patterns of God's own inner-trinitarian life and rightly expands beyond the sermon to include faithful action and service. The proclamation of the church in mission includes the whole scope of the church's identity as the body of Christ, its response to the grace of God and its participation in God's own mission. This means that the church's proclamation is its whole coherent response to and identity in the call of God to participate in communion with God. This coherent response includes the central tasks of preaching, teaching and evangelism as well as the visible practices and patterns of the church. It includes patterns of faithfulness and patience in our relationships, our families, our work, our prayer and our suffering. This claim does not diminish the centrality of gospel proclamation in the life of the church but rather sets it in a coherent and compelling framework of the church's mission as a participation in God's own trinitarian mission and goals.

The doctrine of the Trinity has enjoyed a resurgence of interest in the last twenty or thirty years, with a veritable bloom of contributions. Voices as varied as Jürgen Moltmann, Catherine Mowry LaCugna, Elizabeth Johnson, Phil Butin, T. F. Torrance, Alexander Schmemann and Robert Jenson have opened up many issues of trinitarian theology, including all the classic and historical issues as well as contemporary social and political implications.

As one of the contributions of this resurgence, the doctrine of the Trinity is widespread agreement that God's inner life is one of mutuality and reciprocity, a divine life of energy and outpouring. This trinitarian life of God does not hoard, is not tentative or anxious but rather is expansive, creative and giving. Following the Johannine and Pauline witnesses, we affirm that the Father sends the Son and the Son does the Father's will; the Spirit leads the Son and the Son breathes out the Spirit into the disciples.[1] The widespread agreement in trinitarian resurgence continues: not only is the inner divine life characterized this way, as we see witnessed in Scripture, particularly in the Gospel of John and in the life, teachings, death and resurrection of Jesus Christ; the church also is called to reflect and mirror these trinitarian patterns in a rich mosaic of relationships. Marriage, friendship and the patterns and practices of the church are to mirror God's own self at a creaturely level. The Trinity *ad intra* is reflected not only by the Trinity *ad extra* in redemptive history but also by the embodied practices of the church.

This remarkable insight has so many implications, so many ripples spreading out from its vibrant divine center. We are "a people of divinely modeled relationships," Inagrace Dietterich said in *StormFront: The Good News of God*.[2] Trinitarian doctrine has multiple implications for the call

---

[1]Mark Lau Branson, "Ecclesiology and Leadership for the Missional Church," in *The Missional Church in Context: Helping Congregations Develop Contextual Ministry*, ed. Craig Van Gender (Grand Rapids: Eerdmans, 2007), p. 125.
[2]Inagrace Dietterich, "Practices: Reoriented in the Way of Christ," in *StormFront: The Good News of God*, by James V. Brownson et al. (Grand Rapids: Eerdmans, 2003), p. 121.

and identity of the church. The triune God revealed in Scripture and professed by the Christian tradition is the God who calls the church to participate in divine goals and purposes. This fundamental theological affirmation means that the church proclaims the gospel as a visible and contextual participation in the mission of God. It is worth noting that there is no other way to proclaim the gospel: the church is unavoidably contextual and situated. There is no proclamation that is not contextual, not particular, not fully embedded in a particular time, place and people.

Recent trinitarian affirmations, then, make clear the link between God's own life and the proclamation of the church. That link is a participation or a communion. When the church proclaims the gospel, the church participates in God's own life. There is a divinely ordered connection between God's life and our lives of faith. All of the rich Pauline meanings of "in Christ," "in God" and "in the Spirit" flow out from this central trinitarian perspective. The church is concrete, particular and embodied in participation within God's own concrete and particular mission in the world. The church's incarnational presence in the world mirrors God's own incarnational presence in the world in Jesus Christ.

It is a bold claim—that, in proclamation, the church is participating in God's own mission and purposes in the world. In recent years the missional church conversation has taken up this claim with particular interest. "Missional" language is used in such a wide variety of ways, as Todd Billings has noted in a recent *Christianity Today* article, that we need to put some effort into defining terms and describing certain broad impulses.[3]

Missional church theology, following Lesslie Newbigin, David Bosch and others, has articulated the gospel in a way that takes seriously post-Constantinian realities. These realities include increasing pluralism and diversity in what once was a Christianized West; the dislocation of the church from what was its assumed place of influence and power; the secularism, commercialism and individualism of popular culture; and an ex-

---

[3] J. Todd Billings, "What Makes a Church Missional?" in *Christianity Today*, March 2008, pp. 56-59; also see Tony Jones, *The New Christians: Dispatches from the Emergent Frontier* (San Francisco: Jossey-Bass, 2008), for an overview of the emergent church conversation; and Leanne Van Dyk, "The Formation of Vocation—Individual and Institutional," in *The Scope of Our Art: The Vocation of the Theological Teacher*, ed. L. Gregory Jones and Stephanie Paulsell (Grand Rapids: Eerdmans, 2002), pp. 225-39.

panding awareness of how cultural particularity shapes both understanding and articulation of the Christian faith.

The cultural critique is just one part of missional ecclesiology, however. Another key feature is an understanding of God as a "missionary God." This means that God has goals, purposes and intentions that flow from the inner-trinitarian divine life into the world. The church is called by God to participate in the mission of God in the particular time and place where the church is located. The church's guiding narrative is the action of God in the life, death and resurrection of Jesus Christ. On this understanding of God and church, the church is not a service organization or a volunteer society or a place of self-discovery and enhancement or even an evangelizing force. The church is the gathered people who together worship, confess and give witness in word and deed to the reign of God. In concrete, particular, embodied ways, the church lives the reality of God's reign, which has broken into the present in "already, but not yet" forms in advance of its complete fulfillment in God's future. In words, actions and patterns of life, the church bears witness to the promise and hope of God's restoration of shalom in the new heaven and the new earth.

The missional church perspective is seen more clearly in a series of three contrasts. First, the church does not so much have a mission but participates in God's mission. This participation grounds and authenticates the mission that the church then lives out in word and deed. Second, mission is not primarily an activity of the church, but an attribute of God. In other words, there is a church because there is the mission of God that calls the church to mission. Third, the church does not independently take up the task of saving the world; rather, the church participates in the mission of the Father through the Son and the Spirit for the healing of the world. These contrasts highlight the divine initiative of mission and the church's participation and response to God's mission.

One potential error in a missional church perspective is the assumption that the call of the church is identical to the *missio Dei*, the mission of God. After all, if the church's mission is to participate in God's mission, then the church's mission must *be* God's mission. A careful missional ecclesiology avoids this error. The church participates in the mission of God but does not circumscribe it. God's purposes in and for the world are larger than the church and may, in God's good will and timing, include intentions that work outside of the church. We see this sort of pattern throughout Scripture: God's intentions and gracious initiatives pull in persons and even creatures outside of the covenant community. This list would certainly include Melchizedek, Rahab, Ruth, the people of Nineveh, Balaam's donkey, Naaman, the Queen of Sheba, the Ethiopian eunuch.

The church's mission, then, is a subset of a larger divine mission. It is part of God's mission to the world and not the entirety of God's work in the world. The steps or links from the Trinity to the church's mission and proclamation are mapped out in missional theology. God the Father sends the Son; God the Father and the Son send the Spirit; the Father, Son and Spirit send the church to take up and participate in God's own mission.

Further insights into the link between Trinity and mission can be seen in an examination of the distinction of divine persons. The first person of the Trinity is, as P. T. Forsyth once said, "the first missionary."[4] God the Father sent forth the Son in human form as the basis and fulfillment of mission. The second person of the Trinity is Lord in the form of humility, lowliness, suffering and service. His mission is our reconciliation and the pattern of our own mission. The third person of the Trinity is closely linked and identified with the Son. The mission of the Spirit is to equip and endorse the Son, to make all things new, to give life and breath to all creation, to unite us with Christ, to draw all creation toward the fulfillment of God's shalom.[5] The distinction of trinitarian persons highlights particular aspects of the divine mission, but the unity of the persons results in a coherent and mutual divine mission in the church, in the world and in creation.

The contribution that missional church theology has made to theological conversation in recent years, then, includes at least these two emphases: a contextual critique of the many cultures that encounter the gospel and an understanding of God as a missionary God, who is out ahead of the church in the world and calls the church to participate in divine goals and purposes. These two characteristic emphases can and must inform congrega-

---

[4]P. T. Forsyth, *Missions in State and Church: Sermons and Addresses* (London: Hodder & Stoughton, 1908), p. 270.
[5]John Thompson, *Modern Trinitarian Perspectives* (Oxford: Oxford University Press, 1994), pp. 70-72.

tional life, theological education, preaching, evangelism, proclamation, pastoral care and every practice of ministry.

A trinitarian and missional perspective on proclamation is particularly important for the commitments of a broad evangelical tradition. What does it mean for the church to participate in the mission of God in its proclamation? Certainly it means that the church witnesses to and proclaims the gospel of salvation. The classic marks of the church as a faithful proclamation of Scripture and a pure administration of the sacraments emphasize this key aspect of the church's participation in God's mission. Both preaching and the sacraments are proclamations of the Word of God, as John Calvin pointed out in his treatment of the sacraments.[6] This is because both "set forth" Christ and both unite the believer to Christ, through the power of the Holy Spirit. The church participates in the triune God's mission when it faithfully communicates the gospel and calls for a believing response.

Witness is certainly at the center of proclamation. Preaching, teaching, evangelism and catechesis are all familiar modes of this form of proclamation. In moments of vivid encounter, the power of the proclamation of the Word of God by a human speaker is dramatically displayed. In those moments, we not only receive the Word of God preached in verbal form; we also are enfolded by the presence and reality of God. The sermon and other forms of witness proclaim the message of salvation in Jesus Christ. When Peter addressed the Pentecost crowd, he said to them, "Men of Judea and all who live in Jerusalem, let this be known to you, and listen to what I say" (Acts 1:14 NRSV). Here are words of witness and proclamation in the straightforward sense of a message carried and then delivered. A full understanding of witness, however, would not be complete without a stress on the divine grace that precedes, accompanies and follows the proclaimed Word and brings us into the life of God and God's mission for the world.

An affirmation of God's self-revelation as triune is critical at this point. The confident and vigorous Christian confession is that what happens in the sermon—and what happens throughout the worship service—is our participation, through the Holy Spirit, in Jesus Christ's communion with

---

[6]John Calvin, *Institutes of the Christian Religion*, Library of Christian Classics, trans. Ford Lewis Battles, ed. John T. McNeill (Philadelphia: Westminster Press, 1960), 4.17.

God the Father.[7] Not only is God present with us in witness—in the proclamation of sermon and the communion of worship—but also we are present with God within God's own trinitarian life. James Torrance said, "Jesus Christ is the leader of our worship, the high priest who forgives us our sins and leads us into the holy presence of the Father."[8] He also emphasized that our participation in the life of God in worship—including the sermon—is an event of grace. This is not something we do out of effort or natural capacity. It is God's act of free grace to bring us into the koinonia of God in worship.

Another approach to the question of how it is that the church participates in the mission of God is to propose that the church's "proclamation" is a term that extends beyond the sermon or the evangelistic message. On this approach, proclamation has several forms, which ripple out from its center as witness to Jesus Christ to include other forms of participation in the mission of God.

One such form in an expanded understanding of Christian proclamation is authentic and coherent patterns of Christian life. This expansion of the more familiar form of proclamation as sermon or other verbal forms is an implication of a trinitarian understanding of God's identity and mission. It also has deep confirmation in the experience of Christian believers. Missionaries, for example, know that "living saved" is a form of proclamation. One of my colleagues was a missionary among the Mayan people of Chiapas, Mexico, for more than thirty years. When his family arrived in Chiapas, the indigenous people there were highly suspicious and initially felt threatened. My colleague and his family simply settled in, learned the language, learned the customs of that community and exhibited acceptance and hospitality. Several years passed before the gospel was actually preached—but the gospel certainly was proclaimed in the authentic and coherent patterns of Christian life. These patterns are not human inven-

---

[7]James Torrance develops this trinitarian understanding of Christian worship in his book *Worship, Community and the Triune God of Grace* (Downers Grove, Ill.: InterVarsity Press, 1996). John Calvin's theology has a theme of sacramental union with Jesus Christ by the power of the Holy Spirit in the presence of the Father. It is a trinitarian sacramental theology with an ascent motif; the believer ascends in union with Christ to where Christ is, at the right hand of the Father. See especially Calvin's *Institutes* 4.17.18; 4.17.31.

[8]Torrance, *Worship, Community*, p. 57.

tions; they flow from inner-trinitarian patterns of acceptance and hospitality. In this way my colleague and his family proclaimed the grace and love of God in visible actions.

You will remember the maxim attributed to Francis of Assisi: "Preach the gospel at all times. If necessary, use words." I have always reacted negatively at some visceral level to that little maxim for theological reasons connected with this topic of Trinity and proclamation. Although the saying affirms the proclamation of visible actions, it diminishes the proclamation of speech and completely misses the integration and common trinitarian basis of both. As it turns out, Franciscan scholars have discovered that this maxim has no origin in Francis. It is almost certainly a case of mistaken attribution. What we *can* take from this saying is that the proclamation of Jesus Christ happens in authentic and coherent visible practices and that these practices have their basis and source in the practices of the triune God.

The proposal that visible practices are a form of Christian proclamation is perhaps viewed by some as a confusion of categories. For these, verbal proclamation is intended to evoke conversion. Discipleship is intended to follow in a life of service and obedience to God. Such a clear distinction between conversion and service, however, reinforces the tendency in evangelicalism toward an emphasis on propositional beliefs and personal morality.[9] A clear demarcation between proclamation and service is not intended to suppress the importance of service and embodied practices of faith, but it often has. Robert Jenson remarks, "Much of modern life assumes that there is not, in fact, anything we must say to each other that could not in principle be said by sentences."[10] He then makes the extended claim that the sacraments are "visible words" that speak, by the grace of God, because of their embodied nature. A closer link between speech and action, between preaching and practices, makes the claim that faithful Christian response to the gospel of Jesus Christ is both proclamation and service and, furthermore, that there is a trinitarian basis to both.

---

[9]George Hunsberger, "Evangelical Conversion Toward a Missional Ecclesiology," in *Evangelical Ecclesiology: Reality or Illusion?* ed. John G. Stackhouse Jr. (Grand Rapids: Baker Academic, 2003), p. 125.

[10]Robert W. Jenson, *Visible Words: The Interpretation and Practice of Christian Sacraments* (Philadelphia: Fortress, 1978), p. 16.

If the church broadens its understanding of proclamation to include patterns of faithful practices, then conversion would imply not only proper beliefs and a moral lifestyle but also a pattern of Christian life that anticipates and seeks the reign of God. A believing community that expresses a deep unity of the proclamation of witness and service embodies the gospel in particular and concrete ways. Such a community has a vision that is "characterized every day by its march to the cadence of a drummer others cannot hear, its loyalty to a Lord others may not recognize, its distinct life as a community oriented to a future others cannot believe will be the future of the world. It means being a distinct community that at many points looks odd to onlookers but in which the 'healing of the nations' is already showing up."[11]

In contemporary North American culture, a deep skepticism regarding the church and its structures can be answered when the church is seen as real people living as though the gospel narrative is truth.[12] Lesslie Newbigin said that the congregation is the "hermeneutic of the gospel," the interpretative key of the good news. This means that how the church lives out the patterns of God's reconciling actions toward the world in Jesus Christ *speaks* the gospel in faithful actions.[13]

This second main form of proclamation, visible practices, is seen in countless ways of Christian service, care and compassion. Christian service has a long and persistent record in the history of Christian faithfulness. It includes the authentic and coherent practices of hospitality, presence and listening. But it also includes practicing nonviolent resistance, seeking justice, taking up the cause of the poor and widow and orphan, visiting the prisoner, caring for the sick. Service can certainly include verbal preaching and worship as well as the practices and patterns of life. Proclamation both in verbal forms, typically understood to be the preaching of the gospel, and in service forms are at their best when authentically integrated. Verbal pro-

---

[11]Hunsberger, "Evangelical Conversion," p. 125.

[12]In recent years this skepticism is well documented by sociologists and pollsters such as George Barna. Cf. Robert Wuthnow, *After the Baby Boomers: How Twenty- and Thirty-Somethings Are Shaping the Future of American Religion* (Princeton, N.J.: Princeton University Press, 2007).

[13]Lesslie Newbigin, *The Gospel in a Pluralist Society* (Grand Rapids: Eerdmans, 1989), p. 222.

claimers serve. Servers find opportunities to speak gospel witness. These mutually cohere and support one another, again, in trinitarian patterns of cohesion and support. Service is not an ancillary or secondary form of Christian proclamation. It is an integrated proclamation of the gospel and participation in the life of God. When the church proclaims in this sense, as well, the church takes up the mission of God.

Still another example of visible practices is ordinary faithfulness in the daily patterns of life. We sometimes miss this. When we affirm—and we do—that preaching and worship and building homes in distressed urban areas and medical missionary trips all proclaim the gospel and participate in the mission of God, we have thereby left out a lot of our day-to-day lives. Are we proclaiming the gospel and participating in the mission of God when we play a game with our children? Or fix dinner? Or plant a garden? Or go out with friends? Are these ordinary, day-in and day-out patterns of our lives also included in proclamation and participation?

Amy Plantinga Pauw recently gave a series of lectures exploring this issue from the perspective of the Wisdom books in the Bible, particularly Proverbs and Ecclesiastes. The ordinary observations on life in the book of Proverbs dealing with family harmony or disharmony, friendships, parenting, tasks and toils—along with the recognition that life is puzzling, unpredictable and fleeting in the book of Ecclesiastes—this is the stuff of the Wisdom literature in Scripture. So much of our lives is taken up in just these sorts of things: getting out of bed in the morning and interacting with our families or roommates; going to work or school; encountering a supervisor, a professor, a waiter, a librarian, a student, a waitress, a clerk, a mechanic; and numerous other small, seemingly insignificant matters. We chop onions, peel carrots, scoop ice cream. We run the vacuum cleaner or the dishwasher. We pick up Legos or dry cleaning or pizza. Do all these things count in our lives?

The Wisdom literature in the Scripture, says Plantinga Pauw, speaks a resounding "yes" to that question. All these small, daily things do count. In fact, they have the capacity for gospel proclamation because they are visible practices of the virtues that characterize the inner-divine life of the Trinity. The virtues of patience, hospitality, deference and self-giving love are divine virtues that are practiced day in and day out in these quotidian patterns. When we take up these practices, we participate in God's own life and proclaim in these daily patterns the life of God.

If Christian proclamation is limited to verbal witness to the gospel of Jesus Christ, then these daily patterns of ordinary life seem to lack deep meaning and connection to Christian faith. But the Wisdom literature of Scripture takes great interest in these ordinary patterns of life. In trinitarian and missional perspective, if proclamation is understood as rich and varied patterns and practices in the community of faith that mirror the trinitarian life and the mission of God, then much thicker descriptions of Christian proclamation are possible.

One congregation in Oakland, California, took up a study of the Beatitudes, another example of Wisdom literature, and asked themselves, in small-group settings, "What kind of people do we need to be for this text to make sense?" Theologian and pastor Mark Lau Branson was part of that congregation and said, "Over those next months, as we held before God our marriages, our money, our sorrows and sins, our neighbors and society, we found ourselves with new clarity and new energy."[14] When a congregation seeks to live in the pattern of the Beatitudes, that pattern becomes a proclamation for the world.

The day-to-day patterns of our lives are usually so ordinary and repetitive that we fail to recognize them as visible proclamation. But Proverbs, Ecclesiastes and the Beatitudes all recognize the day-to-day rhythm of our lives as part of our proclamation. Sermons can be memorable and life changing. Running a food pantry can be a clear expression of the gospel. But the steady rhythms of parenting or marriage or friendship are deeply formative and unmistakably proclamatory.

An astounding sidebar to this insight regarding the day-to-day patterns of our lives as part of our proclamation and participation is that creation, too, joins in this proclamation and participation. Human beings are not the only creatures that are called to participate in God's mission in the world. Creation itself is called to participate in God's mission. So the ordinary patterns of birds and flowers and wildebeests and whales also proclaim and participate. This lovely theme is summarized by John Calvin in his under-

---

[14]Mark Lau Branson, "Ecclesiology and Leadership for the Missional Church," p. 101.

standing of creation as a "theater of God's glory."

If we understand the patterns of daily life as a part of the proclamation of Christian life, we need to expand our metaphors. We are accustomed to the image of journey or road to describe faithful Christian living. We follow, we travel, we journey. Yes, we do. But we also rest in comfort and peace, we tend patiently, we—in one of John Calvin's favorite images—repose in God. The wisdom-based images expand our understanding of faithfulness and obedience in Christian life. The images of the psalms, as well, include both journey and rest. We "walk in the law of the Lord" (Ps 119:1 ESV) but are also encouraged to "be still, and know that I am God" (Ps 46:10 ESV). In both of these responses of faith, we participate in God's own life and proclaim in word and deed.

We have explored several understandings of the proclamation of the church—from preaching and worship, to service and hospitality and patterns of faithfulness. The perspective I propose is that the proclamation of the church is a participation in the mission of God and in the inner-trinitarian life. Mission is not a project or a goal. The mission of the church is nothing less than taking up divine work. Our response is broken and flawed and partial, to be sure, but the trinitarian source of the church's proclamation is a sure hope that nothing is wasted: no kind word, no honest testimony, no patient effort. It is taken up, all of it, into God's own purposes for the restoration of shalom.

11

What to Do with Our
Renewed Trinitarian Enthusiasm

Forming Trinitarian Piety and Imagination
Through Worship and Catechesis

JOHN D. WITVLIET

ASSESSING THE TRINITARIAN RENAISSANCE

In the aftermath of various death-of-God theologies in the 1960s, an astonishing trinitarian renaissance has taken hold in many Christian traditions.[1]
Theologians have rediscovered the compelling beauty of a theological vision centered around not a Divine Rambo or "Will-to-Power," but rather
"Being-in-Communion." Theologians have rediscovered the astonishing
beauty of Jesus' high-priestly prayer and the profound fellowship that God's
life not only models for us but also empowers in and through us. Theologians have rediscovered the parsimonious way that the doctrine of the Trinity simultaneously resists individualism, Pelagianism, deism and a host of
sub-Christian accounts of humanity, salvation and eschatology. So pervasive is the recent trinitarian renaissance that we now have a shelf of books
written to summarize all this recent work.[2]

---

[1]This includes but is not limited to works by Orthodox theologians Vladimir Lossky and
John Zizioulas; Roman Catholic theologians Karl Rahner, Leonardo Boff, William Hill,
Walter Kasper and Catherine Mowry LaCugna; and Protestant theologians Jürgen Moltmann, Colin Gunton, Geoffrey Wainwright, Thomas Torrance, James Torrance, Robert
Jenson, Eberhard Jüngel, William Placher, Mark Heim, Kevin Vanhoozer, Alister McGrath
and many others.
[2]I am thinking of a procession of analytical summaries that run from John Thompson, *Modern Trinitarian Perspectives* (New York: Oxford University Press, 1994) to Veli-Matti Kärk-

Yet throughout this period there have been persistent complaints about the lack of trinitarian awareness or piety for vast numbers of ordinary Christians. Lesslie Newbigin contended that "the ordinary Christian in the Western world who hears or reads the word 'God' does not immediately and inevitably think of the triune Being—Father, Son, and Spirit . . . [but rather] of a supreme monad."[3] William Placher suggests, "In contemporary American society the dominant images of divinity and success and community are in some respects radically un-Christian. It cannot be taken for granted that Christians generally remember or ever understood the sort of God in whom we believe and the sort of people we are therefore called to be."[4] Similarly, Christian Smith, in his large-scale study of North American youth, concludes that their theological vision is best described as "moralistic therapeutic deism."[5]

This lack of trinitarian awareness is also often reflected in Christian worship. Though trinitarian doxologies persist in the official liturgical texts of many denominations, the doctrine of the Trinity seems to have little bearing on how a good deal of worship is enacted. As George Stroup asks, "If the claim that God is triune is indeed at the heart of the Christian understanding of God, then why is there so little evidence of that conviction in the liturgies of many Christian churches?"[6] Similarly, Lester Ruth, in his study of the seventy-five most sung contemporary worship songs, concludes: "On the whole, there are few trinitarian aspects within this body of contemporary worship music."[7]

While there may be no definitive way to calculate the precise extent of trinitarian conviction among contemporary Christians, these observations should, at minimum, lead every theologian, pastor, professor and teacher to ask about the state of theological imagination in the parts of the body of

---

käinen, *The Trinity: Global Perspectives* (Louisville, Ky.: Westminster John Knox, 2007).
[3]Lesslie Newbigin, *The Open Secret*, rev. ed. (Grand Rapids: Eerdmans, 1995), p. 27.
[4]William Placher, *Narratives of a Vulnerable God* (Louisville, Ky.: Westminster John Knox, 1994), p. 140.
[5]Christian Smith, *Soul Searching* (New York: Oxford University Press, 1995), p. 162.
[6]George Stroup, "The Worship of the Triune God," *Reformed Liturgy and Music* 17 (1983): 160.
[7]Lester Ruth, "Lex Amandi, Lex Orandi: The Trinity in the Most-Used Contemporary Christian Worship Songs," in *The Place of Christ in Liturgical Prayer: Trinity, Christology, and Liturgical Theology*, ed. Bryan D. Spinks (Collegeville, Minn.: Liturgical Press, 2008), pp. 342-59. See also Robin Parry, *Worshipping Trinity: Coming Back to the Heart of Worship* (Carlisle, U.K.: Paternoster, 2005).

Christ they serve. For myself, I am haunted and challenged by a former student who confessed, "I've professed the Trinity before, but I now see that I've basically worshiped and lived as a unitarian. The church failed to explain to me what the Trinity is, and why it matters." Based on conversations with colleagues in several traditions, it seems safe to conclude that this student speaks for hundreds if not thousands of students in congregations, colleges and even seminaries, who live, work and pray as functional deists within otherwise orthodox traditions and institutions.

In this context, my goal is to jump-start a conversation about how we as teachers, pastors and theologians can more winsomely, passionately and effectively invite our students into the vibrant world of trinitarian life, belief, perception and practice. I am not merely talking about helping students to understand how the doctrine of the Trinity can be coherent—the implicit and all-too-limited goal of some theological classrooms. Rather, my goal is to invite them to experience a kind of theological conversion that will help them construe the world in a trinitarian rather than a deistic way. The transformation of the imagination here is not unlike a two-dimensional creature discovering three-dimensional space, as vividly portrayed in the novel and film *Flatland*.[8]

Christian theologians have a remarkable opportunity to serve God's people with a renewed vision for the triune beauty of God's own life and the trinitarian dimensions of divine activity, provided we take seriously our calling not merely to speak to each other, but also to engage the church in practices that elicit and sustain trinitarian faith.[9] Two of those fundamental practices are trinitarian worship and trinitarian teaching. What follows are brief summaries of some of the most prominent strands of the church's wisdom on how both worship and teaching ministries form trinitarian piety and imagination.

TRINITARIAN WORSHIP

What does trinitarian worship look like? How would you know that you are worshiping in a congregation that affirms the Trinity?

---

[8]Edwin Abbott, *Flatland* (New York: Dover, 1953).
[9]James J. Buckley and David S. Yeago, eds., *Knowing the Triune God: The Work of the Spirit in the Practices of the Church* (Grand Rapids: Eerdmans, 2001).

Perhaps the most obvious answers are that such a congregation would hear the words "I baptize you in the name of the Father, Son and Holy Spirit" at baptism and would sing "Holy, Holy, Holy, . . . blessed Trinity" or another explicitly trinitarian text. But trinitarian worship does not consist of merely appending a triune formula to conclude a prayer or hymn. It is, rather, a fundamental way of reframing nearly every act of worship— even those that never mention the term *Trinity*. The doctrine of the Trinity is, after all, a map or description of the ultimate reality in which we live, move and have our being—the very nature, being and reality of God. The doctrine of the Trinity is a description of the kind of God the Christians worship. And as with interpersonal relationships on earth, so it is with God in heaven: the kind of being we interact with makes a great deal of difference in how we construe and carry out those interactions. To sense this, consider four distinct, complementary examples of trinitarian theological reasoning, each of which commends particular liturgical practices.[10]

Mediation. First, trinitarian Christians emphasize mediation in worship, amplifying the compelling message that "through [Christ] we . . . have access in one Spirit to the Father" (Eph 2:18 ESV).[11] At the center of a Christian understanding of worship is the notion that God is not only the one to whom our worship is addressed; God is also an agent in making our worship possible. The Holy Spirit inspires our worship and, when we are unable or do not know how to pray, prays for us and through us. Jesus Christ mediates our worship as the high priest who brings our prayers before God and who indeed "ever lives to pray for us" (Heb 7:25, my trans.). This means that the triune God is active in our worship, receiving, inspiring and perfecting our words, thoughts, gestures and actions, a beautiful triune dance that makes our activity in worship not an onerous obligation through

---

[10]I have developed these themes in greater detail in "The Opening of Worship: Trinity," *A More Profound Alleluia: Theology and Worship in Harmony*, ed. Leanne Van Dyk (Grand Rapids: Eerdmans, 2005), pp. 1-27; idem, "The Trinitarian DNA of Christian Worship: Perennial Themes in Recent Theological Literature," *Yale Institute of Sacred Music Colloquium* 2 (2005): 87-105; idem, "Prism of Glory: Trinitarian Worship and Liturgical Piety in the Reformed Tradition," in Spinks, *The Place of Christ in Liturgical Prayer*, pp. 268-99.

[11]This theme is prominent in Philip W. Butin, *Revelation, Redemption, Response: Calvin's Trinitarian Understanding of the Divine-Human Relationship* (New York: Oxford University Press, 1995); and Alan Torrance, *Persons in Communion: An Essay on Trinitarian Description and Human Participation* (Edinburgh: T & T Clark, 1996).

which we hope to reach God, but rather a joyful act of participation in a divine mystery beyond our comprehension.

This concern for mediation is reflected in several tangible practices. For one, Christian prayers frequently conclude with statements of mediation, from the very brief "in Jesus' name" or a more complete "in the name of Jesus, who lives and reigns with you [the Father] and the Spirit, one God now and forever." Hardly a mere formula, these phrases reflect the breathtaking claim that it is God who makes possible our access to God. For another, special prayers called epicletic prayers (from the Greek *epikaleō*, "to call upon") are added to call on God not merely to receive our worship but also to be active in worship. These include prayers for illumination before the reading and preaching of Scripture,[12] which ask for God to help the congregation to receive understanding and spiritual insight, and prayers of consecration or blessing at baptism, the Lord's Supper and other occasions, which ask for the Holy Spirit to inspire and bless the celebration, as well as hundreds of hymns and songs that petition for God be active in our worship (e.g., "Come, Thou almighty King, / Help us thy name to sing"). In sum, trinitarian Christians celebrate and savor the mediatorial agency of Jesus Christ and the Holy Spirit in every aspect of worship.

Relationality. Second, trinitarian worship enacts, reflects and savors the relationality or communion that comprises both divine life and the Christian life. The doctrine of the Trinity offers a vision of each that is fundamentally relational and interpersonal. These twin themes come together in Jesus' high-priestly prayer: "as you, Father, are in me and I am in you, may they also be in us," and "may they be one, as we are one" (Jn 17:21, 22 NRSV).[13] They are memorably expressed in John Newton's much-loved hymn text:

---

[12]For more on this, see Philip Butin's contribution in this volume (chap. 9).

[13]This theme is prominent in Miroslav Volf, *After Our Likeness* (Grand Rapids: Eerdmans, 1998); Lesslie Newbigin, *Household of God* (Cincinnati: Friendship Press, 1953); Stanley Grenz, *The Social God and the Relational Self* (Louisville, Ky.: Westminster John Knox, 2001); John Zizioulas, *Being as Communion* (Crestwood, N.Y.: St. Vladimir's Seminary Press, 1993). There are important and necessary limits to this concern for relationality. Descriptions of divine relationality need to avoid slipping into tritheism or simply projecting onto God some kind of human communitarian ideal. See especially Kathryn Tanner, "Kingdom Come: The Trinity and Politics," *The Princeton Seminary Bulletin* 38, no. 2 (2007): 129-45; and the vigorous discussion between Mark Husbands and John R. Franke in this volume.

May the grace of Christ, our Savior,
and the Father's boundless love,
with the Holy Spirit's favor,
rest upon us from above.

May we now remain in union
with each other and the Lord,
and possess, in sweet communion,
joys that earth cannot afford.

This emphasis on relationality has fueled renewed interest in the metaphor of gift-giving as central to our conception of God and of worship.[14] Christian worship is not obeisance by which we appease a divine tyrant. We do not sing loud or pray hard in order to generate divine favor—a perfect theology of worship if we wanted to worship Baal. Worship, rather, is the joyful and solemn exchange of gifts, not unlike that of the exchange of gifts between young toddlers and loving parents at Christmas.

This emphasis on relationality and gift-giving may be expressed in any number of ways: hymns, prayers and sermons that speak of the relationality of divine life; architecture that emphasizes both the relationality between God and the church and the interpersonal relationality that the church is called to embody; practices that accent the corporate nature of Christian prayer, praise, confession of sin, lament and profession of common faith; sermons that aim at restoration of community; truly common prayers that speak the needs and concerns of communities and all of creation; corporate almsgiving as a basic for-another action of Christian *diakonia;* corporate processes for the creation of liturgical art forms, including textiles, sculpture, stained glass as well as drama and music; and worship that intentionally expresses hospitality to people of all generations, ethnicities and abilities. Trinitarian Christians, in other words, are eager to worship in ways that enhance and deepen the intentionality and joy of communal gift-giving between God and the community, as well as within the community itself.

History. Third, trinitarian worship rehearses and savors God's actions in history as a true and reliable way to understand and speak about God's

---

[14]See R. Kevin Seasoltz, *God's Gift Giving: In Christ and Through the Spirit* (New York: Continuum, 2007); Stephen H. Webb, *The Gifting God: A Trinitarian Ethics of Excess* (New York: Oxford University Press, 1996).

being and character. In contrast to Arianism, the doctrine of the Trinity argues that the real God is not a pristine higher power disconnected from the actions of Jesus Christ and the Holy Spirit. In contrast to Sabellianism, the doctrine of the Trinity contends that God's actions in history are not mere shadows or masks of divine being, but rather are a reliable indicator of God's very nature. The doctrine of the Trinity boldly asserts that Jesus Christ and the Spirit are reliable signs of God's nature, for they themselves are truly divine. In Colin Gunton's words, the doctrine of the Trinity ensures that our thinking about God does not "float off into abstraction from the concrete history of salvation."[15]

All of this makes a great deal of difference for worship, calling for liturgical actions that rehearse narratives of divine action, viewed iconically as reliable windows into divine life. Any unitarian or deistic worshiper can praise God by using timeless divine attributes, speaking of God as beautiful, just or holy. But it takes a trinitarian Christian to praise God not only with attributes, but also in reference to the way those attributes are on full display in the actions of Jesus Christ and the Holy Spirit in history. This historical orientation is also practiced in the openings of prayers that name divine actions (e.g., "O God, who by the leading of a star . . ."), in prayers of thanksgiving that feature psalmlike passages reciting God's actions in history (including prayers of thanksgiving at the Lord's Table) and in the use of the Christian year as a guide to historical commemorations. In worship, trinitarian Christians constantly return to the record of God's actions in history as the basis for praise, thanksgiving, lament and intercession.

An integrated theological vision. Fourth, fully trinitarian worship actively rehearses a balanced and integrated presentation and interpretation of God's actions. One central implication of the doctrine of the Trinity is that the works of God, attributed as they are in scriptural narrative and the Christian tradition to Father, Son and Holy Spirit, are not in any way disjointed or at cross-purposes. The divine economy is not only unimaginably fulsome, but wondrously interrelated.[16]

---

[15]Colin Gunton, *The Promise of Trinitarian Theology* (Edinburgh: T & T Clark, 1991), p. 34.

[16]This theme is prominent in Colin Gunton, *The Triune Creator* (Grand Rapids: Eerdmans, 1998); Adrio König, *Here I Am!* (Grand Rapids: Eerdmans, 1982); A. A. Van Ruler, *Calvinist Trinitarianism* (Lewiston, N.Y.: Edwin Mellen, 1969).

This vision calls for liturgical practices that depict the divine economy as a comprehensive and integrated whole. Otto Weber once argued that a deficient appropriation of the doctrine of the Trinity and an incomplete or unintegrated view of the divine economy has inevitable repercussions in prayer and spirituality: "It is only when we constantly keep the unity of God in his work in view that we can avoid an isolated 'theology of the first article,' or an isolated 'Christocentrism,' or an isolated 'Spiritualization' of theology." In fact, said Weber, "it can be said that at this point the Doctrine of the Trinity gains its most direct relationship to 'piety'; . . . when the Doctrine of the Trinity falls apart or retreats in the consciousness of the Community, then piety becomes one-sided and, measured by the liveliness and the wealth of the biblical witness, is impoverished."[17]

Weber's lament about "one-sided piety" easily translates into significant criteria for liturgy: Christian worship must rehearse and celebrate the full scope of God's actions, doing so in a way that communicates their fundamental unity. Many classical elements of worship aim at presenting the full range of divine activity in a unified way: the grand hymns of the Christian tradition like the Gloria, *Te Deum*, the liturgical creeds, the more comprehensive eucharistic and baptismal prayers, the use of a well-balanced lectionary to ensure a balanced diet of Scripture readings and the Christian year. Thoughtful practitioners of these classic elements take care to ensure that their realization resists any temptation to split creation and redemption, grace and law, the work of Jesus on the cross and the work of the Spirit in the world today—or any other of the many dualisms that regularly plague Christian doctrine, worship and life. Likewise, the most promising forms of contemporary preaching, prayer, music-making and artistic expression aim at this same comprehensive and unified theological vision, however much they may differ in terms of style.

In sum, trinitarian worship is worship that fits with a God whose own being is faithfully and aptly described in trinitarian terms. Worshiping this kind of God should not be done with just any readily available worship technique. It should rather look for approaches that are fitting to address this kind of God, including (a) celebrating and resting in the mediation of-

---

[17]Otto Weber, *Foundations of Dogmatics*, trans. Darrell L. Guder, 2 vols. (Grand Rapids: Eerdmans, 1981), 1:393.

fered by Jesus and the Holy Spirit, (b) savoring the kind of intimate and healthy relationality in divine life that is depicted in the Scriptures and offered to humanity through Jesus, (c) rehearsing the astonishing litany of divine actions in history and (d) perceiving the unity of purpose of divine actions attributed to each divine person. Each of these is a part of a distinctly Christian approach to worship.

One remarkable benefit of this way of worshiping is that both communities and individual worshipers will be formed in a more robust trinitarian faith. Worship practices slowly but surely sculpt the perceptions and intuitions worshipers have about God, as well as the affections they associate with God.[18] Communities and individual worshipers who participate in fully trinitarian worship are formed over time to set aside any vague, hazy, quasi-deist, subtrinitarian way of construing God and to embrace a much more vibrant, grace-filled, life-giving trinitarian way.

TRINITARIAN PEDAGOGY AND CATECHESIS

At the same time, worship is certainly not the only locus for formation. Worship both invites and requires effective teaching or catechesis to ground and deepen participation. Catechesis is as crucial for worship as a docent or guide is for first-time visitors to an art museum or a baseball game. Without instruction, most of us will fail to perceive its full trinitarian beauty. With it, our level of appreciation, engagement and discipleship can be exponentially deeper.

So what are the most promising, faithful, disciplined pedagogical means for transforming the theological imagination on a trinitarian trajectory? Given space constraints, I will assume that most discussions of the Trinity typically include a discussion of the biblical roots of the doctrine, a sketch of how the doctrine emerged in the patristic period and basic descriptions of the most typical problems associated with the doctrine (e.g., modalism, tritheism). I will focus on five classic pedagogical approaches by noteworthy theologians throughout history, approaches that show promise for elic-

---

[18]For a summary of the literature on this theme, see my essay "The Cumulative Power of Transformation in Public Worship," in *Worship That Changes Lives: Multidisciplinary and Congregational Perspectives on Spiritual Transformation*, ed. Alexis Abernethy (Grand Rapids: Baker Academic, 2008).

iting a "*Flatland* kind of theological conversion" in a wide variety of teaching settings.

Teaching toward practice. First, effective teaching about the Trinity unfolds the beauty and mystery of the trinitarian dimension of specific Christian practices. The doctrine of the Trinity is not merely a set of abstract ideas. Rather, it is a description of the reality in which we live, move and have our being. As such, it shapes—indeed, it unsettles and transforms—how we approach basic practices of prayer, Bible reading, evangelism and community life.

In my own teaching, one of the brief passages I have found most helpful in the conversion of theological imagination is a brief passage from C. S. Lewis's *Mere Christianity*. One day in 1943, Lewis had the challenge of explaining the doctrine of the Trinity in a brief radio broadcast over the BBC—a tall order indeed! He met that challenge with this simple paragraph:

> You may ask "If we cannot imagine a three-personal Being, what is the good of talking about Him?" Well, there isn't any good talking about Him. The thing that matters is being actually drawn into that three-personal life, and that may begin any time—tonight, if you like. What I mean is this. An ordinary simple Christian kneels down to say his prayers. He is trying to get into touch with God. But if a Christian, he knows that what is prompting him to pray is also God: God, so to speak, inside him. But he also knows that all his real knowledge of God comes through Christ, the Man who was God—that Christ is standing beside him, helping him to pray, praying for him. You see what is happening. God is the thing to which he is praying—the goal he is trying to reach. God is also the thing inside him which is pushing him on—the motive power. God is also the road or bridge along which he is being pushed to that goal. So that the whole threefold life of the three-personal being is actually going on in that ordinary little bedroom where an ordinary Christian is saying his prayers.[19]

Lewis began with a basic, fundamental practice and then pointed out its often-latent trinitarian dimensions, all with the goal of preparing the listener for an even deeper engagement with the practice.[20]

---

[19]C. S. Lewis, *Mere Christianity* (London: Geoffrey Bles, 1952), book 4, chap. 2.
[20]This pattern bears strong structural similarities to the famous mystagogical sermons of Ambrose, Augustine and Cyril, postexperiential discussions of the sacraments that were intended to deepen listeners' future participation in the sacraments. For more on practice-

This pedagogical approach actually recapitulates the history of the doctrine of the Trinity. The doctrine emerged not merely as a result of abstract metaphysical speculations, but rather as the church's own reflection on how to pray to and worship the one God of Israel in light of the divinity of Jesus and the Holy Spirit.[21] This history can be recapitulated in any congregational or academic theology class when an instructor replaces the usual question "How can we find a coherent account of how three persons can be one God?" with this alternative: "If you begin with a firmly monotheistic faith, how would your prayers change if you believed that Jesus and the Holy Spirit were fully divine?"

Note also that Lewis's teaching here is not merely about specific actions, even such explicit trinitarian actions as ending a prayer "in Jesus' name." Rather, it is about how the pray-er pictures, imagines or experiences God while praying.[22] It is about their all-encompassing theological vision or imagination, what Charles Taylor might call "a social imaginary" or what others might call "a worldview." In its concreteness, practice-oriented teaching need not—indeed, must not—pull back from overarching cosmological or metaphysical claims. Rather, practice-oriented teaching seeks to unveil and interpret how we can participate in practices with a much deeper and more faithful perception of that metaphysical reality.

Lewis's approach to prayer can be replicated with other practices in mind. Baptism is a noteworthy example. Following Matthew 28, the vast majority of Christians baptize "in the name of the Father and of the Son and of the Holy Spirit," and few would ever assent to the notion that this phrase is merely some incantation. In contrast, the wording of the baptis-

---

oriented teaching, see John D. Witvliet, "Teaching Worship as a Christian Practice," in *For Life Abundant: Practical Theology, Theological Education, and Christian Ministry*, ed. Dorothy Bass and Craig Dykstra (Grand Rapids: Eerdmans, 2008), pp. 117-49.

[21]See, e.g., Larry W. Hurtado, *Lord Jesus Christ: Devotion to Jesus in Earliest Christianity* (Grand Rapids: Eerdmans, 2003), for an account of the transformation of prayer in light of New Testament claims about Christ's divinity. Basil's fourth-century treatise *On The Holy Spirit* is a particularly significant source text with respect to the divinity of the Holy Spirit.

[22]On this point, see Gordon D. Fee's description of the dynamics of religious experience that informed Paul's own prototrinitarian writings in "Paul and the Trinity: The Experience of Christ and the Spirit for Paul's Understanding of God," in *The Trinity*, ed. Stephen T. Davis, Daniel Kendall and Gerald O'Collins (New York: Oxford University Press, 1999), pp. 49-72.

mal formula means that Christian identity is bound up fundamentally with each divine person. Hence, Miroslav Volf argues: "As baptism into the triune name attests, beginning the Christian pilgrimage does not mean simply to respond to God's summons but to enter into communion with the triune God; to end the Christian pilgrimage does not mean simply to have accomplished an earthly task but to enter perfect communion with the triune God."[23] This offers a rich pedagogical opportunity. In a pastoral conversation, consider exploring "What does your baptism in the name of the Father, Son and Holy Spirit mean for your identity?"[24] That question has a profoundly existential appeal that invites students to see the implications of the Trinity for their own vocation in the world.

Drawing contrasts. Second, effective trinitarian pedagogy depends on the practice of drawing contrasts. The doctrine of the Trinity was borne out in the process of making distinctions, as patristic thinkers carefully charted a way forward that would preserve monotheism and avoid both modalism and tritheism. Helping students see what is at stake in those distinctions remains a crucial pedagogical task.

Consider one especially instructive example in recent literature. Liturgical theologian Bryan Spinks has recently described the work of Enlightenment theologian Samuel Clarke and his antitrinitarian attempt to edit the Book of Common Prayer in 1724 by deleting all prayers *to* Christ and *to* the Holy Spirit. Indeed, if Jesus and the Holy Spirit are not fully divine, then they are not the proper ones to address in prayer. Clarke replaced the traditional Gloria Patri text ("Glory be to the Father, and to the Son, and to the Holy Ghost") with "Glory be to God, by Jesus Christ, through the heavenly assistance by the Holy Ghost" or "Unto God be glory in the church, by Christ Jesus, throughout all ages, world without end."[25] These proposed Enlightenment alterations—never adopted in the Church of Eng-

---

[23]Miroslav Volf, "Being as God Is: Trinity and Generosity," in *God's Life in Trinity*, ed. Miroslav Volf and Michael Welker (Minneapolis: Fortress, 2006), p. 3. See also Eugene Peterson, *Christ Plays in Ten Thousand Places* (Grand Rapids: Eerdmans, 2005), pp. 301-8.

[24]See also Gordon Mikoski, "Baptism, Trinity, and Ecclesial Pedagogy in the Thought of Gregory of Nyssa," *Scottish Journal of Theology* 59 (2006): 175-82.

[25]Bryan D. Spinks, "The Place of Christ in Liturgical Prayer: What Jungmann Omitted to Say," in *The Place of Christ in Liturgical Prayer*, ed. Bryan D. Spinks (Collegeville, Minn.: Liturgical Press, 2008), p. 15; see also his "Trinitarian Belief and Worship: A Historical Case," in Volf and Welker, *God's Life in Trinity*, pp. 211-22.

land, but still a reliable indicator of where later Unitarians and·some other liberal Protestants headed—essentially reversed the work of fourth-century trinitarian liturgists. This example demonstrates that a theological commitment makes a great deal of difference for the life of prayer.

A rhetoric of doxological abundance. Third, fitting trinitarian teaching is best conveyed through what might be called a "rhetoric of doxological abundance." The doctrine of the Trinity has its roots in scriptural texts that are marked with a kind of overflowing exuberance, an almost breathless energy and wonder at the beauty of God. The blessing of 2 Corinthians 13:13 (NRSV) celebrates "the grace of the Lord Jesus Christ" and "the love of God" and asks that "the communion of the Holy Spirit be with all of you"—speaking not just of one but of all three. Ephesians 3, one of the most exalted passages in the Pauline letters, concludes with the soaring intercession: "I pray that . . . [the Father] may grant that you may be strengthened in your inner being with power through his Spirit, and that Christ may dwell in your hearts through faith" (Eph 3:16-17 NRSV).

A similar wonder-filled tone marks many of the most compelling and instructive treatises on trinitarian theology throughout the church's history, from Gregory of Nyssa and Augustine to Jonathan Edwards and John Owen. In the fourth century, Gregory of Nazianzus introduced one of his reflections on the Trinity with the words, "To speak of the Godhead is, I know, like crossing the ocean on a raft, or like flying to the stars with wings of a narrow span." In the recent trinitarian renaissance, David H. C. Read preached a sermon titled "The Thrill of the Trinity," and Neal Plantinga produced essays with memorable sentences like this: "The Trinity is thus a zestful, wondrous community of divine light, love, joy, mutuality, and verve."[26]

This language is more effusive than it needs to be to merely describe the concepts that comprise the doctrine of the Trinity. But it is, to be sure, an appropriate mode for speaking about the majesty and beauty of God. It is also, for our purposes, one element in effective pedagogy. A significant part of learning has always been achieved through teachers who bear witness to

---

[26]David H. C. Read, "The Thrill of the Trinity," *Pulpit Digest* 71, no. 503 (May-June 1990): 27-30; Cornelius Plantinga Jr., "The Threeness/Oneness Problem of the Trinity," *Calvin Theological Journal* 23 (1988): 50.

the beauty or significance of their subject, who generate a contagious enthusiasm for their material—teachers, that is, who are literally *professors*. While effective teaching should always strive for language that is precise, clear and focused, effective teaching about God should also aspire to language that is evocative, doxological and full of conviction.

Analogies and illustrations as a risky but evocative source of trinitarian imagination. Fourth, teaching on the doctrine of the Trinity proceeds best through cautious use of multiple, complementary analogies in order to engage students' imagination. Marguerite Shuster is right to note the perils of using of trinitarian analogies and illustrations in both teaching and preaching: "Not only is the Trinity unique, but it is essentially without analogy, and hence makes it problematic to find compelling illustrative material."[27] And indeed, the history of trinitarian teaching features a long parade of mildly or not-so-mildly heretical analogies and illustrations, which veer alternatively between modalism and tritheism, unsatisfying analogies that compare the Trinity to water, ice and steam, or an apple's skin, meat and core.

This concern could well lead thoughtful teachers to simply shun all analogies, with the possible exception of the one scripturally authorized analogy of the Trinity, which is the eschatological church (see Jn 17:22). Yet the vast majority of front-line theologians in the church's history have resisted this minimalist approach. And there are good educational reasons for doing so. In the words of educational philosopher Elliot Eisner, "The process of representation stabilizes ideas and images, makes the editing process possible, provides the means for sharing meaning, and creates the occasion for discovery."[28] Comparison and analogies remain pedagogically crucial.

Further, the Bible itself offers a helpful model for how images, metaphors and illustrations can function in depicting divine life. The Bible depicts the mystery of God's own being through the use of multiple complementary metaphors (e.g., rock, king, shepherd). It describes the atonement as a conquest, a sacrifice and a propitiation. Each metaphor by itself is in-

---

[27]Marguerite Shuster, "Preaching the Trinity," in Davis, Kendall and O'Collins, *The Trinity*, p. 371.

[28]Elliot W. Eisner, *The Arts and the Creation of Mind* (New Haven: Yale University Press, 2002), p. 239.

complete. A combination of metaphors helps us to grasp new aspects of a given truth claim and also sharpens our sense of which aspects of any specific metaphor are untrue.

The same is true for trinitiarian analogies, depictions and illustrations. Thinking of the Trinity as a family falls off into tritheism. Thinking of the Trinity as three faculties of a single person falls off into modalism. While Rublev's *Icon of the Trinity* (c. 1411) captures trinitarian hospitality in a remarkable way, it could—if left uncorrected—foster a kind of unreflective tritheism. Masaccio's famous *Trinity* (1427-1428) captures the trinitarian mediation of worship well but could, if left uncorrected, foster an imbalanced view of the importance of each member of the Trinity.[29] Taken together, each iconic image and analogy offers an aspect of truth and helps to point out the inadequacies of the other.

In recent work, Jeremy Begbie's analysis of musical categories for theological discourse is especially pedagogically fruitful. Begbie argues that while traditional teaching metaphors and artistic images are important, musical modes of expression also have much to offer us:

> What could be more apt than to speak of the Trinity as a three-note chord, a resonance of life; Father, Son, and Spirit mutually indwelling, without mutual exclusion, and yet without merger, each occupying the same space, "sounding through" one another, yet irreducibly distinct, reciprocally enhancing, and establishing one another as other? . . . The overlapping of musical sounds, though in important respects dissimilar to the space of Father, Son, and Holy Spirit, can nonetheless serve to embody concretely something of that trinitarian space, the space in which we are invited to share, and embody it in ways that would seem to be unique for this art form.[30]

This musical image for the Trinity offers a dynamic rather than a static feel, an aesthetic dimension not found in some descriptions and a vision of "mutual indwelling" that is not possible to convey in other modes of discourse. Begbie's analogy offers rich potential for inviting students to perceive God and God's relations to the world in a trinitarian way.

---

[29]For more on this theme, see David Brown, "The Trinity in Art," in Davis, Kendall and O'Collins, *The Trinity*, pp. 329-56.

[30]Jeremy Begbie, *Resounding Truth: Christian Wisdom in the World of Music* (Grand Rapids: Baker Academic, 2007), pp. 293-94.

An epicletic pedagogy. Fifth and finally, teaching trinitarian theology is most fittingly done in an epicletic way: with prayers for the Holy Spirit to give insight to the beauty and nature of God. Trinitarian theology is built, in part, on the claims that true theological knowledge arrives through what "God has revealed to us through the Spirit" and that "no one comprehends what is truly God's except the Spirit of God" (1 Cor 2:10-11 NRSV). In light of this, it would be ironically contradictory to teach in a way that assumes that clever teaching or heroic student effort can, by themselves, generate theological knowledge and wisdom. Insight about the Trinity, just like trinitarian worship, is truly a gift we receive. We pray for it, hope for it, await it, but we do not produce it.[31] The agency in true trinitarian learning is the Holy Spirit.[32]

Several classic trinitarian sources embody this pedagogy by including prayers inside longer analytic passages, seamlessly moving from third-person descriptions of God to second-person engagement with God. Gregory Nazianzus opens one reflection on the Trinity with this prayer: "Enlighten my mind and loosen my tongue, Spirit of God, and I will sound aloud the trumpet of truth, so that all who are united to God may rejoice with their whole heart." Hilary of Poitier interrupts his treatise with a prayer: "May I worship you, the Father of us all, and your Son together with you and may I be counted worthy to receive your Holy Spirit who through your only Son proceeds from you."[33] John Calvin spoke of the "inner illumination of the Holy Spirit" as fundamental to all genuine knowledge of God.[34] It might seem hard to imagine a divinity school lec-

---

[31]This sensibility is developed in a provocative way by Stephen H. Webb, "The Voice of Theology: Rethinking the Personal and the Objective in Christian Pedagogy," *Journal of the American Academy of Religion* 65, no. 4 (1997): 763-81.
[32]This claim is developed in a much more thorough way as the foundation for an extended trinitarian philosophy or theology of education by Robert W. Pazmiño, *God Our Teacher: Theological Basics in Christian Education* (Grand Rapids: Baker Academic, 2001); Peter C. Hodgson, *God's Wisdom: Toward a Theology of Education* (Louisville, Ky.: Westminster John Knox, 1999); and Debra Dean Murphy, *Teaching That Transforms: Worship as the Heart of Christian Education* (Grand Rapids: Brazos, 2004).
[33]Gregory of Nazianzus, *Poems* 1.3; and Hilary of Poitier, *The Trinity* 12.55-56, with translation from *Benedictine Daily Prayer: A Short Breviary*, compiled and edited by Maxwell E. Johnson and the monks of St. John's Abbey (Collegeville, Minn.: Liturgical Press, 2007), p. 1631.
[34]John Calvin, *Institutes of the Christian Religion*, ed. John T. McNeill (Philadelphia: Westminster Press, 1960), I.VII.4.

ture or a congregational educational session on the Trinity consisting entirely of a prayer, or of a prayer filling in the content of an academic journal article in theology. Yet Christian teaching in each setting can grow by including significant prayers for the Spirit's instruction, by naming the limits of human knowing and by regular reminders that we teach and learn *coram Deo*, before the face of God.

To conclude: the Christian tradition includes not only rich discourse about trinitarian theology, but also rich resources for practicing trinitarian worship and for teaching the trinitarian theology in evocative and compelling ways. In a world filled with deistic inclinations, any trinitarian renaissance must not be limited to the world of theological discourse; it must also extend into worship and catechesis of all kinds of ordinary communities. The next generation of trinitarian theologians, pastors and teachers will do well to invest their lives in discerning faithful, resourceful and effective ways of forming trinitarian piety and imagination in Christian communities through worship and teaching. May God's Spirit bless us in this life-giving work.

Contributors

Philip W. Butin is president and professor of theology at San Francisco Theological Seminary. He has authored such books as *Revelation, Redemption, and Response: Calvin's Trinitarian Understanding of the Divine-Human Relationship* (Oxford University Press, 1995) and *The Trinity* (Geneva Press, 2001). He has also cochaired and taught in the New Mexico Ecumenical Institute for Ministry, a theological institute for lay ministry training.

John R. Franke is the Lester and Kay Clemens Professor of Missional Theology at Biblical Seminary in Philadelphia. He is the author of *Beyond Foundationalism: Theology in a Postmodern Context* (Westminster John Knox, 2001), *The Character of Theology: An Introduction to Its Nature, Task, and Purpose* (Baker Academic, 2005) and *Barth for Armchair Theologians* (Westminster John Knox, 2006).

Edith M. Humphrey is the William F. Orr Professor of New Testament at Pittsburgh Theological Seminary. She is the author of a number of books, including *Ecstasy and Intimacy: When the Holy Spirit Meets the Human Spirit* (Eerdmans, 2005) and *And I Turned to See the Voice: The Rhetoric of Vision in the New Testament* (Baker Academic, 2007).

Mark Husbands is the Leonard and Marjorie Maas Associate Professor of Reformed Theology at Hope College and was assistant professor of theology at Wheaton College from 2001-2007. Among his coedited works are *The Beauty of God: Theology and the Arts* (InterVarsity Press, 2007), *Women, Ministry and the Gospel: Exploring New Paradigms* (InterVarsity Press, 2007) and *The Community of the Word: Toward an Evangelical Ecclesiology* (InterVarsity Press, 2005).

Keith E. Johnson is national director of theological education for the U.S. campus ministry of Campus Crusade for Christ. He also serves as a guest professor of systematic theology at Reformed Theological Seminary and has authored several articles on the Trinity and the theology of religions.

Robert K. Lang'at is currently university provost at Kabarak University in Kenya, where he was previously the head of the Department of Biblical Studies and Education. He has also served as an adjunct professor at West Africa Theological Seminary and assistant academic dean at Wesley Biblical Seminary. He has authored a number of articles on holiness theology in the African context.

David Lauber is assistant professor of theology at Wheaton College and the author of *Barth on the Descent into Hell: God, Atonement, and the Christian Life* (Ashgate, 2004).

Gordon T. Smith is presently the president of reSource Leadership International and was formerly the academic vice president and dean of Regent College. His published books include *The Voice of Jesus: Discernment, Prayer and the Witness of the Spirit* (InterVarsity Press, 2003), *Beginning Well: Christian Conversion and Authentic Transformation* (InterVarsity Press, 2001), *Courage and Calling: Embracing Your God-Given Potential* (InterVarsity Press, 1999) and *A Holy Meal: The Lord's Supper in the Life of the Church* (Baker, 2005).

Daniel J. Treier is associate professor of theology at Wheaton College and the author or coeditor of several books, including most recently *Introducing Theological Interpretation of Scripture: Recovering a Christian Practice* (Baker Academic, 2008).

Leanne Van Dyk is dean and vice president of academic affairs and professor of Reformed theology at Western Theological Seminary. Dr. Van Dyk serves on the editorial board of *Perspectives: A Journal of Reformed Thought* and the *Scottish Journal of Theology*. She has authored *The Desire of Divine Love: John McLeod Campbell's Doctrine of the Atonement*

(Peter Lang, 1995) and edited *A More Profound Alleluia: Theology and Worship in Harmony* (Eerdmans, 2005).

Kevin J. Vanhoozer is currently Research Professor of Systematic Theology at Trinity Evangelical Divinity School, having previously served as Senior Lecturer in Theology and Religious Studies at New College of the University of Edinburgh. Dr. Vanhoozer recently edited the *Dictionary for Theological Interpretation of the Bible* (Baker, 2005) and *Everyday Theology: How to Read Cultural Texts and Influence Trends* (Baker, 2007). He won the *Christianity Today* best theological book award for his work *The Drama of Doctrine: A Canonical-Linguistic Approach to Christian Theology* (Westminster John Knox, 2005).

John D. Witvliet is director of the Calvin Institute of Christian Worship and is professor of theology, music and worship at Calvin College and Calvin Theological Seminary. He is author of *The Biblical Psalms in Christian Worship: A Brief Introduction and Guide to Resources* (Eerdmans, 2007) and *Worship Seeking Understanding: Windows into Christian Practice* (Baker Academic, 2003), as well as coauthor of *Proclaiming the Christmas Gospel: Ancient Sermons and Hymns for Contemporary Christian Inspiration* (Baker, 2004).

Name and Subject Index

Scripture Index